JavaScript Application Design

JavaScript
Application Design

A Build First Approach

NICOLAS BEVACQUA

MANNING

SHELTER ISLAND

For online information and ordering of this and other Manning books, please visit
www.manning.com. The publisher offers discounts on this book when ordered in quantity.
For more information, please contact

>   Special Sales Department
>   Manning Publications Co.
>   20 Baldwin Road
>   PO Box 761
>   Shelter Island, NY 11964
>   Email: orders@manning.com

Manning Publications Co.
20 Baldwin Road
PO Box 761
Shelter Island, NY 11964

Development editor:	Susan Conant
Technical development editor:	Douglas Duncan
Copyeditor:	Katie Petito
Proofreader:	Alyson Brener
Technical proofreaders:	Deepak Vohra
	Valentin Crettaz
Typesetter:	Marija Tudor
Cover designer:	Marija Tudor

ISBN: 9781617291951
Printed in the United States of America
1 2 3 4 5 6 7 8 9 10 – EBM – 20 19 18 17 16 15

To Marian, for withstanding the birth of this book,
your unconditional love, and your endless patience.

I love you!

Will you marry me?

brief contents

contents

foreword

The process of designing a robust JavaScript web app has gone through a roaring renaissance in recent years. With the language being used to develop increasingly ambitious apps and interfaces, this is the perfect time for *JavaScript Application Design*. Through concise examples, lessons learned from the field, and key concepts for scalable development, Nico Bevacqua will give you a whirlwind tour of taking the process and design of your apps to the next level.

This book will also help you craft build processes that will save you time. Time is a key factor in staying productive. As web app developers, we want to make the most of ours, and a Build First philosophy can help us hit the ground running with clean, testable apps that are well structured from the get-go. Learning process workflow and how to manage complexity are fundamental cornerstones of modern JavaScript app development. Getting them right can make a massive difference in the long run.

JavaScript Application Design will walk you through automation for the front end. It covers everything from avoiding repetitive tasks and monitoring production builds to mitigating the cost of human error through a clean tooling setup. Automation is a big factor here. If you aren't using automation in your workflow today, you're working too hard. If a series of daily tasks can be accomplished with a single command, follow Nico's advice and spend the time you save improving the code quality of your apps.

Modularity is the final crucial concept that can assist with building scalable, maintainable apps. Not only does this help ensure that the pieces composing our application can be more easily tested and documented, it encourages reuse and focus on quality. In *JavaScript Application Design*, Nico expertly walks you through writing modular JavaScript components, getting asyncronous flow right, and enough client-side MVC for you to build an app of your own.

Strap on your seatbelts, adjust your command line, and enjoy a ride through the process of improving your development workflow.

ADDY OSMANI
SENIOR ENGINEER
WITH A PASSION FOR DEVELOPER TOOLING
GOOGLE

preface

Like most people in our field, I've always been fascinated with problem solving. The painful thrill of hunting for a solution, the exhilarating relief of having found a fix—there's nothing quite like it. When I was young I really enjoyed strategy games, such as chess, which I've played ever since I was a kid; StarCraft, a real-time strategy game I played for 10 years straight; and Magic: The Gathering, a trading card game that can be described as the intersection between poker and chess. They presented plenty of problem-solving opportunities.

At primary school I learned Pascal and rudimentary Flash programming. I was psyched. I would go on and learn Visual Basic, PHP, C, and start developing websites, reaping the benefits of a masterful handle on `<marquee>` and `<blink>` tags, paired with a modest understanding of MySQL; I was unstoppable, but my thirst for problem solving didn't end there, and I went back to gaming.

Ultima Online (UO), a massively multiplayer online role-playing game (no wonder they abbreviate that as MMORPG), wasn't any different than other games that got me hooked for years. Eventually I found out that there was an open source[1] implementation of the UO server, which was named RunUO and written entirely in C#. I played on a RunUO server where the administrators had no programming experience. They slowly started trusting me to handle minor bug fixes by literally emailing source code files back and forth. I was hooked. C# was a wonderful, expressive language, and the open source software for the UO server was amicable and inviting—you didn't even

---

[1] You can check out the RunUO website at runuo.com, although the project isn't maintained anymore.

need an IDE (or even need to know what that was) because the server would compile script files dynamically for you. You'd be essentially writing a file with 10 to 15 lines in it, inheriting from the `Dragon` class, and adding an intimidating text bubble over their head, or overriding a method so they'd spit more fireballs. You'd learn the language and its syntax without even trying, simply by having fun!

Eventually, a friend revealed that I could make a living out of writing C# code: "You know, people actually pay you to do that," he said. That's when I started developing websites again, except I wasn't using only Front Page and piles of `<marquee>` tags or Java applets for fun anymore. It still feels like a game to me, though.

A few years ago I read *The Pragmatic Programmer*[2], and something clicked. The book has a lot of solid advice, and I can't recommend it highly enough. One thing that particularly affected me: the authors advocate you get out of your comfort zone and try something you've been meaning to do but haven't gotten around to. My comfort zone was C# and ASP.NET at that point, so I decided to try Node.js, an unmistakably UNIX-y platform for JavaScript development on the server side, certainly a break from my Microsoft-ridden development experience so far.

I learned a ton from that experiment and ended up with a blog[3] where I'd write about everything I learned in the process. About six months later I'd decided that I'd put my years of experience in C# design into a book about JavaScript. I contacted Manning, and they jumped at the opportunity, helping me brainstorm and turn raw ideas into something more deliberate and concise.

This book is the result of many hours of hard work, dedication, and love for the web. In it, you'll find practical advice about application design, process automation, and best practices that will improve the quality of your web projects.

---

[2] *The Pragmatic Programmer: From Journeyman to Master* by Andrew Hunt and David Thomas (Addison Wesley, 1999) is a timeless classic you should seriously consider reading.

[3] You can read my blog, "Pony Foo," at ponyfoo.com. I write articles about the web, performance, progressive enhancement, and JavaScript.

acknowledgments

You wouldn't be holding this book in your hands if it weren't for everyone who supported and endured me throughout the writing process. I can only hope that those who deserve acknowledgment the most, my friends and family, already know that I can't put into words how thankful I am for their love, understanding, and frequent reassurance.

Many more people contributed—directly or indirectly—a great deal of wisdom and inspiration to this book.

The open source JavaScript community is an endless spring of insight, encouragement, and selfless contributions. They have opened my eyes to a better approach to software development, where collaboration isn't only possible, but actively encouraged. Most of these people have contributed indirectly by evangelizing for the web, maintaining blogs, sharing their experience and resources, and otherwise educating me. Others have contributed directly by developing tools discussed in the book. Among these individuals are Addy Osmani, Chris Coyier, Guillermo Rauch, Harry Roberts, Ilya Grigorik, James Halliday, John-David Dalton, Mathias Bynens, Max Ogden, Mikeal Rogers, Paul Irish, Sindre Sorhus, and T.J. Holowaychuk.

There are also many book authors and content distributors who have influenced and motivated me to become a better educator. Through their writing and sharing, these people have significantly helped shape my career. They include Adam Wiggins, Alan Cooper, Andrew Hunt, Axel Rauschmayer, Brad Frost, Christian Heilmann, David Thomas, Donald Norman, Frederic Cambus, Frederick Brooks, Jeff Atwood, Jeremy Keith, Jon Bentley, Nicholas C. Zakas, Peter Cooper, Richard Feynmann, Steve Krug, Steve McConnell, and Vitaly Friedman.

XX   ACKNOWLEDGMENTS

Susan Conant, my developmental editor at Manning, deserves to be singled out. She held this book to the greatest standard of quality I could possibly create, and it's in much better shape than it would've been if not for her. On top of that, she had to hand-hold me through the delicate and intimate process of writing my first book. Through her relentless, yet gentle, guidance she helped shape my lumps of ideas into a book that I'm not afraid to publish. I've become a better writer because of her, and I'm grateful for that.

She wasn't alone in that endeavor. All of the staff at Manning wanted this book to be the best that it could be. The publisher, Marjan Bace—along with his editorial collective—are to be thanked for that. Valentin Crettaz and Deepak Vohra, the technical proofreaders, were not only instrumental in ensuring the code samples were consistent and useful, but provided me with great feedback as well.

There are also the hordes of anonymous souls that were willing to read through the manuscript, leaving their impressions and helping improve the book. Thanks to the MEAP readers who posted corrections and comments in the Author Online forum, and to the reviewers who read the chapters at various stages of development: Alberto Chiesa, Carl Mosca, Dominic Pettifer, Gavin Whyte, Hans Donner, Ilias Ioannou, Jonas Bandi, Joseph White, Keith Webster, Matthew Merkes, Richard Harriman, Sandeep Kumar Patel, Stephen Wakely, Torsten Dinkheller, and Trevor Saunders.

Special thanks to Addy Osmani for contributing the foreword, and to everyone else who played a part. Even if they didn't make the keystrokes themselves, they played an instrumental role in getting this book published, and one step closer to you.

about this book

Web development has grown out of proportion, and today it's hard to imagine a world without the web. The web is famously fault tolerant. While traditional programming teaches us that missing a semicolon, forgetting to add a closing tag, or declaring invalid properties will have crippling consequences, the same cannot be said about the web. The web is a place where it's okay to make mistakes, yet there's increasingly less room for error. This dichotomy stems from the fact that modern web applications are an order of magnitude more complex than they used to be. During the humble beginnings of the web, we would maybe modestly make a minor change in web pages using JavaScript; whereas on the modern web, entire sites are rendered in a single page, powered by JavaScript.

JavaScript Application Design is your guide to a better modern web development experience, one where you can develop maintainable JavaScript applications as you would if you were using any other language. You'll learn how to leverage automation as a replacement for tedious and repetitive error-prone processes, how to design modular applications that are easy to test, and how to test them.

Process automation is a critical time-saver across the board. Automation in the development environment helps us focus our efforts on thinking, writing code, and debugging. Automation helps ensure our code works after every change that we publish to version control. It saves time when preparing the application for production by bundling, minifying assets, creating spritesheets, and adding other performance optimization techniques. It also helps with deployments by reducing risk and automating away a complicated and error-prone process. Many books discuss processes and automation when it comes to back-end languages, but it's much harder to find material on the subject when it comes to JavaScript-driven applications.

The core value of *JavaScript Application Design* is quality. Automation gives you a better environment in which to build your application, but that alone isn't enough: the application itself needs to be quality conscious as well. To that end, the book covers application design guidelines, starting with a quick rundown of language-specific caveats, teaching you about the power of modularity, helping you untangle asynchronous code, develop client-side MVC applications, and write unit tests for your JavaScript code.

This book relies on specific tools and framework versions, as books about web technologies usually do, but it separates library-specific concerns from the theory at hand. This is a concession to the fact that tooling changes frequently in the fast-paced web development arena, but design and the processes behind tooling tend to have a much slower rhythm. Thanks to this separation of concerns, I hope this book stays relevant for years to come.

Road map

JavaScript Application Design is broken into two parts and four appendixes. The first part is dedicated to the Build First approach, what it is, and how it can aid your everyday job. This part covers process automation in detail, from everyday development to automated deployments, as well as continuous integration and continuous deployments; it spans 4 chapters.

- Chapter 1 describes the core principles that drive Build First, and the different processes and flows you can set up. It then introduces the application design guidelines that we'll discuss throughout the book and lays the foundation for the rest of the book.
- In chapter 2 you learn about Grunt, and how you can use it to compose build flows. Then we look at a few different build tasks that you can easily perform using Grunt.
- Chapter 3 is all about environments and the development workflow. You'll learn that not all environments are born the same, and how you can prioritize debugging and productivity in the development environment.
- Chapter 4 walks you through the release flow and discusses deployments. You'll learn about a few more build tasks that are geared toward performance optimization, and discover how to perform automated deployments. You'll also learn how to hook up continuous integration and how to monitor your application once in production.

While part 1 is focused on building applications using Grunt, appendix C teaches you to choose the best build tool for the job. Once you've read past part 1, you'll go into the second part of the book, which is dedicated to managing complexity in your application designs. Modules, MVC, asynchronous code flows, testing, and a well-designed API all play significant roles in modern applications and are discussed in the next chapters.

- Chapter 5 focuses on developing modular JavaScript. It starts by expressing what constitutes a module and how you can design applications modularly and lists the benefits of doing so. Afterward, you'll get a crash course on lexical scoping and related quirks in the JavaScript language. Later you get a rundown of the major ways to attain modularity: RequireJS, CommonJS, and the upcoming ES6 module system. The chapter concludes by going over different package management solutions such as Bower and npm.

- In chapter 6 you learn about asynchronous code flows. If you ever descend into callback hell, this may be your way out. This chapter discusses different approaches to deal with complexity in asynchronous code flows, namely callbacks, Promises, events, and ES6 generators. You'll also learn how to do proper error handling under each of those paradigms.

- Chapter 7 starts by describing MVC architectures, and then ties them specifically to the web. You'll learn how you can use Backbone to develop rich client-side applications that separate concerns using MVC. Later, you'll learn about Rendr, which can be used to render Backbone views on the server side, optimizing the performance and accessibility of your applications.

- In chapter 8, now that your applications are modular, clean-cut, and maintainable, you'll take the next logical step and look into testing your applications in different ways. To this end we'll go over an assortment of JavaScript testing tools and get hands-on experience using them to test small components. Then we'll go back to the MVC application built in chapter 7 and add tests to it. You won't be doing unit testing only, you'll also learn more about continuous integration, visual testing, and measuring performance.

- Chapter 9 is the last chapter of the book, and it's dedicated to REST API design. This is the layer where the client side interacts with the server, and it sets the scene for everything that we do in the application. If the API is convoluted and complicated, chances are the application as a whole will be as well. REST introduces clear guidelines when designing an API, making sure the API is concise. Last, we'll look at consuming these services in the client side in a conventional manner.

The appendixes can be read after you're done with the book, but you'll probably get the most value from them by reading them if you get stuck with the areas they cover, as they contain answers to questions you might have. Throughout the book, you'll be pointed to the appendixes where it makes sense to expand a little on one of these subjects.

- Appendix A is a soft introduction to Node.js and its module system, CommonJS. It'll help you troubleshoot your Node.js installation and answer a few questions on how CommonJS works.

- Appendix B is a detailed introduction to Grunt. Whereas the chapters in part I only explain what's absolutely necessary about Grunt, the appendix covers its inner workings in more detail, and will be handy if you're serious about developing a full-blown build process using Grunt.

- Appendix C makes it clear that this book is in no way married to Grunt, and lists a couple of alternatives, Gulp and `npm run`. The appendix discusses the pros and cons of each of the three tools, and leaves it up to you to determine which one (if any) fits your needs best.
- Appendix D presents a JavaScript quality guide containing a myriad of best practices you may choose to follow. The idea isn't to force those specific guidelines down your throat, but rather to arm you with the idea that consistency is a good thing to enforce throughout a code base when working in a development team.

Code conventions and downloads

All source code is in `fixed-size width font like this`, and sometimes grouped under named code listings. Code annotations accompany many of the listings, highlighting important concepts. The source code for this book is open source and publicly hosted on GitHub. You can download it by visiting github.com/buildfirst/buildfirst. The online repository will always have the most up-to-date version of the accompanying source code. While source code might only be discussed at a glance in the book, it's better documented in the repository, and I encourage you to check out the commented code there, if you run into trouble.

You can also download the code from the publisher's website at www.manning .com/JavaScriptApplicationDesign.

Author Online

Purchase of *JavaScript Application Design* includes free access to a private web forum run by Manning Publications, where you can make comments about the book, ask technical questions, and receive help from the author and from other users. To access the forum and subscribe to it, point your web browser to www.manning.com/JavaScriptApplicationDesign. This page provides information on how to get on the forum once you are registered, what kind of help is available, and the rules of conduct on the forum.

Manning's commitment to our readers is to provide a venue where a meaningful dialogue between individual readers and between readers and the author can take place. It is not a commitment to any specific amount of participation on the part of the author, whose contribution to the book's forum remains voluntary (and unpaid). We suggest you try asking the author some challenging questions, lest his interest stray!

The Author Online forum and the archives of previous discussions will be accessible from the publisher's website as long as the book is in print.

about the author

Nicolas Bevacqua is an active member of the open source JavaScript community, a freelance web developer, an occasional public speaker, and a passionate writer. He maintains many open source projects and blogs about the web, performance, progressive enhancement, and JavaScript development at ponyfoo.com. Nico currently lives in Buenos Aires, Argentina, with his beautiful girl-friend, Marian.

about the cover illustration

The figure on the cover of *JavaScript Application Design* is captioned "Winter Habit of a Kamtchadal in 1760." The Kamchatka Peninsula is the eastern-most part of Russia, lying between the Pacific Ocean to the east and the Sea of Okhotsk to the west. The illustration is taken from Thomas Jefferys' *A Collection of the Dresses of Different Nations, Ancient and Modern*, London, published between 1757 and 1772. The title page states that these are hand-colored copperplate engravings, heightened with gum arabic. Thomas Jefferys (1719–1771) was called "Geographer to King George III." He was an English cartographer who was the leading map supplier of his day. He engraved and printed maps for government and other official bodies and produced a wide range of commercial maps and atlases, especially of North America. His work as a mapmaker sparked an interest in local dress customs of the lands he surveyed and mapped; they are brilliantly displayed in this four-volume collection.

Fascination with faraway lands and travel for pleasure were relatively new phenomena in the eighteenth century and collections such as this one were popular, introducing both the tourist as well as the armchair traveler to the inhabitants of other countries. The diversity of the drawings in Jefferys' volumes speaks vividly of the uniqueness and individuality of the world's nations centuries ago. Dress codes have changed, and the diversity by region and country, so rich at one time, has faded away. It is now often hard to tell the inhabitant of one continent from another. Perhaps, trying to view it optimistically, we have traded a cultural and visual diversity for a more varied personal life—or a more varied and interesting intellectual and technical life.

At a time when it is hard to tell one computer book from another, Manning celebrates the inventiveness and initiative of the computer business with book covers based on the rich diversity of national costumes two and a half centuries ago, brought back to life by Jefferys' pictures.

Part 1

Build processes

The first part of this book is dedicated to build processes and provides a practical introduction to Grunt. You'll learn the why, how, and what of build processes, both in theory and in practice.

In chapter 1, we go over what the Build First philosophy entails: a build process and application complexity management. Then, we'll start fiddling with our first build task, using lint to prevent syntax errors in our code.

Chapter 2 is all about build tasks. You'll learn about the various tasks that comprise a build, how to configure them, and how to create your own tasks. In each case, we'll take a look at the theory and then walk through practical examples using Grunt.

In chapter 3, we'll learn how to configure application environments while keeping sensitive information safe. We'll go over the development environment workflow, and you'll learn how to automate the build step itself.

Chapter 4 then describes a few more tasks we need to take into account when releasing our application, such as asset optimization and managing documentation. You'll learn about keeping code quality in check with continuous integration, and we'll also go through the motions of deploying an application to a live environment.

Introduction to Build First

This chapter covers

- Identifying problems in modern application design
- Defining Build First
- Building processes
- Managing complexity within applications

Developing an application properly can be hard. It takes planning. I've created applications over a weekend, but that doesn't mean they were well-designed. Improvisation is great for throw-away prototypes and great when concept-proofing an idea; however, building a maintainable application requires a plan, the glue that holds together the features you currently have in mind and maybe even those you might add in the near future. I've participated in countless endeavors where the application's front-end wasn't all it could be.

Eventually, I realized that back-end services usually have an architect devoted to their planning, design, and overview—and often it's not one architect but an entire team of them. This is hardly the case with front-end development, where a developer is expected to prototype a working sketch of the application and then asked to

3

run with it, hoping that the prototype will survive an implementation in production. Front-end development requires as much dedication to architecture planning and design as back-end development does.

Long gone are the days when we'd copy a few snippets of code off the internet, paste them in our page, and call it a day. Mashing together JavaScript code as an afterthought no longer holds up to modern standards. JavaScript is now front and center. We have many frameworks and libraries to choose from, which can help you organize your code by allowing you to write small components rather than a monolithic application. Maintainability isn't something you can tack onto a code base whenever you'd like; it's something you have to build into the application, and the philosophy under which the application is designed, from the beginning. Writing an application that isn't designed to be maintainable translates into stacking feature after feature in an ever-so-slightly tilting Jenga tower.

If maintainability isn't built in, it gets to a point where you can't add any more pieces to the tower. The code becomes convoluted and bugs become increasingly hard to track down. Refactoring means halting product development, and the business can't afford that. The release schedule must be maintained, and letting the tower come crashing down is unacceptable, so we compromise.

1.1   *When things go wrong*

You might want to deploy a new feature to production, so humans can try it out. How many steps do you have to take to do that? Eight? Five? Why would you risk a mistake in a routine task such as a deployment? Deploying should be no different than building your application locally. One step. That's it.

Unfortunately that's rarely the standard. Have you faced the challenging position I've found myself in of having to take many of these steps manually? Sure, you can compile the application in a single step, or you might use an interpreted server-side language that doesn't need any pre-compilation. Maybe later you need to update your database to the latest version. You may have even created a script for those updates, and yet you log into your database server, upload the file, and run the schema updates yourself.

Cool, you've updated the database; however, something's not right and the application is throwing an error. You look at the clock. Your application has been down for more than 10 minutes. This should've been a straightforward update. You check the logs; you forgot to add that new variable to your configuration file. Silly! You add it promptly, mumbling something about wrestling with the code base. You forget to alter the config file before it deploys; it slipped your mind to update it before deploying to production!

Sound like a familiar ritual? Fear not, this is an unfortunately common illness, spread through different applications. Consider the crisis scenarios described next.

1.1.1 *How to lose $172,222 a second for 45 minutes*

I bet you'd consider losing almost half a billion dollars a serious issue, and that's exactly what happened to Knight's Capital.[1] They developed a new feature to allow stock traders to participate in something called the Retail Liquidity Program (RLP). The RLP functionality was intended to replace an unused piece of functionality called Power Peg (PP), which had been discontinued for close to nine years. The RLP code reused a flag, which was used to activate the PP code. They removed the Power Peg feature when they added RLP, so all was good. Or at least they thought it was good, until the point when they flipped the switch.

Deployments had no formal process and were executed by hand by a single technician. This person forgot to deploy the code changes to one of their eight servers, meaning that in the case of the eighth server, the PP code, and not the RLP feature, would be behind the activation flag. They didn't notice anything wrong until a week later when they turned on the flag, activating RLP on all servers but one, and the nine-year-old Power Peg feature on the other.

Orders routed through the eighth server triggered the PP code rather than RLP. As a result, the wrong types of orders were sent to trading centers. Attempts to amend the situation only further aggravated it, because they removed the RLP code from the servers which did have it. Long story short, they lost somewhere in the vicinity of $460 million in less than an hour. When you consider that all they needed to do to avoid their downfall was have a more formal build process in place, the whole situation feels outrageous, irresponsible, and, in retrospect, easily averted. Granted, this is an extreme case, but it boldly illustrates the point. An automated process would have increased the probability that human errors could be prevented or at least detected sooner.

1.1.2 *Build First*

In this book, my goal is to teach you the Build First philosophy of designing for clean, well-structured, and testable applications before you write a single line of code. You'll learn about process automation, which will mitigate the odds of human error, such as those leading to Knight's Capital's bankruptcy. Build First is the foundation that will empower you to design clean, well-structured, and testable applications, which are easy to maintain and refactor. Those are the two fundamental aspects of Build First: process automation and design.

To teach you the Build First approach, this book will show you techniques that will improve the quality of your software as well as your web development workflow. In Part 1, we'll begin by learning how to establish build processes appropriate for modern web application development. Then, you'll walk through best practices for productive day-to-day development, such as running tasks when your code changes, deploying applications from your terminal by entering a single command, and monitoring the state of your application once it's in production.

---

[1] For more information about Knight's Capital, see http://bevacqua.io/bf/knight.

The second part of the book—managing complexity and design—focuses on application quality. Here I give you an introduction to writing more modular Java-Script components by comparing the different options that are currently available. Asynchronous flows in JavaScript tend to grow in complexity and length, which is why I prepared a chapter where you'll gain insight into writing cleaner asynchronous code while learning about different tools you can use to improve that code. Using Backbone as your gateway drug of choice, you'll learn enough about MVC in JavaScript to get you started on the path to client-side MVC. I mentioned testable applications are important, and while modularity is a great first step in the right direction, testing merits a chapter of its own. The last chapter dissects a popular API design mentality denominated REST (Representational State Transfer), helping you design your own, as well as delving into application architecture on the server side, but always keeping an eye on the front end. We'll begin our exploration of build processes after looking at one more crisis scenario Build First can avert by automating your process.

1.1.3 *Rites of initiation*

Complicated setup procedures, such as when new team members come onboard, are also a sign you may be lacking in the automation department. Much to my torment, I've worked on projects where getting a development environment working for the first time took a week. A full week before you can even begin to fathom what the code does.

Download approximately 60 gigabytes worth of database backups, create a database configuring things you've never heard of before, such as collation, and then run a series of schema upgrade scripts that don't quite work. Once you've figured that out, you might want to patch your Windows Media Player by installing specific and extremely outdated codecs in your environment, which will feel as futile as attempts to cram a pig into a stuffed refrigerator.

Last, try compiling the 130+ project monolith in a single pass while you grab a cup of coffee. Oh, but you forgot to install the external dependencies; that'll do it. Nope, wait, you also need to compile a C++ program so codecs will work again. Compile again, and another 20 minutes go by. Still failing? Shoot. Ask around, maybe? Well, nobody truly knows. All of them went through that excruciating process when they started out, and they erased the memory from their minds. Check out the wiki? Sure, but it's all over the place. It has bits of information here and there, but they don't address your specific problems.

The company never had a formal initiation workflow, and as things started to pile up, it became increasingly hard to put one together. They had to deal with giant back-ups, upgrades, codecs, multiple services required by the website, and compiling the project took half an hour for every semi-colon you changed. If they'd automated these steps from the beginning, like we'll do in Build First, the process would've been that much smoother.

Both the Knight's Capital debacle and the overly complicated setup story have one thing in common: if they'd planned ahead and automated their build and deployment processes, their issues would've been averted. Planning ahead and automating the processes surrounding your applications are fundamental aspects of the Build First philosophy, as you'll learn in the next section.

1.2 *Planning ahead with Build First*

In the case of Knight's Capital, where they forgot to deploy code to one of the production web servers, having a single-step deployment process that automatically deployed the code to the whole web farm would've been enough to save the company from bankruptcy. The deeper issue in this case was code quality, because they had unused pieces of code sitting around in their code base for almost 10 years.

A complete refactor that doesn't provide any functional gains isn't appealing to a product manager; their goal is to improve the visible, consumer-facing product, not the underlying software. Instead, you can continuously improve the average quality of code in your project by progressively improving the code base and refactoring code as you touch it, writing tests that cover the refactored functionality, and wrapping legacy code in interfaces, so you can refactor later.

Refactoring won't do the trick on its own, though. Good design that's ingrained into the project from its inception is much more likely to stick, rather than attempts to tack it onto a poor structure as an afterthought. Design is the other fundamental aspect of the book, along with build processes mentioned previously.

Before we dive into the uncharted terrains of Build First, I want to mention this isn't a set of principles that only apply to JavaScript. For the most part, people usually associate these principles with back-end languages, such as Java, C#, or PHP, but here I'm applying them to the development process for JavaScript applications. As I mentioned previously, client-side code often doesn't get the love and respect it deserves. That often means broken code because we lack proper testing, or a code base that's hard to read and maintain. The product (and developer productivity) suffers as a result.

When it comes to JavaScript, given that interpreted languages don't need a compiler, naive developers might think that's justification enough to ditch the build process entirely. The problem when going down that road is that they'll be shooting in the dark: the developer won't know whether the code works until it's executed by a browser, and won't know whether it does what it's expected to, either. Later on, they might find themselves manually deploying to a hosting environment and logging into it remotely to tweak a few configuration settings to make it work.

1.2.1 *Core principles in Build First*

At its core, the Build First approach encourages establishing not only a build process but also clean application design. The following list shows at a high level what embracing the Build First approach gives us:

- Reduced error proclivity because there's no human interaction
- Enhanced productivity by automating repetitive tasks
- Modular, scalable application design

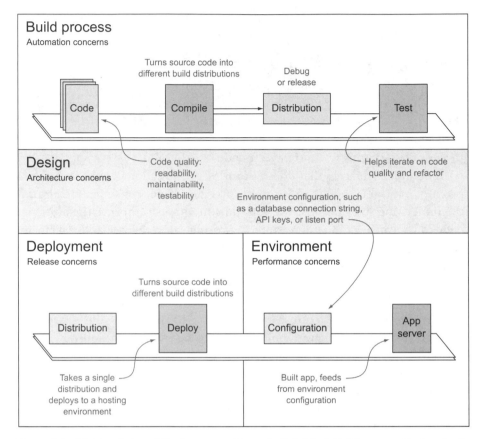

Figure 1.1   High-level view of the four areas of focus in Build First: Build process, Design, Deployment, and Environment

- Testability and maintainability by shrinking complexity
- Releases that conform to performance best practices
- Deployed code that's always tested before a release

Looking at figure 1.1, starting with the top row and moving down, you can see

- Build process: This is where you compile and test the application in an automated fashion. The build can be aimed at facilitating continuous development or tuned for maximum performance for a release.
- Design: You'll spend most of your time here, coding and augmenting the architecture as you go. While you're at it, you might refactor your code and update the tests to ensure components work as expected. Whenever you're not tweaking the build process or getting ready for a deployment, you'll be designing and iterating on the code base for your application.
- Deployment and Environment: These are concerned with automating the release process and configuring the different hosted environments. The

deployment process is in charge of delivering your changes to the hosted environment, while environment configuration defines the environment and the services—or databases—it interacts with, at a high level.

As figure 1.1 illustrates, Build First applications have two main components: the processes surrounding the project, such as building and deploying the application, and the design and quality of the application code itself, which is iteratively improved on a daily basis as you work on new features. Both are equally important, and they depend on each other to thrive. Good processes don't do any good if you're lacking in your application design. Similarly, good design won't survive crises such as the ones I described previously without the help of decent build and deployment procedures.

As with the Build First approach, this book is broken into two parts. In part 1, we look at the build process (tuned for either development or release) and the deployment process, as well as environments and how they can be configured. Part 2 delves into the application itself, and helps us come up with modular designs that are clear and concise. It also takes us through the practical design considerations you'll have to make when building modern applications.

In the next two sections, you'll get an overview of the concepts discussed in each part of the book.

1.3 Build processes

A build process is intended to automate repetitive tasks such as installing dependencies, compiling code, running unit tests, and performing any other important functions. The ability to execute all of the required tasks in a single step, called a *one-step build*, is critical because of the powerful opportunities it unveils. Once you have a one-step build in place, you can execute it as many times as required, without the outcome changing. This property is called *idempotence*: no matter how many times you invoke the operation, the result will be the same.

Figure 1.2 highlights in more detail the steps that make up the automated build and deployment processes.

Pros and cons of automating your build processes

Possibly the most important advantage to having an automated build process is that you can deploy as frequently as needed. Providing humans with the latest features as soon as they're ready allows us to tighten the feedback loop through which we can gain better insights into the product we should be building.

The main disadvantage to setting up an automated process is the time you'll need to spend putting the process together before you can start seeing the real benefits, but the benefits—such as automated testing, higher code quality, a leaner development workflow, and a safer deployment flow—far outweigh the effort spent putting together that process. As a general rule, you'll set up the process once and then replay it as much as you'd like, tweaking it a little as you go.

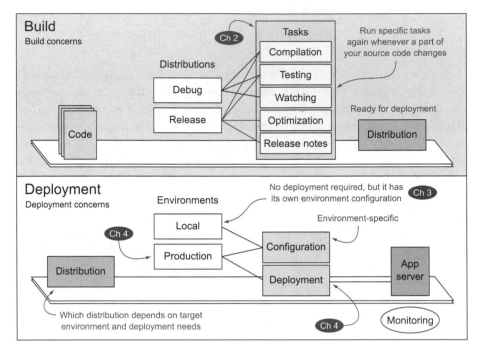

Figure 1.2   High-level view of the processes in Build First: Build and Deployment

BUILD

The top of figure 1.2 zooms in on the build portion in the build process workflow (shown back in figure 1.1), detailing the concerns as you aim for either development or release. If you aim for development, you'll want to maximize your ability to debug, and I bet you'll like a build that knows when to execute parts of itself without you taking any action. That's called *continuous development* (CD), and you'll learn about it in chapter 3. The release distribution of a build isn't concerned with CD, but you'll want to spend time optimizing your assets so they perform as fast as possible in production environments where humans will use your application.

DEPLOYMENT

The bottom of figure 1.2 zooms into the deployment process (originally shown in figure 1.1), which takes either the debug or release *distribution* (what I call distinct process flows with a specific purpose throughout the book) and deploys it to a hosted environment.

This package will work together with the environment-specific configuration (which keeps secrets, such as database connection strings and API keys, safe, and is discussed in chapter 3) to serve the application.

Part 1 is dedicated to the build aspect of Build First:

- Chapter 2 explains build tasks, teaching you how to write tasks and configure them using Grunt, the task runner you'll use as a build tool throughout part 1.

- Chapter 3 covers environments, how to securely configure your application, and the development work flow.
- Chapter 4 discusses tasks you should perform during release builds. Then you'll learn about deployments, running tests on every push to version control, and production monitoring.

BENEFITS OF A BUILD PROCESS

Once you're done with part 1, you'll feel confident performing the following operations on your own applications:

- Automating repetitive tasks such as compilation, minification, and testing
- Building an icon spritesheet so that HTTP requests for iconography are reduced to a single one. Such spriting techniques are discussed in chapter 2, as well as other HTTP 1.x optimization tricks, as a means to improve page speed and application delivery performance.
- Spinning up new environments effortlessly and neglecting to differentiate between development and production
- Restarting a web server and recompiling assets automatically whenever related files change
- Supporting multiple environments with flexible, single-step deployments

The Build First approach eliminates manual labor when it comes to tedious tasks, while also improving your productivity from the beginning. Build First acknowledges the significance of the build process for shaping a maintainable application iteratively. The application itself is also built by iteratively chipping away at its complexity.

Clean application design and architecture are addressed in part 2 of this book, which covers complexity management within the application, as well as design considerations with a focus on raising the quality bar. Let's go over that next.

1.4 *Handling application complexity and design*

Modularization, managing dependencies, understanding asynchronous flow, carefully following the right patterns, and testing are all crucial if you expect your code to work at a certain scale, regardless of language. In part 2 you'll learn different concepts, techniques, and patterns to apply to your applications, making them more modular, focused, testable, and maintainable. Figure 1.3, viewed from the top down, shows the progression we'll follow in part 2.

MODULARITY

You'll learn how to break your application into components, break those components down into modules, and then write concise functions that have a single purpose inside those modules. Modules can come from external packages, developed by third parties, and you can also develop them yourself. External packages should be handled by a package manager that takes care of versioning and updates on your behalf, which eliminates the need to manually download dependencies (such as jQuery) and automates the process.

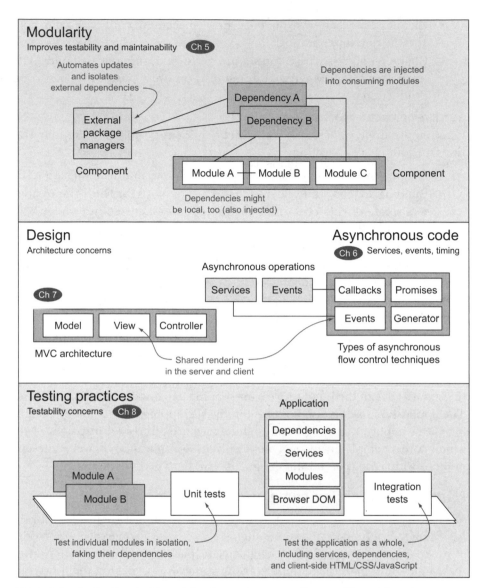

Figure 1.3   Application design and development concerns discussed in part 2

As you'll learn in chapter 5, modules indicate their dependencies (the modules they depend upon) in code, as opposed to grabbing them from the global namespace; this improves self-containment. A module system will take advantage of this information, being able to resolve all of these dependencies; it'll save you from having to maintain long lists of <script> tags in the appropriate order for your application to work correctly.

DESIGN

You'll get acquainted with separation of concerns and how to design your application in a layered way by following the Model-View-Controller pattern, further tightening the modularity in your applications. I'll tell you about shared rendering in chapter 7, the technique where you render views on the server side first, and then let the client side do view rendering for subsequent requests on the same single-page application.

ASYNCHRONOUS CODE

I'll teach you about the different types of asynchronous code flow techniques, using callbacks, Promises, generators, and events and helping you tame the asynchronous beast.

TESTING PRACTICES

In chapter 5 we discuss everything about modularity, learn about closures and the module pattern, talk about module systems and package managers, and try to pinpoint the strengths found in each solution. Chapter 6 takes a deep dive into asynchronous programming in JavaScript. You'll learn how to avoid writing a callback soup that will confuse you a week from now, and then you'll learn about the Promise pattern and the generators API coming in ES6.

Chapter 7 is dedicated to patterns and practices, such as how to best develop code, whether jQuery is the right choice for you, and how to write JavaScript code you can use in both the client and the server. We'll then look at the Backbone MVC framework. Keep in mind that Backbone is the tool I'll use to introduce you to MVC in JavaScript, but it's by no means the only tool you can use to this end.

In chapter 8 we'll go over testing solutions, automation, and tons of practical examples of unit testing client-side JavaScript. You'll learn how to develop tests in JavaScript at the unit level by testing a particular component and at the integration level by testing the application as a whole.

The book closes with a chapter on REST API design, and the implications of consuming a REST API in the front end, as well as a proposed structure to take full advantage of REST.

PRACTICAL DESIGN CONSIDERATIONS

The book aims to get you thinking about practical design considerations made when building a real application, as well as deciding thoughtfully on the best possible tool for a job, all the while focusing on quality in both your processes and the application itself. When you set out to build an application, you start by determining the scope, choosing a technology stack, and composing a minimum viable build process. Then you begin building the app, maybe using an MVC architecture and sharing the view rendering engine in both the browser and the server, something we discuss in chapter 7. In chapter 9 you'll learn the important bits on how to put an API together, and you'll learn how to define backing services that will be used by both the server-side view controllers and the REST API.

Figure 1.4 is an overview of how typical Build First applications may be organized.

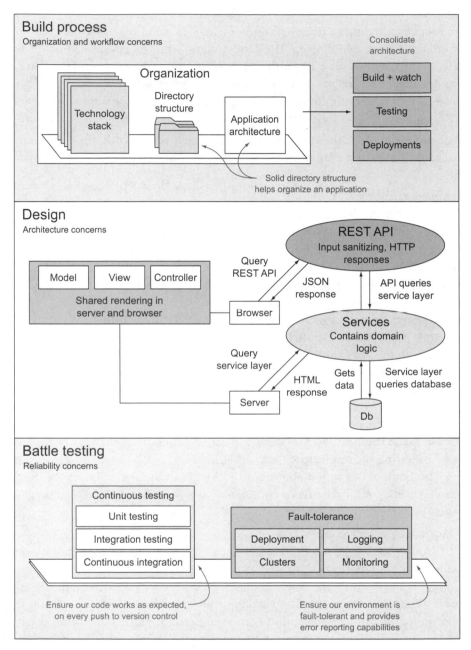

Figure 1.4 Pragmatic architectural considerations

BUILD PROCESS

Beginning at the upper left, figure 1.4 outlines how you can start by composing a build process which helps consolidate a starting point for your architecture, by deciding how to organize your code base. Defining a modular application architecture is the key to a maintainable code base, as you'll observe in chapter 5. The architecture is then consolidated by putting in place automated processes that provide you with continuous development, integration, and deployment capabilities.

DESIGN AND REST API

Designing the application itself, including a REST API that can effectively increase maintainability, is only possible by identifying clear cut components with clear purposes so they're orthogonal (meaning that they don't fight for resources on any particular concern). In chapter 9 we'll explore a multi-tiered approach to application design which can help you quickly isolate the web interface from your data and your business logic by strictly defining layers and the communication paths between those layers.

BATTLE TESTING

Once a build process and architecture are designed, battle testing is where you'll get drenched in reliability concerns. Here you'll plumb together continuous integration, where tests are executed on every push to your version control system, and maybe even continuous deployments, making several deployments to production per day. Last, fault tolerance concerns such as logging, monitoring, and clustering are discussed. These are glanced over in chapter 4, and help make your production environment more robust, or (at worst) warn you when things go awry.

All along the way, you'll write tests, adjust the build process, and tweak the code. It will be a terrific experiment for you to battle test Build First. It's time you get comfortable and start learning specifics about the Build First philosophy.

1.5 *Diving into Build First*

Quality is the cornerstone of Build First, and every measure taken by this approach works toward the simple goal of improving quality in both your code and the structure surrounding it. In this section, you'll learn about code quality and setting up lint, a code quality tool, in your command line. Measuring code quality is a good first step toward writing well-structured applications. If you start doing it early enough, it'll be easy to have your code base conform to a certain quality standard, and that's why we'll do it right off the bat.

In chapter 2, once you've learned about lint, I'll introduce you to Grunt, the build tool you'll use throughout the book to compose and automate build processes. Using Grunt allows you to run the code quality checks as part of a build, meaning you won't forget about them.

Grunt: the means to an end

Grunt is used intensively in part 1 and in some of part 2 to drive our build processes. I chose Grunt because it's a popular tool that's easy to teach and satisfies the most needs:

- It has full support for Windows.
- Little JavaScript knowledge is required and it takes little effort to pick up and run.

> **(continued)**
>
> It's important to understand that Grunt is a means to an end, a tool that enables you to easily put together the build processes described in this book. This doesn't make Grunt the absolute best tool for the job, and in an effort to make that clear, I've compiled a comparison between Grunt and two other tools: *npm, which is a package manager that can double as a lean build tool, and *Gulp, a code-driven build tool that has several conventions in common with Grunt.
>
> If you're curious about other build tools such as Gulp or using npm run as a build system, then you should read more about the topic in appendix C, which covers picking your own build tool.

Lint is a code-quality tool that's perfect for keeping an interpreted program—such as those written in JavaScript—in check. Rather than firing up a browser to check if your code has any syntax errors, you can execute a lint program in the command line. It can tell you about potential problems in your code, such as undeclared variables, missing semicolons, or syntax errors. That being said, lint isn't a magic wand: it won't detect logic issues in your code, it'll only warn you about syntax and style errors.

1.5.1 *Keeping code quality in check*

Lint is useful for determining if a given piece of code contains any syntax errors. It also enforces a set of JavaScript coding best practice rules, which we'll cover at the beginning of part 2, in chapter 5, when we look at modularity and dependency management.

Around 10 years ago Douglas Crockford released JSLint, a harsh tool that checks code and tells us all the little things that are wrong with it. Linting exists to help us improve the overall quality of our code. A lint program can tell you about the potential issues with a snippet, or even a list of files, straight from the command line, and this has the added benefit that you don't even have to execute the code to learn what's wrong with it. This process is particularly useful when it comes to JavaScript code, because the lint tool will act as a compiler of sorts, making sure that to the best of its knowledge your code can be interpreted by a JavaScript engine.

On another level, linters (the name given to lint programs) can be configured to warn you about code that's too complex, such as functions that include too many lines, obscure constructs that might confuse other people (such as `with` blocks, `new` statements, or using `this` too aggressively, in the case of JavaScript), or similar code style checks. Take the following code snippet as an example (listed as ch01/01_lint-sample in the samples online):

```
function compose_ticks_count (start) {
  start || start = 1;
  this.counter = start;
  return function (time) {
    ticks = +new Date;
    return ticks + '_'  + this.counter++
  }
}
```

Figure 1.5   Lint errors found in a code snippet.

Plenty of problems are readily apparent in this small piece, but they may not be that easy to spot. When analyzed through JSLint, you'll get both expected and interesting results. It'll complain that you must declare your variables before you try to use them, or that you're missing semicolons. Depending on the lint tool you use, it might complain about your use of the `this` keyword. Most linters will also complain about the way you're using `||` rather than using a more readable `if` statement. You can lint this sample online.[2] Figure 1.5 shows the output of Crockford's tool.

In the case of compiled languages, these kinds of errors are caught whenever you attempt to compile your code, and you don't need any lint tools. In JavaScript, though, there's no compiler because of the dynamic nature of the language. This is decidedly powerful, but also more error-prone than what you might expect from compiled languages, which wouldn't even allow you to execute the code in the first place.

Instead of being compiled, JavaScript code is interpreted by an engine such as V8 (as seen in Google Chrome) or SpiderMonkey (the engine powering Mozilla Firefox).

---

[2]   Go to http://jslint.com for the online sample. This is the original JavaScript linter Crockford maintains.

Where other engines do compile the JavaScript code, most famously the V8 engine, you can't benefit from their static code analysis outside the browser.[3] One of the perceived disadvantages of dynamic languages like JS is that you can't know for sure whether code will work when you execute it. Although that's true, you can vastly diminish this uncertainty using a lint tool. Furthermore, JSLint advises us to stay away from certain coding style practices such as using `eval`, leaving variables undeclared, omitting braces in block statements, and so on.

Has your eye caught a potential problem in the last code snippet function we looked at? Check out the accompanying code sample (chapter 1, 01_lint-sample) to verify your answer! Hint: the problem lies in repetition. The fixed version is also found in the source code example; make sure to check out all that good stuff.

Understanding the source code that comes with this book

The source code included with this book has many nuggets of information, including a tweaked version of the linting example function, which passes the lint verification, fully commented to let you understand the changes made to it. The sample also goes on to explain that linters aren't bulletproof.

The other code samples in the book contain similar pieces of advice and nuggets of information, so be sure to check them out! Samples are organized by chapter, and they appear in the same order as in the book. Several examples are only discussed at a glance in the book, but all of the accompanying code samples are fully documented and ready to use.

The reason for this discrepancy between code in the book and the source code is that sometimes I want to explain a topic, but there may be too much code involved to be included in the book. In those cases, I didn't want to drift too much from the concept in question, but still wanted you to have the code. This way you can focus on learning while reading the book, and focus on experimenting when browsing the code samples.

Linting is often referred to as the first test you should set up when writing JavaScript. Where linters fail, unit tests come in. This isn't to say that using linters is unnecessary, but rather, that linting alone is insufficient! Unit testing helps ensure your code behaves the way you expect it to. Unit testing is discussed in chapter 8, where you'll learn how to write tests for the code you develop throughout part 2, which is dedicated to writing modular, maintainable, and testable JavaScript code.

Next up, you'll start putting together a build process from scratch. You'll start small, setting up a task to lint the code, then running it from the command line, similar to how the process looks if you use a compiler; you'll learn to make a habit of running the build every time you make a change and see whether the code still

---

[3] You can see Node.js, a server-side JavaScript platform that also runs on V8, in effect in the console instead, but by the time V8 detects syntax issues, it'll be too late for your program, which will implode. It's always best to lint first, regardless of the platform.

"compiles" against the linter. Chapter 3 teaches you how to have the build run itself, so you don't have to repeat yourself like that, but it'll be fine for the time being.

How can you use a lint tool such as JSLint straight in the command line? Well, I'm glad you asked.

1.5.2 *Lint in the command line*

One of the most common ways to add a task to a build process is to execute that task using a command line. If you execute the task from the command line, it'll be easy to integrate it to your build process. You're going to use JSHint[4] to lint your software.

JSHint is a command line tool that lints JavaScript files and snippets. It's written in Node.js, which is a platform for developing applications using JavaScript. If you need a quick overview of Node.js fundamentals, refer to appendix A, where I explain what modules are and how they work. If you want a deeper analysis of Node.js, refer to *Node.js in Action* by Mike Cantelon et al. (Manning, 2013). Understanding this will also be useful when working with Grunt, our build tool of choice, in the next chapter.

Node.js explained

Node is a relatively new platform you've surely heard of by now. It was initially released in 2009, and it follows event-driven and single-threaded patterns, which translates into high-performing concurrent request handling. In this regard, it's comparable to the design in Nginx, a highly scalable multi-purpose—and very popular—reverse proxy server meant to serve static content and pipe other requests to an application server (such as Node).

Node.js has been praised as particularly easy to adopt by front-end engineers, considering it's merely JavaScript on the server side (for the most part). It also made it possible to abstract the front end from the back end entirely,[a] only interacting through data and REST API interfaces, such as the one you'll learn to design and then build in chapter 9.

---

[a] For more information on abstracting the front end from the back end, see http://bevacqua.io/bf/node-frontend.

NODE.JS AND JSHINT INSTALLATION

Here are the steps for installing Node.js and the JSHint command-line interface (CLI) tool. Alternative Node.js installation methods and troubleshooting are also offered in appendix A.

1 Go to http://nodejs.org, as shown in figure 1.6, and click on the INSTALL button to download the latest version of node.
2 Execute the downloaded file and follow the installation instructions.

---

[4] For more information on JSHint, see http://jshint.com.

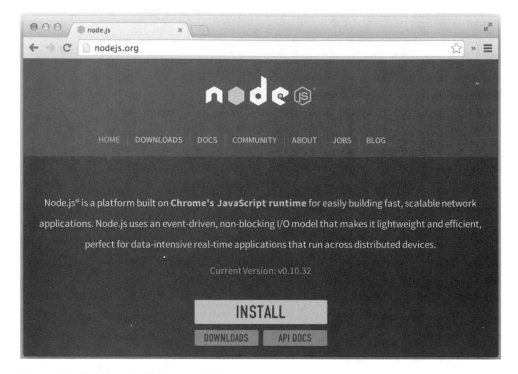

Figure 1.6   The http://nodejs.org website

You'll get a command-line tool called npm (Node Package Manager) for free, as it comes bundled with Node. This package manager, npm, can be used from your terminal to install, publish, and manage modules in your node projects. Packages can be installed on a project-by-project basis or they can be installed globally, making them easier to access directly in the terminal. In reality, the difference between the two is that globally installed packages are put in a folder that's in the PATH environment variable, and those that aren't are put in a folder named node_modules in the same folder you're in when you execute the command. To keep projects self-contained,

```
○ ○ ○   nico@ubuntu: ~

» npm install -g jshint --loglevel warn
/home/nico/.nvm/v0.10.23/bin/jshint -> /home/nico/.nvm/v0.10.23/lib/node_modules/
jshint/bin/jshint
jshint@2.4.0 /home/nico/.nvm/v0.10.23/lib/node_modules/jshint
├── console-browserify@0.1.6
├── underscore@1.4.4
├── shelljs@0.1.4
├── minimatch@0.2.14 (sigmund@1.0.0, lru-cache@2.5.0)
├── htmlparser2@3.3.0 (domelementtype@1.1.1, domutils@1.1.6, domhandler@2.1.0, re
adable-stream@1.0.17)
└── cli@0.4.5 (glob@3.2.7)
»
```

Figure 1.7   Installing jshint through npm

local installs are always preferred. But in the case of utilities such as the JSHint linter, which you want to use system-wide, a global install is more appropriate. The `-g` modifier tells npm to install `jshint` globally. That way, you can use it on the command line as `jshint`.

1 Open your favorite terminal window and execute `npm install -g jshint`, as shown in figure 1.7. If it failed, you may need to use `sudo` to get elevated privileges; for example, `sudo npm install -g jshint`.

2 Run `jshint --version`. It should output the version number for the `jshint` program, as shown in figure 1.8. It'll probably be a different version, as module versions in actively developed packages change frequently.

```
nico@ubuntu: ~

» jshint --version
jshint v2.4.0

»
```

Figure 1.8   Verifying `jshint` works in your terminal

The next section explains how to lint your code.

LINTING YOUR CODE

You should now have `jshint` installed on your system, and accessible in your terminal, as you've verified. To lint your code using JSHint, you can change directories using `cd` to your project root, and then type in `jshint .` (the dot tells JSHint to lint all of the files in the current folder). If the operation is taking too long, you may need to add the `--exclude node_modules` option; this way you'll only lint your own code and ignore third-party code installed via `npm install`.

When the command completes, you'll get a detailed report indicating the status of your code. If your code has any problems, the tool will report the expected result and line number for each of those problems. Then it will exit with an error code, allowing you to "break the build" if the lint fails. Whenever a build task fails to produce the expected output, the entire process should be

```
nico@ubuntu: ~/nico/git/buildfirst/ch01/01_lint-sample
  latest    ~/nico/git/buildfirst/ch01/01_lint-sample
» jshint .
sample.js: line 2, col 18, Bad assignment.
sample.js: line 2, col 18, Expected an assignment or function
call and instead saw an expression.
sample.js: line 2, col 19, Missing semicolon.
sample.js: line 2, col 20, Expected an assignment or function
call and instead saw an expression.
sample.js: line 5, col 18, Missing '()' invoking a constructor

sample.js: line 6, col 41, Missing semicolon.
sample.js: line 7, col 4, Missing semicolon.

sample.jslint.js: line 8, col 3, Possible strict violation.

8 errors
  latest    ~/nico/git/buildfirst/ch01/01_lint-sample
»
```

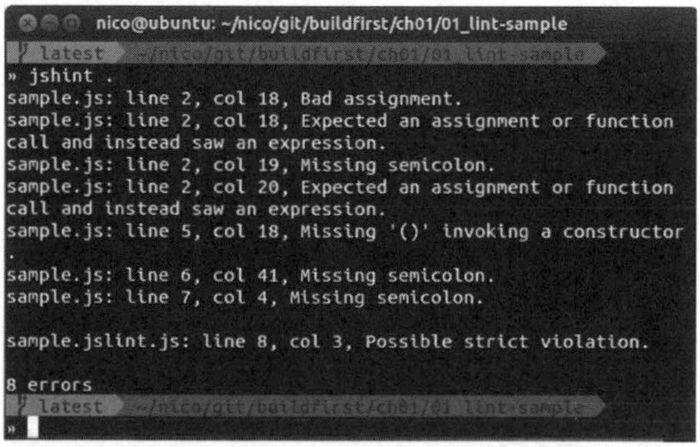

Figure 1.9   Linting with JSHint from your terminal

aborted. This presents a number of benefits because it prevents work from continuing if something goes wrong, refusing to complete a build until you fix any issues. Figure 1.9 shows the results of linting a snippet of code.

Once JSHint is all set, you might be tempted to call it a day, because it's your only task; however, that wouldn't scale up nicely if you want to add extra tasks to your build. You might want to include a unit testing step in your build process; this becomes a problem because you now have to run at least two commands: jshint and another one to execute your tests. That doesn't scale well. Imagine remembering to use jshint and half a dozen other commands complete with their parameters. It would be too cumbersome, hard to remember, and error prone. You wouldn't want to lose half a billion dollars, would you?

Then you better start putting your build tasks together, because even if you only have a single one for now, you'll soon have a dozen! Composing a build process helps you think in terms of automation, and it'll help you save time by avoiding repetition of steps.

Every language has its own set of build tools you can use. Most have a tool that stands out and sees far wider adoption than the rest. When it comes to JavaScript build systems, Grunt is one of the most popular tools, with thousands of plugins (to help you with build tasks) to pick from. If you're writing a build process for another language, you'll probably want to research your own. Even though the build tasks in the book are written in JavaScript and use Grunt, the principles I describe should apply to almost any language and build tool.

Flip over to chapter 2 to see how you can integrate JSHint into Grunt, as you begin your hands-on journey through the land of build processes.

1.6   Summary

This chapter serves as an overview of the concepts you'll dig into throughout the rest of the book. Here are highlights about what you've learned in this chapter:

- Modern JavaScript application development is problematic because of the lack of regard given to design and architecture.
- Build First is a solution that enables automated processes and maintainable application design, and encourages you to think about what you're building.
- You learned about lint and ran code through a linter, improving its code quality without using a browser.
- In part 1 you'll learn all about build processes, deployments, and environment configuration. You'll use Grunt to develop builds, and in appendix C you'll learn about other tools you can use.
- Part 2 is dedicated to complexity in application design. Modularity, asynchronous code flows, application and API design, and testability all have a role to play, and they come together in part 2.

You've barely scratched the surface of what you can achieve using a Build First approach to application design! We have much ground to cover! Let's move to chapter 2, where we'll discuss the most common tasks you might need to perform during a build and go over implementation examples using Grunt.

Composing build
tasks and flows

This chapter covers

- Understanding what should happen in a build
- Learning about key build tasks
- Using Grunt to run key tasks
- Configuring a build flow using Grunt
- Creating your own Grunt tasks

In the previous chapter you got a quick overview of what the Build First approach looks like, and you glanced at a lint task. In this chapter, we'll go over common build tasks and a few more advanced ones. I'll uncover the use cases and reasoning behind each of them, and we'll look at how to implement them in Grunt. Learning the theory might sound dull, but it's particularly important if you use a task runner other than Grunt, as I'm sure you will eventually.

Grunt is a configuration-driven build tool that helps set up complex tasks easily—if you know what you're doing. Using Grunt, you'll compose workflows, such as those I described in chapter 1, which could be tuned for development productivity or optimized for releases. Similarly, Grunt helps with deployment procedures, which you'll analyze in chapter 4.

This chapter focuses on build tasks rather than trying to teach you everything about Grunt. You can always learn to use a new tool, as long as you understand the concepts underlying its goals, but you can't learn to use other tools properly if you don't understand those underlying concepts. If you want a deeper understanding of Grunt itself, check out appendix B. Reading that appendix isn't instrumental to understanding this chapter; however, it does define the Grunt features you'll use throughout part 1.

We'll begin this chapter with a quick introduction to Grunt and its core concepts; then you'll spend the rest of the chapter learning about build tasks and using a few different tools. We'll look at preprocessing (per Manning MOS) tasks such as compiling code into another language, postprocessing (per Manning MOS) tasks such as asset minification and image spriting, and code integrity tasks such as running JavaScript unit tests and linting CSS code. Then you'll learn how to write your own build tasks in Grunt, and you'll look at a case study on writing your own set of database schema update tasks, complete with rollbacks!

Let's get started!

2.1 *Introducing Grunt*

Grunt[1] is a task runner that helps you execute commands, run JavaScript code, and configure different tasks with the configuration written entirely in JavaScript. Grunt borrows its build concepts from Ant, and allows you to define your flows using JavaScript.

Figure 2.1 dissects Grunt at a high level, showing how it can be configured and what the key players are in defining a build task.

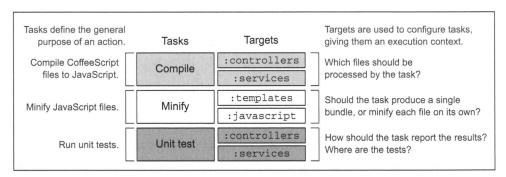

Figure 2.1 Grunt at a glance: tasks and targets are combined in configuration.

- *Tasks* perform an action.
- *Targets* help define a context for those tasks.
- *Task configuration* allows you to determine options for a particular task-target combination.

[1] Learn more about Grunt at http://bevacqua.io/bf/grunt. You should also take a look at appendix B.

Grunt tasks are configured in JavaScript and most of the configuring can be done by passing an object to the `grunt.initConfig` method, describing the files affected by the task, and passing in a few options to tweak the behavior for a particular task target.

In the case of a unit testing task, you might have a target that runs only a few tests for local development, or you may want to execute all the tests you have before a production release.

Figure 2.2 illustrates what task configuration looks like in JavaScript code, detailing the `grunt.initConfig` method and its conventions. Wildcards can be used when enumerating files, and using these patterns is called *globbing*; we'll examine globbing in detail in section 2.2.2.

Tasks can be imported from *plugins*, which are Node modules (well-designed and self-contained pieces of code) containing one or more Grunt tasks. You only need to figure out what configuration to apply to them, and that's it; the task itself is handled by the plugin. You'll use plugins heavily throughout this chapter.[2]

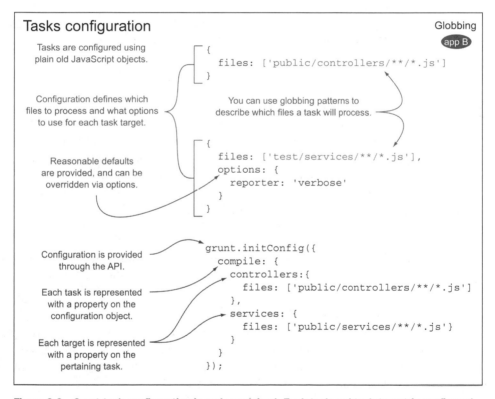

Figure 2.2 Grunt task configuration in code explained. Each task and task target is configured individually.

---

[2] You can search for Grunt plugins online at http://gruntjs.com/plugins.

You can also create your own tasks, as you'll investigate in sections 2.4 and 2.5. Grunt comes with a CLI (command-line interface) named grunt, which provides a simple interface to execute build tasks straight from the command line. Let's install that.

2.1.1 Installing Grunt

You should already have npm, the package manager that comes with Node, from the JSHint lint tool installation in Chapter 1. Getting started with Grunt is simple. Type the following into your terminal, and it will install the grunt[3] CLI for you:

```
npm install -g grunt-cli
```

The -g flag indicates the package should be installed globally; that lets you execute grunt in your terminal, regardless of the current working directory.

> **Find the accompanying annotated samples**
>
> Check out the full working example in the accompanying source code. You'll find it in the 01_intro-to-grunt folder, under the ch02 directory. The rest of the samples for this chapter can also be found in the ch02 directory. Most of them contain code annotations that can help you understand the sample if you're struggling with it.

You'll need to take one additional step, which is creating a package.json manifest file. These files describe Node projects. They indicate a list of packages the project depends upon, as well as metadata such as the project name, version, description, and homepage. For Grunt to work in your project, you need to add it as a development dependency in your package.json. It should be a development dependency because you won't use Grunt anywhere other than your local development environment. You can create a bare minimum package.json file containing the following JSON code, and you should place it in your project root directory:

```
{}
```

That'll be enough. Node Package Manager (npm) can add the dependency to your package.json as long as the file exists and it contains a valid JSON object, even if it's an empty {} object.

INSTALLING GRUNT LOCALLY

Next up, you need to install the grunt package. This time, the -g modifier won't do any good, because it needs to be a local install, not a global one[4]—that's why you created the package.json file. Use the --save-dev modifier instead, to indicate the module is a development dependency.

---

[3] Learn more about Grunt at http://bevacqua.io/bf/grunt.

[4] Grunt requires you to make a local install for the Grunt package and any task plugins. This keeps your code working across different machines, because you can't include global packages in your package.json manifest.

The command looks like this: `npm install --save-dev grunt`. After `npm` completes the installation, your `package.json` manifest will look like the following code:

```
{
  "devDependencies": {
    "grunt": "~0.4.1"
  }
```

In addition, the Grunt module will be installed to a `node_modules` directory inside your project. This directory will contain all the modules you'll use as part of your Grunt setup, and they'll be declared in the package manifest as well.

CREATING A GRUNTFILE.JS

The last step is creating a `Gruntfile.js` file. Grunt uses this file to load any tasks that are available and configure them with any parameters you need. The following code shows the bare minimum `Gruntfile.js` module:

```
module.exports = function (grunt) {
  grunt.registerTask('default', []); // register a default task alias
};
```

Please note a few things about that innocent-looking file. Grunt files are Node modules that subscribe to the CommonJS Modules spec,[5] so the code you write in each file isn't immediately accessible to others. The local `module` object is the implicit object, rather than a global object like `window` in the browser. When you import other modules, all you get is the public interface exposed in `module.exports`.

> **Node modules**
>
> You can learn more about Common.JS, the spec behind Node.js modules, in appendix A, which covers these modules. It will also be discussed in chapter 5, when we talk about modularity. Appendix B expands on appendix A, reinforcing your understanding of Grunt.

The `grunt.registerTask` line, in the previous code snippet, tells Grunt to define a default task that will be executed when you run `grunt` in the command line without any arguments. The array indicates a task alias, which will run all the tasks named in the array, if there are any. For instance, `['lint', 'build']` would run the lint task and then run the build task.

Running the `grunt` command at this point won't achieve anything, because the only task you've registered is an empty task alias. You must be eager to set up your first Grunt task, so let's do that.

---

[5] Read the Common.JS module specification at http://bevacqua.io/bf/commonjs.

2.1.2   *Setting up your first Grunt task*

The first step in setting up a Grunt task is installing a plugin that does what you need; then you add configuration to the code, and you're set up to run the task.

Grunt plugins are usually distributed as npm modules, which are pieces of Java-Script code someone published so you can use them. We'll start by installing the JSHint plugin for Grunt, which will allow you to run JSHint using Grunt. Note that the jshint CLI tool you installed in chapter 1 is completely unnecessary here; the Grunt plugin contains everything you need to run the task without the jshint CLI. The command shown below will fetch the JSHint Grunt plugin from the npm registry, install it to the node_modules directory, and add it to your package.json file as a development dependency:

```
npm install --save-dev grunt-contrib-jshint
```

Next you need to tweak your Gruntfile, telling Grunt to lint the Gruntfile itself, because it's JavaScript. You also need to tell it to load the JSHint plugin package, which contains the task that sets up the linting, and update your default task, so you can lint your code using grunt in your command line. The following listing (named ch02/01_intro-to-grunt in the code samples) shows how you can configure your Gruntfile.

Listing 2.1   Example Gruntfile.js

```
                                             ⟵ Exported function gets a grunt argument.
module.exports = function (grunt) {
    grunt.initConfig({                        ⟵ Tasks are configured using initConfig,
        jshint: ['Gruntfile.js']                passing an object that describes them.
    });
    grunt.loadNpmTasks('grunt-contrib-jshint');
    grunt.registerTask('default', ['jshint']);   ⟵ Create a default alias, which
};                                                  will run the jshint task.
```

Plugins need to be loaded individually into Grunt.

Whenever you install a package, you'll need to load it in the Gruntfile, using grunt.loadNpmTasks, as in listing 2.1. It'll load the tasks in the package so you can configure and execute them. Then you need to configure the tasks, which can be done by passing an object to grunt.initConfig. Each task plugin you use needs configuration, and I'll teach you how to configure each one as we go through them. Lastly, I've updated the default alias to run the jshint task. The default alias defines what tasks are executed when grunt is executed without task arguments. Here's a screenshot of the output.

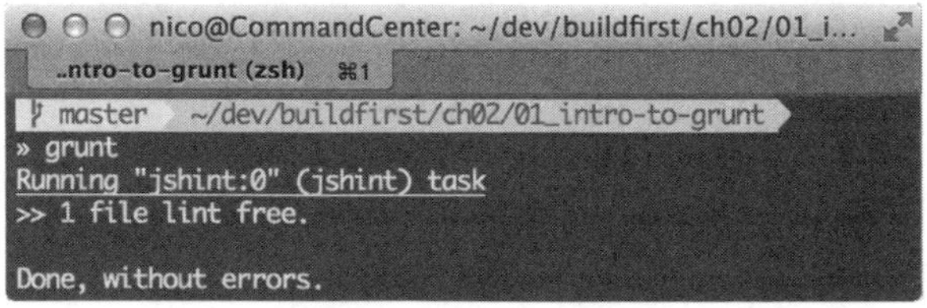

Figure 2.3   **Our first Grunt task and its output. Our code is lint-free, meaning it doesn't contain any syntax errors.**

2.1.3   *Using Grunt to manage the build process*

You're pretty much in the same position as you were at the end of chapter 1, where you could lint your JavaScript, except that you're not. Grunt will help you put together the full-blown build process that's at the heart of the Build First philosophy. With relative ease, you can focus on different tasks, depending on whether you're building for local development or diagnostics, or building the end product humans will ultimately consume. Let's examine a few properties found in build tasks.

The lint task you set up will serve as the basis for a much more powerful build, as you expand your understanding throughout part 1 of the book. This task innocently shows off one of the fundamental properties of build tasks: in the vast majority of cases, they'll be *idempotent*—repeated execution of a task shouldn't produce different results. In the case of the lint task, that might mean getting the same warnings every time, as long as you don't change the source code. More often than not, build tasks are a function of one or many provided input files. The idempotence property, when paired with the fact that you shouldn't perform any operations by hand, translates into more consistent results.

CREATING WORKFLOWS AND CONTINUOUS DEVELOPMENT

Tasks in your build are meant to follow a clearly defined set of steps to achieve a specific goal, such as preparing a release build. This is called a workflow, as mentioned in chapter 1. Certain tasks may be optional for a particular workflow, while others might be instrumental. For instance, you have no incentive to optimize images, so they become smaller when working in your local development environment. Because it won't yield any noticeable performance gains, it's perfectly fine to skip that task in that case. Regardless of whether your workflow is meant for development or release, you'll probably want to make sure to look out for issues with a lint task.

Figure 2.4 will help you understand the development, release, and deployment pieces involved in a build process: how they relate to each other, and how they come together when composing different workflows.

DEVELOPMENT FLOW

With only a glance at the top row of the figure, you can already see that productivity and watching for changes are the key aspects of a development flow, while they're completely unnecessary during the release flow, and perhaps even an obstacle. You may also notice that both flows produce a built application, although the one built during development is geared towards continuous development, as we'll examine in depth in chapter 3.

RELEASE FLOW

In the release flow, we're concerned with performance optimization and building a well-tested application overall. Here we'll run a slightly modified version of the development flow, where reducing the byte size of our application is at a premium.

DEPLOYMENT FLOW

The deployment flow doesn't build the application at all. Instead, it reuses the build distribution prepared in one of the other two flows, and delivers it to a hosting environment. You'll learn all about the deployment flow in chapter 4.

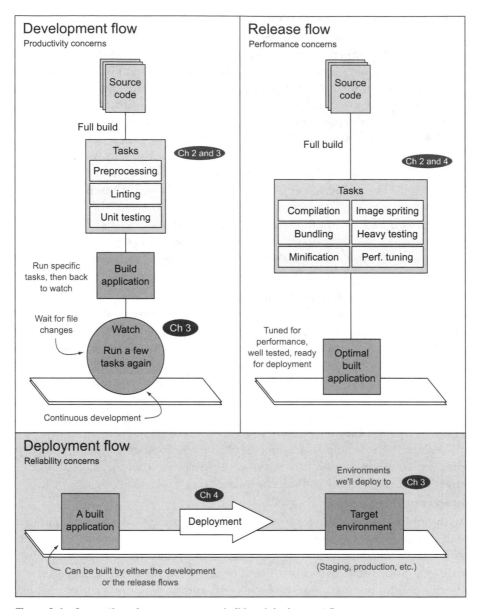

Figure 2.4   Separation of concerns across build and deployment flows

Any reasonable build flow needs to be automated every step of the way; otherwise you won't meet the goal of increasing productivity and reducing error proclivity. During development, you should switch between your text editor and your browser, without having to execute a build by yourself. This is called *continuous development*, because the friction introduced by going into the shell and typing something to compile your application is removed. You'll learn how to accomplish this using file watches and other mechanisms in chapter 3. Deploying the application should be separate from the build flow, but it should also be automated; this enables you to build and deploy the application in a single step. Similarly, serving your application should be strictly separate from the build process.

In the next section, we'll dive head first into build tasks using Grunt. Namely, we'll start with preprocessing tasks such as taking LESS, a language that can be compiled into CSS, and postprocessing tasks, such as bundling and minifying, which help you optimize and fine-tune for releases.

2.2 Preprocessing and static asset optimization

Whenever we talk about building a web application, we need to talk about preprocessing. Often, you'll find yourself using languages that aren't natively supported by internet browsers because they help you wrap away repetitive work by providing features not available to plain CSS (such as vendor prefixing), HTML, or JavaScript.

The point here isn't for you to learn LESS, a CSS preprocessor introduced in the following section, or even to learn CSS. Great resources are tailored to teach you that. The point is to make you aware of the glaring benefits of resorting to preprocessing languages. Preprocessing isn't about CSS. *Preprocessors* help transform source code in a language into various target languages. For instance, the more powerful and expressive LESS language can be transformed into native CSS at build time. Reasons to use preprocessors may vary, but they can be categorized as more productivity, less repetition, or having a more pleasant syntax.

Postprocessing tasks such as minification and bundling are mostly meant to optimize a build for release purposes, but they're related to preprocessing closely enough that they all belong in the same conversation. We'll go over preprocessing, using LESS, and then we'll dabble with globbing, a file path pattern-matching mechanism used in Grunt, before we move on to bundling and minification, which will tune your application's performance for adequate human consumption.

By the end of the section you'll have a much clearer picture of how assets can be preprocessed by using a different, more suitable language, and how they can be postprocessed, improving the performance to make the experience easier on humans.

2.2.1 Discussing preprocessing

Language preprocessors are fairly common in web development nowadays. Unless you've been living under a rock for the last decade, you probably understand that preprocessors help you write cleaner code, as you first learned with lint in chapter 1, but require extra work to become useful. Plainly put, when you write code in a language that translates into another one, *preprocessing* is the translation step.

You might not want to write code in the target language for several reasons: maybe it's too repetitive, too error-prone, or you just don't like that language. That's where these higher-level languages, tuned to keeping your code concise and simple, come into play. Writing code in one of these higher-level languages comes at a price, though: browsers don't understand them. Therefore, one of the most common build tasks you'll encounter in front-end development is compiling that code down into something a browser understands, namely JavaScript and CSS styles.

Sometimes, preprocessors also offer practical benefits over the "native" languages of the web (HTML, CSS, and JavaScript). For example, several CSS preprocessors provide the necessary tools so you don't need to target each browser. By removing these browser inconsistencies, preprocessing languages increase your productivity and make it less tedious to do your job.

LESS IS MORE

Take LESS, for example. LESS is a powerful language that allows you to write code using a variant on CSS that follows the DRY (Don't Repeat Yourself) principle of application design, because it helps you write code that's less repetitive. In plain CSS, you often end up repeating yourself again and again, writing the same value for all the different vendor prefixes out there to maximize browser support of a style rule you want to apply.

To illustrate the point, take the `border-radius` CSS property, used whenever you want to style an element with rounded borders. The following listing is how you might write them using plain CSS.

Listing 2.2   Rounded borders in plain CSS

```
.slightly-rounded {
 -webkit-border-radius: 2px;            Certain browsers require "vendor
 -moz-border-radius: 2px;               prefixes" to apply certain styles.
 border-radius: 2px;
 background-clip: padding-box;          Helps prevent the background from
}                                       leaking outside rounded borders
.very-rounded {
 -webkit-border-radius: 16px;
 -moz-border-radius: 16px;              The issue only worsens as
 border-radius: 16px;                   you factor in more stylings.
 background-clip: padding-box;
}
```

That might be fine for a one-time rule, but for properties such as `border-radius`, it quickly becomes unacceptable to write such plain CSS, because this scenario occurs too often. LESS allows you to code in a way that's easier to write, read, and maintain. In this use case, you can set up a `.border-radius` reusable function, and the code becomes something like the following listing.

Listing 2.3   Rounded borders using LESS

```
.border-radius (@value) {              This is a reusable function,
 -webkit-border-radius: @value;        or a "mixin," in LESS slang.
 -moz-border-radius: @value;
 border-radius: @value;
 background-clip: padding-box;
}
```

```
.slightly-rounded {
  .border-radius(2px);
}
.very-rounded {
  .border-radius(16px);
}
```

◁— **Use the function passing the radius value.**

◁— **Use the function again to set the border-radius multiple times.**

LESS and similar tools boost your productivity by allowing you to reuse snippets of CSS code.

LESS DRY IS BETTER THAN MORE WET

As soon as you need to use the `border-radius` property in more than one place, you'll reap the benefits of not writing everything twice (WET). By following the DRY principle, you avoid listing all four properties any time you need to specify a border. Instead, you can declare a border by reusing the `.border-radius` LESS mixin.

Preprocessing plays a key role in a lean development workflow: now you don't have to use all the vendor prefixes everywhere you want to use this rule, and you can update the prefixes in a single place, making your code more maintainable. LESS enables you to take this even further, if you want to cleanly separate static rules from the variables that affect them. Without LESS, a typical CSS design style sheet excerpt might look like the following code:

```
a {
  background-color: #FFC;
}
blockquote {
  background-color: #333;
  color: #FFC;
}
```

LESS allows you to use variables so you don't have to copy and paste colors everywhere. Properly naming these variables also helps you to easily identify the colors by scanning the style sheet.

USING LESS VARIABLES

Using LESS, you could set up variables for the colors and avoid potential mistakes such as updating a color in one place but forgetting to update other occurrences. This also enables you to keep colors and other variable elements of your design together. The following code shows how it might look using LESS:

```
@yellowish: #FFC;
a {
  background-color: @yellowish;
}
blockquote {
  background-color: #333;
  color: @yellowish;
}
```

◁— **Declaring variables helps locate and replace colors, preventing mistakes.**

Using a variable is as simple as referencing it.

This way you can keep your code DRY, as I mentioned at the beginning of section 2.2. Following the Don't Repeat Yourself principle here is particularly useful because you avoid copying and pasting color codes, and that saves you the potential trouble of mistyping one. In addition, languages such as LESS (SASS, Stylus, and so on) provide functions to derive other colors, such as a darker green, a more transparent white, and other amusing color math.

Now, let's turn our attention to compiling the LESS code into CSS within a Grunt task.

2.2.2 *Doing LESS*

As we discussed earlier in the chapter, Grunt tasks consist of two different components—the task and the configuration:

- The *task* itself is the single most important component: this is the code that will be executed by Grunt when you run a build, and generally you can find a plugin that does what you need.
- The *configuration* is an object you can pass to `grunt.initConfig`. Almost every Grunt task needs configuration.

As you progress through the rest of this chapter, you'll see how to set up the configuration in each case. To compile LESS files with Grunt so you can serve CSS directly, you're going to use the `grunt-contrib-less` package. Remember when you installed the JSHint plugin? Same thing here! Only the package name changes, because you're going to use a different plugin now. To install it, run the following in your terminal:

```
npm install grunt-contrib-less --save-dev
```

This plugin provides a task named `less`, and you can load it in your `Gruntfile.js` like so:

```
grunt.loadNpmTasks('grunt-contrib-less');
```

From now on, I'll omit the `npm install` and `grunt.loadNpmTasks` bits in the examples, for brevity. You still need to run `npm install` to fetch the packages and load the plugins in your Gruntfiles! In any case, you can look for the full examples for each case in the accompanying source code files.

Setting up the build task is straightforward: you specify the output filename and provide it with the path to the source used to generate your CSS file. This example can be found as ch02/02_less-task in the code samples.

```
grunt.initConfig({
  less: {
    compile: {
      files: {
        'build/css/compiled.css': 'public/css/layout.less'
      }
    }
  }
});
```

The last piece of the puzzle for executing a task is invoking `grunt` from the command line. In this case, `grunt less` in your terminal should do the trick. Explicitly declaring a target is usually recommended. In this case, you could do that by typing `grunt less:compile`. If you don't provide a target name, all targets get executed.

Consistency in grunt configuration

Before we go any further, I want to mention a nicety you'll enjoy as part of using Grunt. Task configuration patterns don't vary all that much when jumping from task to task, particularly when using tasks supported by the Grunt team itself. Even those you might find on `npm` are pretty consistent with each other, as far as configuration goes. As you'll learn throughout the chapter, the different tasks I'll show you are configured similarly, even if they provide a wide array of operations in a versatile way.

Running the `less:compile` build target in Grunt will now compile `layout.less` into `compiled.css`. You could also declare an array of input files, rather than using only one. This will result in a bundled file, which will contain the CSS for all of the LESS input files. We'll cover bundling in full later on; bear with me. The following listing is an example.

Listing 2.4 Declaring an array of input files

```
grunt.initConfig({
  less: {
    compile: {
      files: {
        'build/css/compiled.css': [
          'public/css/layout.less',
          'public/css/components.less',
          'public/css/views/foo.less',
          'public/css/views/bar.less'
        ]
      }
    }
  }
});
```

Listing each file individually is okay, but you could also use a pattern language called globbing and avoid enumerating hundreds of files, as I'll explain next.

MASTERING GLOBBING PATTERNS

You could further improve the configuration shown in the previous code with a nice perk of using Grunt that's called globbing. *Globbing*[6] is a file path matching mechanism that will help you include or exclude files using file path patterns. It's particularly useful because you don't have to maintain a list of all the files in your assets folder, which helps you avoid common mistakes such as forgetting to add a new style sheet to the list.

---

[6] The Grunt website has valuable insight into how globbing works. Go to http://bevacqua.io/bf/globbing.

Globbing might also come in handy if you want to exclude individual files from a build task, such as those provided by a third party. The following code shows a few globbing patterns you might find useful:

```
[
 'public/*.less',
 'public/**/*.less',
 '!public/vendor/**/*.less'
]
```

Note the following about the previous code:

- The first pattern will match any file with a LESS extension in the `public` folder.
- The second pattern does much the same, except that it matches files that might be in subfolders of `public` of any nesting level thanks to the special `**` pattern.
- As you might've guessed, the last pattern works the same way as the second one does, except that the `!` at the beginning indicates that matched files should be excluded from the results.

Globbing patterns work in the order they're presented, and they can be mixed with regular file paths too. Globbing patterns will result in arrays containing the path for all matching files.

Taking globbing patterns into consideration, our latest `less:compile` configuration might be refactored a little further, becoming a simplified version:

```
grunt.initConfig({
  less: {
    compile: {
      files: {
        'build/css/compiled.css': 'public/css/**/*.less'
      }
    }
  }
});
```

Before moving on, let me remind you that in this particular case `less` is the build task and `compile` is a build target for that task, which offers configuration specific to that target. You could easily provide different targets for the `less` task by adding other properties to the `less` object, like you did in the `compile` task target in the configuration you're handing over to `initConfig`. For instance, you could have a `compile_mobile` target which would create the CSS assets targeting mobile devices, and a `compile_desktop` target that would compile assets targeting desktop browsers.

It should be noted that as a side effect of using a globbing pattern to compile LESS using this task, your CSS will be bundled into a single file, regardless of how many files are used in the source code. So, let's look into asset bundling now, a postprocessing task that will help you improve a site's performance by reducing the amount of HTTP requests against it.

2.2.3   *Bundling static assets*

I've hinted at what bundling accomplishes, and you might've heard about it before embarking on this enlightening adventure of ours. It's okay if you've never heard of bundling before; it's not a hard concept to wrap your head around.

Asset bundling is a fancy name for putting everything together before you hand it over to your clients. It's like the difference between going to the store for a single grocery item and coming back home, only to go back to the grocery store to get another item on the list again and again, and going to the grocery store once and buying all of your groceries at one time.

Handing over everything in a single HTTP response reduces transactional network costs and benefits everyone. The payload might become larger, but it saves clients many unnecessary network trips to your server, which incur associated networking costs such as latency, the TCP and TLS handshakes, and so on. If you'd like to learn more about the underlying internet protocols (TCP, TLS, UDP, HTTP, and so on), I highly recommend *High Performance Browser Networking* by Ilya Grigorik (O'Reilly Media, 2013).

In so many words, then, asset bundling consists of literally appending each of your files at the end of the previous one. In this way, you might bundle together all of your CSS or all of your JavaScript. Fewer HTTP requests yields better performance, and that's reason enough to warrant a static asset bundling build step. Figure 2.5 examines the

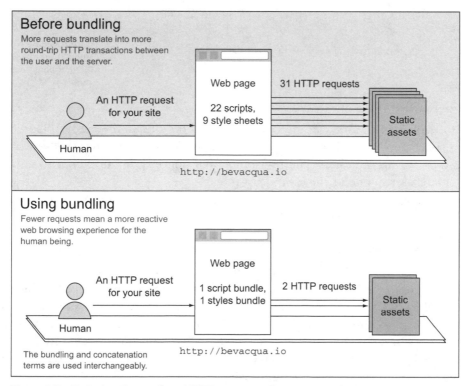

Figure 2.5   Reducing the number of HTTP requests with asset bundling

interaction between a human and a site that uses a bundle, and one that doesn't, and how each affects network connections.

As shown in the figure, before bundling the browser has to make many more HTTP requests to fetch a site's resources, while after bundling only a single request suffices to fetch every bundle (containing the many different files that make up your application's logic).

Many preprocessors include the option to bundle your assets together in a single file, and you already experienced that in the demonstration of `less:compile`, where you bundled many assets into one.

BUNDLING IN THE WILD

Using the `grunt-contrib-concat` package, you can easily set up build targets to put together any number of files using the globbing patterns I described previously, and in a fashion that you might already be comfortable with. Throughout the book, the terms concatenation and bundling are used interchangeably. The following listing (listed as ch02/03_bundle-task in the accompanying code samples) describes how to configure the `concat` task.

Listing 2.5   Configuring the concatenation task

```
grunt.initConfig({                    concat property indicates you're
  concat: {                           configuring the concat task.
    js: {          #B
      files: {
        'build/js/bundle.js': 'public/js/**/*.js'      Output will be written to
      }                                                'build/js/bundle.js', taking
    }                                                  the globbing pattern
  }                                                    'public/js/**/*.js' as source.
});
```

Inside the concat object, each property indicates configuration for a task target.

Unsurprisingly, the `concat:js` task will take all the files in the `public/js` folder (and its subfolders, recursively) and bundle them together, writing the results to `build/js/bundle.js`, as indicated. The transition from one task to another is so natural that sometimes you won't believe how easy it is.

One more thing to keep in mind when dealing with static assets during builds is minification. Let's move onto that topic.

2.2.4   *Static asset minification*

Minification resembles concatenation in that it ultimately attempts to reduce the strain on network connections, but it applies a different approach. Rather than mashing all the files together, minifying consists of removing white space, shortening variable names, and optimizing the syntax tree of your code to produce a file which, while functionally equivalent to what you wrote, will be significantly smaller in file size at the cost of becoming nearly unreadable. This shrinking caters to your goal of improving performance, as explained in figure 2.6.

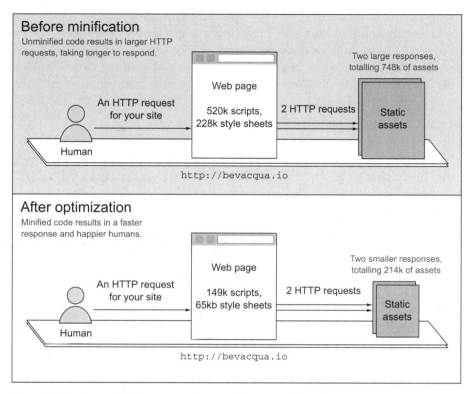

Figure 2.6   Reducing HTTP response length with asset minification

As you can see in the figure, the minified version of your static assets is much smaller, resulting in faster downloads. When combined with GZip[7] compression on your server-side platform of choice, the minified bundle becomes drastically smaller than the source code.

The obfuscation side effect might make you feel like it's "safe enough" for you to put anything in your JavaScript code, since it will become harder to read, but it won't matter how much you obfuscate your client-side code; people can always decode what you're doing in it if they try hard enough. The corollary is to never trust clients and always put sensitive code in your back end instead.

Bundling can be combined with minification, as they're completely *orthogonal* (meaning they don't run into each other). One puts files together and the other reduces each file's footprint, but these tasks play well together because they don't overlap in functionality.

Bundling and minification can also be performed in either order, and the result will be pretty much the same: a single, compressed file best suited for release and

---

[7]   Visit http://bevacqua.io/bf/gzip for more information on enabling GZip compression on your favorite back-end server.

hardly useful to your development efforts. While minification and bundling are undoubtedly important for your human-facing application, they get in the way of the productive, continuous development approach we strive for in our daily development flow, because they make debugging harder. That's why it's important you keep these tasks clearly separated in your build process, so that you can execute them in the appropriate environment without hindering your development productivity.

REVIEWING AN ASSET MINIFICATION EXAMPLE

Let's get into an asset minification example (labeled ch02/04_minify-task in the samples), which you could then serve to real humans. Many asset minification options exist. In your example, you'll use the `grunt-contrib-uglify` package meant to minify JavaScript files. After installing it from npm and loading the plugin, you can set it up as shown in the following listing.

Listing 2.6   Asset minification configuration

The uglify property indicates you're configuring the uglify task.

Inside the uglify object, each property indicates configuration for a task target.

```
grunt.initConfig({
  uglify: {
    cobra: {
      files: {
        'build/js/cobra.min.js': 'public/js/cobra.js'
      }
    }
  }
});
```

Output is written to 'build/js/cobra.min.js', using 'public/js/cobra.js' as source.

That setup will help minify `cobra.js`, doing `grunt uglify:cobra`. What if you want to minify what you bundled together in the previous step, further improving the performance of your application? That's a matter of taking the concatenated file created in listing 2.6 and minifying it, as shown in the following listing (labeled ch02/05_bundle-then-minify in the samples).

Listing 2.7   Asset minification after bundling

The uglify property indicates you're configuring the uglify task.

Inside the uglify object, each property indicates configuration for a task target.

```
grunt.initConfig({
  uglify: {#A
    bundle: {
      files: {
        'build/js/bundle.min.js': 'build/js/bundle.js'
      }
    }
  }
});
```

Output is written to 'build/js/bundle.min.js', using the bundle built by concat:js as source.

Putting those two steps together is a matter of running both tasks in sequence. For that purpose, you might use the `grunt` command `grunt concat:js uglify:bundle`, but this also might be an ideal scenario in which to introduce task aliases.

A *task alias* is a group of any number of tasks that are often executed as part of the same step and that are related to each other. Tasks in an alias should preferably depend on each other to produce a more meaningful output, as this would make them easier to follow and more semantic. Task aliases are also great for declaring workflows.

In Grunt, you can set up task aliases easily in one line, as I'll demonstrate below. You can also provide an optional description argument; this will be displayed when executing `grunt --help`, but it's mostly helpful for describing why that alias was put together, for developers browsing your code:

```
grunt.registerTask('js', 'Concatenate and minify static JavaScript assets',
    ['concat:js', 'uglify:bundle']);
```

Now you can treat `assets` as any other Grunt task, and `grunt assets` will perform both concatenation and minification.

I have a bonus task you can implement on your static asset during builds to improve your application's performance. It's similar in spirit to bundling, but it covers images. This operation results in sprite maps and is a concept that's been around for far longer than minifying or concatenation.

2.2.5 *Implementing image sprites*

Sprites consist of taking many images and building a large file that contains all of them. Instead of referencing each individual file, you use the `background-position`, `width`, and `height` CSS properties to choose the image you want from the sprite. Think of image sprites as asset bundling but for images.

Spriting is a technique that originated in game development many years ago, and it's still used today. Many graphics get crammed into a single image, significantly improving the performance of games. In the web realm, spriting is most useful for iconography or any kind of small images.

Maintaining the spritesheet and the CSS that goes with it by yourself is work. Particularly if you're cutting and pasting, keeping your icons and the spritesheet in sync is tedious. That's where Grunt comes in as the knight in shining armor, ready to save the day. When it comes to setting up image sprites, npm has options ready for you to start automating your CSS spritesheet generation processes. For the purposes of this self-contained example, I'll refer to the `grunt-spritesmith` Grunt plugin. If you have issues installing the plugin, refer to the code samples for troubleshooting. Its configuration is similar to what you're already accustomed to:

```
grunt.initConfig({
  sprite: {
    icons: {
      src: 'public/img/icons/*.png',
      destImg: 'build/img/icons.png',
      destCSS: 'build/css/icons.css'
    }
  }
});
```

By now, you can safely assume that the `src` property takes any kind of glob patterns. The `destImg` and `destCSS` properties will map to the files where your spritesheet will be generated, along with the CSS file that should be used to render the sprited images in your HTML. Once you have both the CSS and your newly created spritesheet, you can add icons to your site simply by creating HTML elements and assigning the different sprite CSS classes to those elements. CSS is used to "crop" different parts of the image, effectively taking only the relevant portion of the image used for the desired icon.

Perceived performance on the web

I can't stress enough how important a role asset bundling, minification, and even spriting play when it comes to release builds. Images typically make up most of the footprint for web applications today. Reducing the number of requests to your server using these techniques provides you with an immediate performance boost that doesn't require more expensive hardware. A similar case can be made for reducing the byte size of the responses by minifying and/or compressing them.

SPEED MATTERS

Speed is a fundamental, defining factor of the web. Responsiveness, or at least *perceived* responsiveness, has a tremendous impact on the user experience (UX). Perceived responsiveness is now more important than ever; this is what the user perceives as speed, even though technically it might take even longer to fulfill a request. As long as you display immediate feedback for their actions, users will perceive your application as "faster." This is what you see every day on Facebook or Twitter when you submit a new post, and it's immediately added to the list, even though its data is still being sent to their servers.

Numerous experiments have demonstrated how important it is to provide swift and reliable services. Two experiments in particular, performed by Google and Amazon, respectively, come to mind.

In 2006, Marissa Mayer was Google's vice president for UX. She ran an experiment after collecting feedback from a group of users who wanted to see more results per page in their searches. The experiment increased the number to 30 search results per page. Traffic and revenue from customers in the experimental group who got more results per page dropped by 20%.

Marissa explained that they found an uncontrolled variable. The page with 10 results took .4 seconds to generate. The page with 30 results took .9 seconds. Half a second delay caused a 20% drop in traffic. Half a second delay killed user satisfaction.[8]

Amazon conducted a similar experiment, progressively delaying their website's responsiveness on purpose during split tests. Even the slightest delay resulted in significant drops in sales.

[8] You can find a detailed article about the subject here: http://bevacqua.io/bf/speed-matters.

JUDGING PERCEIVED RESPONSIVENESS VS. ACTUAL SPEED
On the opposite end of the spectrum, we meet perceived speed. You can increase perceived speed by providing instant feedback (as if the action was successful) to user interaction, even when the task itself might take a few seconds to process. This kind of fast-forwarding is always well received by humans.

Now that we've talked about speeding up network access to your assets, and the build tasks relevant to compiling these assets, as well as the performance implications of different approaches and techniques, let's slow down for a minute and start talking code quality. Until now, we've paid only a little attention to the quality of your code, so let's turn to the kind of tasks you should perform in that regard. You have a good idea what preprocessing and post-processing tasks are, how they work, and how to apply them.

We first talked about code quality in chapter 1, when you integrated lint into your build. Cleaning up after yourself is important if you want to preserve the idempotence property. Similarly, linting your code and running tests are paramount for keeping your code quality standards high.

Now, let's go a little deeper and find out how to better integrate these tasks into a real build process.

2.3 *Setting up code integrity*

Keep in mind a few tasks when it comes to code integrity:

- First and foremost, we should talk about cleaning up after ourselves. Whenever our builds start, they should clean up the build artifacts they generate. This helps us achieve idempotency, where executing a build many times always results in the same output.
- We'll go over lint again, adding to what we explored near the end of chapter 1, making sure that our code doesn't contain any syntax errors whenever we run a build.
- We'll talk briefly about setting up a test runner so that you can automate code tests, which we'll go over in future chapters.

2.3.1 *Cleaning up your working directory*

After you're done with a build, your *working directory* will generally be in a dirty state, because you'll have generated content that's not part of your source code. You want to make sure your working directory is always in the same state whenever you run a build, so you get the same results every time. To ensure this, it's generally good practice to clean up generated files before running any other tasks.

> **WORKING DIRECTORY**   Working directory is fancy talk for the root directory for your code base during development. It's often best to use a subdirectory to aggregate the compiled results of your builds, such as a directory named `build`. This helps you keep your source code cleanly separated from build artifacts.

After your release, your servers will use the results of your build, and you shouldn't change its output except by performing another release. Running build tasks after the deployment is complete would be as bad as manually executing those tasks, as you'd reintroduce the human factor. As a general rule, if something doesn't feel clean, it probably isn't clean enough and should be revised.

> **Isolating build output**
>
> While we're on the topic of code integrity, I believe it's important to highlight something that you might've noticed from the examples I've presented so far. I strongly recommend you follow the practice of strictly separating build-generated content from source code. It's sufficient to put generated content in a `build` directory. Benefits include the ability to remove generated content without hesitation, the ability to easily ignore the folder with globbing patterns, browsing generated content in one place, and perhaps even more importantly, making sure you don't accidentally delete source code.

Tasks that generate content but clean up preexisting build artifacts whenever they're run are happily idempotent: running them infinite times doesn't affect their behavior; the result is always the same. The cleanup step is a required property for build tasks to become idempotent, granting them the consistency of always producing the same output. That being said, let's see what the cleanup task configuration might look like in Grunt. You'll use the `grunt-contrib-clean` package, which provides a `clean` task you can use. This task (available as ch02/07_clean-task in the samples) is as simple as it gets: you provide target names, and then you can remove specific files or entire folders that you specify using a globbing pattern. See the following code for an example:

```
grunt.initConfig({
  clean: {
    js: 'build/js',            Removing generated content can be
    css: 'build/css',          as easy as deleting a directory.
    less: 'public/**/*.css'    It can also be as hard as deleting
  }                            specific files, if source and
});                           destination are mixed together.
```

The first two, `build/js` and `build/css`, show how simple it can be to pick generated content and remove it, as long as it's clearly separated from source code. On the other hand, the third example shows how messy it becomes when the source code lives in the same directory as the build-generated content. Furthermore, if you isolate your generated content to one folder, then you could easily exclude that folder from your version control system more conveniently.

2.3.2 *Lint, lint, lint!*

We already went over the benefits of linting in the previous chapter, but let's look at the configuration for your lint task again. Keep in mind you were using the `grunt-contrib-jshint` package here. You can configure it as shown in the following code (sample ch02/08_lint-task):

```
grunt.initConfig({
  jshint: {
    client: [
      'public/js/**/*.js',
      '!public/js/vendor'
    ]
  }
});
```

It's important to consider third-party (someone else's) code as outside of our efforts' reach. You wouldn't unit test third-party code. Similarly, it's not your job to lint their code, either. If you weren't putting generated content in a separate folder, you'd also have to exclude it from your JSHint profile. That's yet another benefit of strictly separating build artifacts from the general population (your source files).

Lint is often considered the first line of defense when it comes to maintaining a reasonable level of code quality in JavaScript. You should still write unit tests on top of what lint is capable of for reasons I'll explain below, and you guessed it, there's a task for that.

2.3.3 *Automating unit testing*

One of the most important steps to automate during build is unit testing. Unit tests make sure the individual components in your code base work appropriately. A popular flow for developing an application that's well tested is the following:

- Write tests for something you want to implement (or change).
- Run those tests and see them fail.
- Implement your changes to the code.
- Run the tests again.

If a test failed, keep coding until all tests pass, and finally go back to write new tests. This process is called *Test-Driven Development* (TDD). We'll go deeper into unit testing in chapter 8. This is a topic that warrants a more dedicated section, so we'll postpone the discussion of setting up the Grunt task to run unit tests.

The key takeaway for now is that unit tests must be automated. Tests that aren't run often are nearly useless, so the build process should trigger them before deploys and probably during your local builds, too. Taking that into account, you'll also want your unit tests to run as quickly as possible, so they don't cripple the performance of your builds. A commonly cited principle is "Test early; test often."

NOTE The different packages we've seen so far only expose a single Grunt task you can use, but that's not a constraint Grunt itself imposes. You can include as many custom tasks in your packages as you deem necessary. This is usually done by package authors on purpose. npm packages are commonly modular in their design, because they're designed to do exactly one thing extremely well.

You've spent most of this chapter learning how to use build tasks that other people wrote. Let's turn our attention to writing your own build tasks, which comes in handy whenever the existing task plugins you find on npm don't satisfy your needs.

2.4   *Writing your first build task*

Even though Grunt has an active community around it that provides many high-quality npm modules, you'll certainly come across the need to write your own tasks. Let's go over how that process looks, using an example. We've covered tasks loaded from npm and setting up task aliases. The simplest way to create a task is using the `grunt.registerTask` method. Indeed, that's the same method you used to register aliases in section 2.2.4 when we looked at minification, but instead of passing in a list of tasks that compose your task, you'll pass in a function instead.

The following listing (which can be found as ch02/09_timestamp-task in the samples) shows how to create a simple build task that creates a file with a timestamp, which you could then use as a unique identifier somewhere else in the application.

> **Listing 2.8   A time-stamping task**

```
grunt.registerTask('timestamp', function() {
  var options = this.options({              Take configuration and provide
    file: '.timestamp'                       sensible default values in case
  });                                        they're not configured.
  var timestamp = +new Date();
  var contents = timestamp.toString();      Cast date into a UNIX timestamp.

  grunt.file.write(options.file, contents);   Create a file in the location provided
});                                           by the task configuration.
```

By default, the timestamp will be created in a file named `.timestamp`; however, because you're using `this.options`, users can change that to use another file name by providing one when configuring the task, as shown in the following code:

```
grunt.initConfig({
  timestamp: {
    options: {
      file: 'your/file/path'
    }
  }
});
```

In essence, this is the only requirement to write custom build tasks. Grunt has an extensive API that abstracts away common functionality, enabling you to easily address configuration, perform I/O operations, execute tasks, and perform tasks asynchronously. Luckily, the API is well documented, so check it out on their website.[9]

For an all-encompassing analysis of Grunt, head to appendix B. The `timestamp` task was mightily trivial. Let's look at a real Grunt task you might want to implement.

---

[9] You can find Grunt's documentation at http://bevacqua.io/bf/grunt.

2.5 *Case study: database tasks*

As you've seen, developing your own build tasks isn't that complicated; however, it's important to identify whether a task has already been developed for your task runner of choice (Grunt in our case) before setting out to reinvent the wheel all by yourself! Most task runners offer some sort of search engine for plugins, so be sure to look online before sitting down to write your own tasks. Now, let's look at the case of database schema updates and how you can help automate them in a build. There aren't many plugins out there that do this specific sort of thing, so we're better off developing our own.

Database case study code

Note that the code for this particular case hasn't been included in the text of the book. Instead, you'll find a fully working example in the accompanying code listings, labeled ch02/10_mysql-tasks.[a]

Before you look at the code, read this section in the book to find out what the code is, what it does, and why.

---

[a] The code sample for the database tasks can be found online at http://bevacqua.io/bf/db-tasks.

Database migrations are one of those tasks that are complicated to set up, but after you have, you'll wonder how you managed to keep applications together without the automated process.

The general concept is that you start with the original database schema designed for the application. As time goes by, you'll probably make adjustments to the schema: maybe you'll add a table, remove unnecessary fields, change constraints, and so on.

These schema updates are more often than not shamelessly done by hand, typically using the excuse that they're too sensitive to automate. We do them by hand and waste tons of time. It's easy to make mistakes in the process, wasting even more time. Needless to say, this becomes unbearable in larger development teams.

TWO-WAY SCHEMA CHANGES

I propose that an automated set of tasks should gracefully handle migrations in both directions: upgrade and rollback. If you build them carefully enough, you can even integrate them into an automated process. The line of thinking is you should apply these schema changes only within these tasks, and never directly on the database. When you adopt that line of thinking, consider two additional tasks: creating the database from the ground up, and seeding it with data to aid in your development workflow. These tasks would allow you to manage your database directly from the command line, easily creating new instances, changing the schema, populating with data, and rolling back changes.

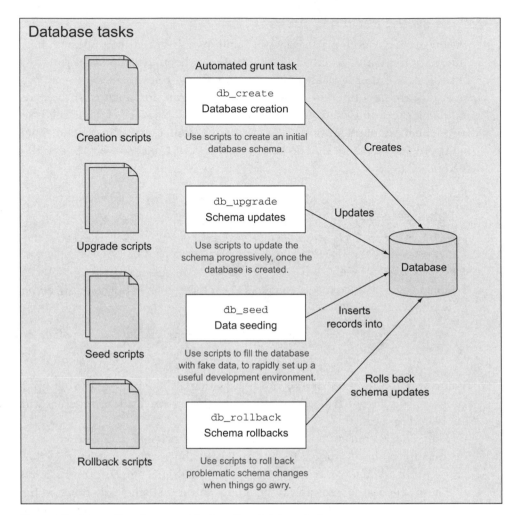

Figure 2.7   Interaction of proposed tasks with a database instance

Figure 2.7 summarizes these steps, consolidating them as Grunt tasks, and also explains how they could interact with a given database.

Taking a close look at the figure, you'll notice there's a flow to it:

- Create the database once.
- Run schema update scripts whenever new ones come out.
- Seed your development database once.
- Run rollback scripts as an extra layer of security in case something goes wrong.

Using db_create, you can create a database instance, and that's it. It shouldn't recreate the database if it already exists, to avoid errors. It won't write anything to the schema yet: tables, views, procedures, and such, are part of the next step.

The `db_upgrade` task will run the upgrade scripts that haven't yet been executed. You'll want to check the accompanying source code for this chapter to learn how it works.[10] In simple terms, you create a table where you can keep track of the upgrade scripts that were applied; then you check if unapplied scripts exist and execute those, updating your tracking records as you go along.

HAVING A BACKUP PLAN
When things go awry, `db_rollback` will take the last upgrade script applied and execute its downgrade counterpart. It then updates the tracking table by deleting the last record, so that you can effectively go back and forth in your schema with upgrades and rollbacks, by using these two tasks. Keep in mind that while `db_upgrade` executes all of the unapplied upgrade scripts, `db_rollback` only downgrades the last one that's still applied.

Last, the `db_seed` task is used to insert records you can play with in your development environment. This one will be crucial in making it dead simple to set up new developers with a working environment by running Grunt tasks exclusively. These tasks would look something like those in figure 2.7.

At this point, you should be comfortable enough to go through the fully documented code listing for database tasks (which is ch02/10_mysql-tasks in the samples), and get a sense of how it could be implemented.[11]

In upcoming chapters, you'll see different ways of configuring tasks such as this one to avoid relying on a configuration file directly. Rather, you'll learn how to use environment variables and encrypted JSON configuration files to store your environment configuration.

2.6   *Summary*

You've learned a lot about build tasks! Let's go over a quick recap:

- A build process should facilitate everything that's needed to produce a fully configured environment that's ready and can do its job.
- The different tasks in a build are clearly separated, and similar tasks are grouped together under task targets.
- Primary tasks that comprise a build include static asset compilation and optimization, linting, and running unit tests.
- You've learned how to write your own build tasks and studied how to approach the automated database schema updates.

Armed with the knowledge you've garnered, we'll switch gears in the two upcoming chapters and expand your understanding of how to target different environments, namely local development and release servers, and you'll learn best practices that you can apply to maximize productivity and performance.

---

[10] The code sample for the database tasks can be found online at http://bevacqua.io/bf/db-tasks.
[11] You can dig through the Chapter 2 code samples, and look for the one named 10_mysql-tasks.

Mastering environments and
the development workflow

3

This chapter covers

- Creating build distributions and workflows
- Setting up application environments
- Building secure environment configuration
- Automating first-time setup
- Using Grunt for continuous development

We spent the last chapter going over what to do and what not to do during builds. We covered build tasks and configured different targets in them. I also hinted at how your workflow differs according to whether you build your application for debug or release distributions; these differences in your build workflow, based on either debug or release goals of your target environment, are called *build distributions.*

Understanding the interaction between development, staging, and production environments and build distributions is vital to creating a build process that can be used regardless of environment, allowing you to develop your application in a setting loyal to what your end users will see, but that can still be debugged with ease. Additionally, this understanding will allow you to create middle-tier environments, which are instrumental to robust deployment mechanisms, which we'll discuss in the next chapter.

In this chapter we'll start off learning what we mean by environments and distributions, and I'll propose a typical configuration that should suffice for most use cases, where you'll have your

- Local development environment, used to improve the application on a daily basis
- Staging or testing environment, dedicated to making sure no issues would arise from deploying to production
- Production environment, which is the one customers have access to

Then we'll look at different approaches to take when configuring an application under different contexts. You'll learn how to automate the oftentimes tedious first-time setup, and then have fun setting up a continuous development workflow using Grunt. Let's get started.

3.1 *Application environments*

In the previous chapter we talked a bit about environments, but we didn't detail the options you have when it comes to setting up new ones or how they differ from one another.

The *development environment* is where you spend most of your time, working on a local web server, which is often configured in such a way to allow debugging, reading stack traces, and getting diagnostics more readily than other environments. The development environment is also the environment that's closest to the developers and the source code they write. The application used in this environment is almost always built using the *debug distribution*, which is fancy talk for setting a flag that will allow you to turn on certain capabilities, such as debug symbols, increased logging (or logging verbosity), and so on.

The *staging environment* is where you make sure everything works correctly on a hosted environment and that you can deploy to production with confidence that nothing will break. In the *production environment*, you'll almost always want to build for the release distribution, as that build flow will be designed to optimize your application and squeeze as many bytes as possible out of your static assets.

Now let's look at how you can configure your build distribution for each of these environments, tuning the distribution's output to meet your specific goals: either debug or release.

3.1.1 *Configuring build distributions*

To help understand build distributions, think of application building like working in a bakery. When you're preparing the mixture for a cake, there's a myriad of pans you might use to hold the batter. You can use a standard round cake pan, a square baking dish, a loaf pan, or whatever's available to you. These pans are like tools in the development environment, which would be your kitchen. The ingredients are always the same: flour, butter, sugar, a pinch of salt, cocoa powder, eggs, and half a cup of buttermilk. The ingredients you use to build your cake are akin to assets in your application.

Furthermore, the ingredients are combined into a recipe that indicates how to mix them together: when, in what quantities, and how long you should store the mix in the fridge to get a good consistency before putting it in the oven at a well-defined temperature. Choosing different recipes can result in a spongier cake or a crustier one, the way choosing different distributions results in an application that's easier to debug or performs better.

While you're trying out different ways to put together your mixture, you might change the ingredients (your assets), and maybe even the recipe (your distribution), but you'll still do the work in your kitchen (the development environment).

Eventually you get better at baking, and you attend competitions. You're provided with professional tools in a different setting (a new environment), given guidelines, and expected to bake a cake with what you have. You might pick the ingredients yourself, you might choose to use syrup to give the cake a final touch, and you might want to cook the mixture for a little longer than you do in your own kitchen. These changes to the recipe are influenced by the environment you're working in, as it may affect your decision on what recipe to use, but you can still use *any* recipe you want in *any* environment you see fit!

Note that build distributions are constrained to either debug or release, although you can have any number of different environments configured to use either of those distributions, as you deem necessary. Environments don't have a one-to-one relationship with build distributions. You may have a preferred distribution for each environment, but that doesn't mean the preference is set in stone. For instance, in your development environment you'll typically use the debug distribution, as that yields more productivity in your day-to-day activities. However, you might want to occasionally try the release distribution in your development environment, to be sure it works as expected regardless of the environment, before deploying to production.

DETERMINING WHICH BUILD DISTRIBUTION TO USE

It's hardly possible for you to be ready to bake a cake in any kitchen: different ovens, pans, and skillets might not be the tools you're comfortable with. Similarly, the build process doesn't have much control over which environment it's targeting. But you can determine the appropriate build distribution based on the purpose of the target environment; either

- *Debugging* purposes, where you aim to rapidly develop and debug your application
- *Release* purposes, where your goals are performance and uptime

These purposes determine your build distributions. In your development environment, you'll use a distribution that's better tuned to meet your development needs,

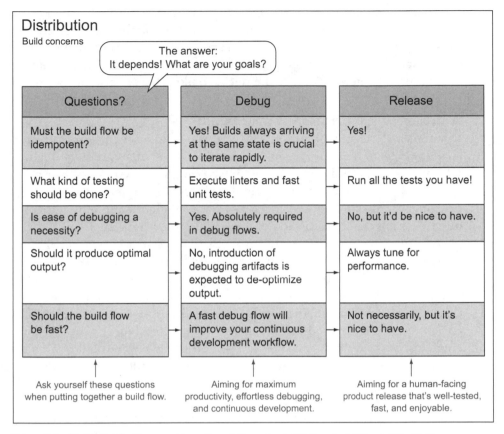

Figure 3.1   Build distributions and how they define your build flow to fulfill specific goals

and that mostly comes down to finding problems and resolving them. This is the debug distribution. Later in the chapter, you'll look at ways to improve the flow to go beyond simple debugging, also enabling true continuous development that runs specific build tasks whenever the code that involves a task changes.

Figure 3.1 displays how build distributions answer questions about the type of goals you want to accomplish, using configuration to define a build flow.

BUILD DISTRIBUTIONS FOR PRODUCTION ENVIRONMENTS

On the farthest end of the spectrum, far from the development environment, you have the *production environment*. Returning to our baking analogy, in this case, you'll aim for high-cnd, quality cakes that paying customers love, and that can only be baked by using the best recipes you have. Production is the environment that ultimately serves the application to real end users, manipulating data they provide.

This is in contrast to the development environment, where you should use mostly fake dummy data, although similar in appearance to real customer data. Production environments will rarely be built with a distribution other than release. This distribution usually regards performance as the most important factor, and as you saw in chapter 2, that might mean minifying and bundling static assets, producing spritesheets out of your icons, and optimizing your images, but we'll cover those topics in chapter 4. Although the production environment shouldn't use debug builds, you should definitely make sure the release build process works in your development environment.

BUILD DISTRIBUTIONS FOR STAGING ENVIRONMENTS

In between development and production, you might have a *staging environment;* its goal would be to replicate, as much as possible, the configuration used in production (although not affecting user data or interacting with services used in production). The staging environment will commonly be hosted somewhere other than on a local machine. Think of this as working as a baker: you might want to bake cakes that hold up to a certain quality, regardless of the kitchen you're working in.

A staging environment might involve working somewhere other than your own kitchen, but it wouldn't be in a restaurant's kitchen, either. Maybe you want to bake a treat for a friend, so you use her kitchen instead. Staging environments attempt to bring production and development to a middle ground, meaning they try to stay as close to both environments as possible. For this purpose they might periodically get a *curated* version of the production database (by curated I mean sensitive data, such as credit cards or passwords, must be stripped off or blanked). You'll pick a distribution for this environment based on what you're testing, but you'll generally default to release, because that's closer to the production environment.

The real purpose of having a staging environment is to allow for quality assurance (QA) engineers, product owners, and others to test the application before it goes live to production. Given that staging is basically the same as production, except it's inaccessible to end users, your team can quickly identify issues in the upcoming release without compromising the production environment, and with certainty that it'll work as expected on a hosted environment.

Let's swim in code for a moment and consider how you can use distributions to approach build configuration so your build tasks adequately portray which build flow (debug or release) they belong to.

DISTRIBUTIONS IN GRUNT TASKS

In chapter 2 we went over a few build tasks and their configurations, but they were mostly standalone and not part of a flow. With build distributions, you'll improve your build process by assigning each task the intent of using it in a given build flow. Are you aiming for debugging quality or smaller file sizes and fewer HTTP requests? Well, if you start using naming conventions in your Grunt tasks and aliases, the answer will become much easier for you to deduce.

As a general rule, I propose you call your build targets `debug` or `release` based on what distribution the task target is geared toward. General purpose tasks such as `JSHint` don't need to abide by this convention, and you can still call your targets names such as `jshint:client`, `jshint:server`, and `jshint:support`. You could use the `support` target for the remainder of the code base, which isn't server- or client-related, but mostly build- or deploy-related.

Considering this convention, you may see yourself having a series of tasks such as `jade:debug` and `less:debug`, which you could then bundle together in a `build:debug` alias. The same could apply to release, clearly separating your build flows in code as well as in your thinking. The following listing (sample 03/01_distribution-config) shows what this would be like in code.

Listing 3.1 Distributed build configuration

```
grunt.initConfig({
  jshint: {
  . client: ['public/js/**/*.js'],
    server: ['server/**/*.js'],
    support: ['Gruntfile.js']
  },
  less: {
    debug: {
      files: {
        'build/css/layout.css': 'public/css/layout.less',
        'build/css/home.css': 'public/css/home.less'
      }
    },
    release: {
      files: {
        'build/css/all.css': [
          'public/css/**/*.less'
        ]
      }
    }
  },
  jade: {
    debug: {
      options: {
        pretty: true
      },
      files: {
        'build/views/home.html': 'public/views/home.jade'
      }
    },
    release: {
      files: {
        'build/views/home.html': 'public/views/home.jade'
      }
    }
  }
});
```

The file found at the path in the value will be compiled into the path in the property.

The less:debug task target compiles LESS files into CSS for development purposes.

The release target is only used during the release build flow.

A globbing pattern compiles all LESS style sheets into a single output CSS file.

Note how jade:debug sets options different from those in release flows.

Using this kind of separation, it's easy to create aliases to build the application for either distribution. Here are a couple of sample aliases:

```
grunt.registerTask('build:debug', ['jshint', 'less:debug', 'jade:debug']);
grunt.registerTask('build:release', ['jshint', 'less:release',
    'jade:release']);
```

You can look for the fully working code listing example in the accompanying source code repository. Remember, these are organized by chapter, so look for the 01_distribution-config folder under chapter 3.

This provides an excellent base for you to build on. You can keep iterating on each of these flows, possibly reusing tasks, such as `jshint` in this example, adding more tasks to both distributions or maybe to one of them in case it only applies to one flow. For example, you'll want to keep tasks such as updating the change log in the release flow, because the product to be released might change across debug builds, and you need to accompany your deployment with documentation about all the changes introduced. We'll come back to the topic, looking at debug distribution-specific tasks later in the chapter. Release-specific tasks are analyzed in chapter 4.

You've now learned what build distributions are and how they define the different flows created when putting together a build process; let's turn our attention to the application configuration within each environment, or what I call environment-level configuration.

3.1.2   *Environment-level configuration*

Environment configuration is separate from build distributions, and the distinction is clear: *build distributions* determine how your application should be built. They shouldn't bear any weight in the application itself, but only affect the build process, or more concretely, the build flow you follow. *Environment configuration*, in contrast, is environment-specific.

Environment-level configuration: what does it include?

Moving forward, whenever I mention configuration in this chapter, I'm referring to environment-level configuration, unless otherwise noted. By *environment-level configuration* I mean values such as

- Database connection strings
- API authentication credentials
- Session encryption secrets
- The port your web server listens on for HTTP requests

These kinds of configuration values tend to contain mostly sensitive data. I strongly discourage merrily packaging these kinds of secrets in plain text along with the rest of your code base. Developers shouldn't have direct access to services, such as your database, and therefore access to user data. It also becomes an attack vector: gaining access to your code repository translates into gaining access into your databases or API secrets, and most frighteningly, accessing your customer's data.

In this respect, an excellent rule of thumb is to develop your applications as if you were developing open source software. You wouldn't push sensitive API keys and database connection strings into your publicly available open source repositories, would you?

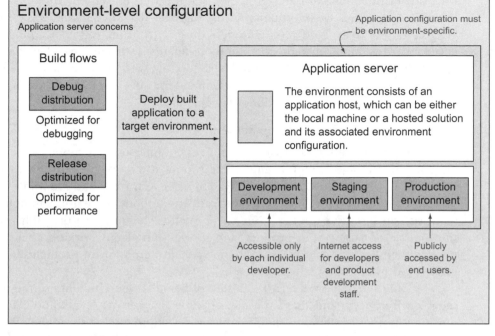

Figure 3.2   Environment-level configuration—environments, configuration, and distributions, coming together in an application. Environment configuration consists of secret credentials and any other configuration that might change across environments.

Figure 3.2 depicts how your application combines build distribution output and environment configuration to serve an application.

BUILD FLOWS

As you can see on the left of the figure, the debug and release distributions only affect the build itself, while environment configuration will affect the application directly, after a build is executed, for either debug or release.

ENVIRONMENT-LEVEL CONFIGURATION

Application configuration must be environment-specific. These environment variables are not to be confused with build distributions, which only affect the build process itself. Application configuration refers to small (and often sensitive) snippets of data such as database connection strings, API keys, encryption secrets, logging verbosity level, and so on.

Although distributions generally don't contain sensitive data, environment-level configuration often does. For example, an environment's configuration might have access credentials to a database instance, an API service such as Twitter's REST API, or maybe a username and a password used to send out emails through IMAP.

But not all environment configuration is sensitive or poses a security threat if leaked. For instance, the application's listening port and the logging verbosity level, which determine how verbose your logger should be, are both environment-specific, but they're not sensitive information in the slightest. That being said, you don't have any reason to treat "safe" configuration differently from sensitive configuration, except that you might include configuration defaults with safe variables, such as the application's listening port. You should never do that with sensitive data.

You'll focus on the development environment for now, and move on to staging and production environments in the following chapter.

3.1.3 *What's so special about development?*

What's so different about local development in comparison with other environments? Well, much, and ideally, not so much. The two most remarkable differences are that this is the environment where you'll spend most of your time, and it doesn't matter if something stops working; you can always fix it, and nobody else is going to notice it. In contrast, you should spend little time in production, because that probably translates into people not using your product, and if something stops working, that won't be good, either. We'll go over measures to mitigate and monitor for problems in release-grade environments in the next chapter.

The Build First approach carries a slew of benefits when it comes to the development environment, and that's the meat of this chapter. We'll talk about tools and mechanisms that are famously helpful during development. Let's save the fun for last; we need to talk about configuration first. We'll go over your options when it comes to managing, reading, and storing the sensitive data of your environment-level configuration in a sensible way, so as not to expose your secrets to potential intruders.

3.2 *Configuring environments*

Until now, you've established that committing sensitive configuration to your repositories in plain text poses a security risk. In this section we'll cover how to manage configuration from different sources, such as a file, the database, or application memory. At the same time, you'll explore different approaches for protecting your configuration data. Please note that the information I'm about to give you isn't limited to Node.js. I picked that platform because I needed to give you a concrete example of how to configure your environment-level variables, and because this is a JavaScript book. That being said, the environment configuration approaches we'll discuss can be applied to applications running on any server-side platform you like.

> **Environment-specific variables**
>
> Environment configuration is changing any variable that could change depending on the environment you run your application in. For example, you might need variables with credentials so you can send emails, and you might want to allow an option to send all emails to a catch-all account for debug environments. API keys to services you consume usually change on a per-environment basis, too. Environment configuration is the place where you should keep all of these settings and credentials so you can adjust them for each environment.

More often than I'd like to admit, I've worked on projects that shamefully broke this configuration principle and contained configuration for all of their environments directly in their repository. Development, staging, production—they all were fair game. Configuration for each of these was maintained in a separate file, and something such as a string that contains "development" governed which of those files was used. This is bad because of a number of problems:

- First, I can't stress enough the importance of not packing credentials to your live environments directly in your repositories. That's exactly the kind of thing that belongs in environment-level configuration.
- Second, you shouldn't have to repeat configuration values for each environment you have, effectively maintaining the same value in multiple different files; this would be WET code. It doesn't scale well when you want to add new environments or configuration values to your application.

I've also participated in endeavors where configuration was tediously manual: you'd get a brand new code base, ask around for a few credentials to get started, and type them into a single configuration file. If you had to deploy, then you'd manually change those same values again to whatever configuration that satisfied the environment you were deploying to. In the previous case, at least you didn't have to change configuration around to get your application to work any time you changed environments. You'd change a magic string, setting it to something such as "staging," and it'd work.

How can you go with that approach without sharing everything with everyone? You might think that's not a big deal; it's not as if you're going to open source your project overnight. But if you're thinking like that, you're missing the point entirely. It's not good practice to give everyone access to potentially sensitive information about your production environment. And there's no reason to—that configuration belongs with that environment, nowhere else.

Open source software

Experimenting in open source projects, something I vigorously encourage you to try, helped me vastly improve over time the techniques and measures I take to protect sensitive data. I started thinking in a "what if a stranger downloaded my code?" kind of way, and it opened my eyes as to what was fine, and what wasn't, when it came to pushing code to my repositories.

Let's start our discussion of configuring environments by talking about waterfall configuration, and then we'll cover different methods you can use to protect it, namely, encryption and environment variables.

3.2.1 Storing configuration in a waterfall

Waterfall is a method for storing your configuration. It's as simple as picking a priority that determines the order of importance of these stores as you merge them together.

Waterfall is useful because it helps your configuration to be divided in different places but still be part of a whole. A few places exist where you can define your configuration; for example

- Plain text directly in your code base, only meant for data that doesn't violate your security
- In encrypted files; it's meant to distribute configuration securely.
- At the machine level, setting operating system environment variables
- Passing command-line arguments to your application at the process level

Keep in mind, you're configuring the environment, regardless of the level at which you do it; thus, all configuration sources must always be accessed from a single point in your application. This configuration root service should be careful to determine which source is most important when providing a requested value. In the list above, I ordered a few potential configuration sources from lowest to highest priority. For example, a command-line argument setting the port number will overwrite the port number stored in a plain text file within the repository.

Clearly these aren't the only places where we can store configuration, but they provide a great starting point for any application. I know I've severely thrashed plain text, but it's okay to have a plain JSON file to set up absolute basics, such as the environment name and the port number. Let's call this one `defaults.json`:

```
{
    "NODE_ENV": "development",
    "PORT": 80
}
```

This is perfectly reasonable as far as plain text goes. I also encourage keeping a second plain text file, which you might call `user.json`, to keep personal configuration you might want to use, but not necessarily commit to modifying the defaults. The `user.json` file is also useful if you need to quickly test with a different configuration:

```
{
    "PORT": 3000
}
```

As long as it's encrypted, sensitive configuration can be checked into source control. I advocate using this kind of configuration to share environment defaults among your developers. The reasoning is that instead of having to redistribute a JSON file every time the defaults change, you distribute the key to decrypt the secure file once, and whenever a change is made it's checked into source control, and the developers can decrypt it using the key they already had.

I should mention that to maximize security, different private keys should be used for each encrypted configuration file. This is particularly important when dealing with one file per environment, because a breach would be chaotic for every environment; in addition, it'll be easier to change the keys if they're only used in one place.

You have a few different ways to safely distribute configuration among your environments; we'll go over a couple of them next. The first one is through encryption, and we'll go over the process of safely encrypting your configuration files using a concrete example. The second alternative is not to distribute environment configuration files with your code base, but rather to store the configuration solely in the target environment. Let's start with security through encryption.

3.2.2 *Using encryption to harden environment configuration security*

To securely transmit configuration within your code base, you need to take a few security measures. First and foremost, you shouldn't commit decrypted configuration files to source control, as this would defeat the entire purpose of encryption. The same holds true for encryption keys: you should keep these somewhere safe, preferably off the cloud altogether—maybe on a USB pen drive. What you should share in your repositories are the encrypted versions of these files and simple command-line tools to decrypt or update their encrypted counterparts. Figure 3.3 describes this flow.

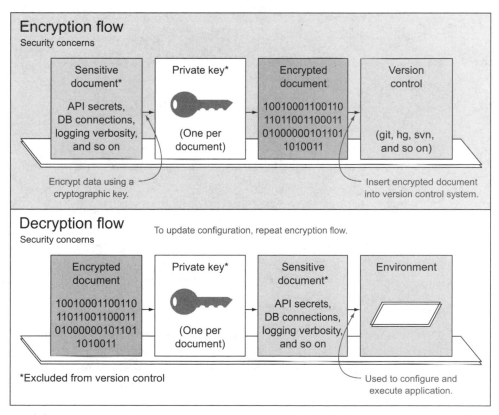

Figure 3.3   Configuration encryption and decryption flows using private RSA keys

To this purpose, you can set up a couple of folders. For example, use `env/private`, where you'll keep the unsecured data that's been decrypted, and `env/secure` to store the encrypted files. Because the `env/private` folder contains sensitive data, it shouldn't be committed to source control systems. Rather, you're going to distribute an encryption key by another means; for example, physically giving it to the interested parties. Then the repository will contain tools (Grunt tasks in your case) to encrypt and decrypt each particular file using its corresponding RSA (an encryption algorithm) key. You'll use three different Grunt tasks for encryption purposes. The first one will generate the private key; the other two will encrypt and decrypt your configuration using that private key.

> ## RSA encryption example
>
> I wrote a fully working example that's available in the accompanying source code listings, named 02_rsa-config-encryption,[a] under ch03. In that example, you'll use the `grunt-pemcrypt` package I wrote, which facilitates the tasks required to deal with encryption and decryption of secure configuration files. We won't deviate into the code itself, because it's fairly straightforward to follow and properly documented.
>
> ———————
> [a] The code example is available online at http://bevacqua.io/bf/secure-config.

To recap RSA encryption

- Create a private key; don't share it with anyone.
- Use it to encrypt your sensitive files.
- Transmit the encrypted file with your code base.
- When you need to update the secure file, update the plain one and encrypt it again.
- When someone else copies your code base, they can't access the encrypted configuration unless you give them the key.

In the next section, let's look at the pros and cons of taking the alternative route: not encrypting your environment-level configuration but also not distributing it (and your sensitive secrets with it) together with the rest of your application's code repository.

3.2.3 *Setting environment-level configuration at the OS level*

When it comes to release environments (staging, production, and anything in between) you might want to configure sensitive values in the environment directly and keep them off your code base. Keeping your configuration off the code base enables you to change it without the need for a full redeployment. Using system-level environment variables is a great way to do that.

This is something I picked up from working with cloud-based hosting solutions (such as Heroku), and it's convenient to set up. An added benefit of using environment variables is that you don't need to touch the code base to change its behavior. The downside is that, similar to your previous approach, you don't have access to most of the configuration when you clone the repository for the first time. An exception to that downside is any unprotected defaults you might have, such as the development environment listen port. That downside, however, is also the goal of taking this route: being unable to deploy a newly cloned repository as is to one of the production environments.

The difference between encrypted file stores and environment-level configuration is that it's more secure not to share anything with your code base at all, even if it's encrypted. But the downside of going the environment variables route is that you still need to get the configuration there.

In the next chapter, I'll introduce Heroku, a cloud hosting Platform as a Service (PaaS) provider, which enables hosting of web applications in the cloud as easily as doing a `git push`. Heroku uses environment variables for your environment configuration, and they thoroughly documented their philosophy (on web application building, architecture, and scaling) and published it on a website called 12factor.net[1] that everyone should read.

For local development, you'll still use a JSON file that doesn't get committed to source control, and it contains what you would've put in the secure JSON file in the previous section. The following is a sample environment JSON file:

```
{
  "NODE_ENV": "development",
  "PORT": 8080,
  "SOME_API_SECRET": "zE1nMDDqkzDbSDX4fS5acCpllk0W9",
  "SOME_API_KEY": "IYOxBMFi34Rkzce7kY4h0GqI"
}
```

If you want to provision new contributors to your project with a copy of the environment file you use locally, consider going the encryption approach for that one file (the `development` configuration), and taking the environment variables approach for hosted environments (those that aren't local to your development machine) to maximize security.

For hosted solutions (such as `staging` or `production`), a different approach takes place. Heroku provides a command-line interface that makes it easy to set environment variables.[2] With the example below, you could set the environment to `staging` so your code can tune the experience to that environment—increased logging, for example, but mostly the same as production:

```
heroku config:add NODE_ENV=staging
```

The command line should have the last say on what values go where, making it easy to enable small modifications to your environment, such as setting a port or the execu-

---

[1] 12 Factor is an excellent guide to robust application development. Check it out at http://bevacqua.io/bf/ 12factor.

[2] Learn more about configuring your Node.js environments with Heroku at http://bevacqua.io/bf/heroku-cli.

tion mode (debug or release). Here's an example of an override that changes the port and the environment:

```
NODE_ENV=production PORT=3000 node app.js-
```

Last, let's go over how you could pull together all the different sources of configuration (environment variables, text files, and command-line arguments) in a way that makes sense.

3.2.4 *Merging configuration as a waterfall in code*

You're ready to glue all this together into pieces of JavaScript. Considering how lazy we are, let's not write much code to accomplish this.

There's an npm module called `nconf` that deals with merging configuration sources together, regardless of what you're using: JSON files, JavaScript objects, environment variables, process arguments, and so on. The following code is an example (labeled ch03/03_merging-config in the samples) of how you could configure `nconf` to use the plain JSON files from section 3.2.2. Note that while the configuration source order in the code listing might seem counterintuitive, `nconf` prioritizes configuration on a "first-come first-served" basis:

```
var nconf = require('nconf');

nconf.argv();
nconf.env();
nconf.file('dev', 'development.json');

module.exports = nconf.get.bind(nconf);
```

After you set up this module, you can use it to get configuration values from any of those stores, in order of appearance:

- First, `nconf.argv()` prioritizes command-line arguments above everything else, as it's the first source we've added. For instance, executing the application with `node app --PORT 80` means that the PORT variable will be assigned that value, regardless of configuration from other sources.
- The `nconf.env()` line tells `nconf` to source configuration from the environment as well. For instance, executing `PORT=80 node app` will set the port to 80, while `PORT=80 node app --PORT 3000` will set the port to 3000, because command-line arguments have more priority than environment variables.
- Last, the `nconf.file()` line sources a JSON file to pull the least important values: these will be overridden by both environment variables and command-line arguments! If you provide a command-line argument such as `--PORT 80`, it won't matter that you had `"PORT": 3000` in your development JSON file; you'll still use port 80. Again, you'll find a complete example in the accompanying source code, also detailing how to use `nconf` when going the Heroku route. This will prove useful in the following chapter, so I'd advise you to read this

chapter to the end and then get up to speed with the code samples if you haven't gone through them yet.

Now that you know how to properly configure builds and environments, we'll head on to the last couple of sections. Before getting to continuous development, let me emphasize a couple of best practices when it comes to setting up environments for the first time.

3.3 *Automating tedious first-time setup tasks*

When setting up your environment for the first time, you've got to think about what you're doing, and you need to automate anything that's plausible to automate. The reason: if you don't automate, it'll translate directly into more work for newcomers. Another reason for preemptively automating these tasks is purely that you can.

In the beginning, it's simple to automate the little stuff one bit at a time. Yet, as the project develops, it becomes daunting and implausible to do so. Your coworkers might be against doing so at this point, and yet setting up a working environment might take you as long as a week. I had this happen to me on a ridiculously huge project I worked on in the past, and management was okay with that. Setting up a local development environment involved

- Reading through a daunting series of poorly written wiki articles
- Installing dependencies by hand
- Applying schema updates by hand
- Applying those updates every morning by hand after getting the latest code
- Installing audio codecs and even proprietary software, such as a specific version of Windows Media Player

After a week all I had to show for it was a "kind-of-working" environment. Three weeks after that I landed another job, because I couldn't bear the manual, laborious work in that project. The driving issue behind this problem is that changing the way an application is built is hard, and not having a straightforward and automated process to set up new environments can become extremely costly down the line, and so cumbersome to change, in fact, that you wouldn't want to bother doing it. The frustration I felt during that experience is one of the root motivators that drove me to Build First, the build-oriented approach I'm pile-driving in this book.

In chapter 2 we covered how to automate our build process, and you even learned how you could automatically create, provision, and update a MySQL database instance (found at ch02/10_mysql-tasks in the samples).[3] Setting up database seeding is complex, as you saw in the sample code, but it can also be rewarding: not having to provide new collaborators with anything other than the code repository, and a few instructions asking them to execute a Grunt task.

---

[3] The database provisioning task examples can be found at http://bevacqua.io/bf/db-tasks.

We've discussed at great length the measures you can take when it comes to configuration, and in that regard all you need to do when setting up a new development environment is get the decryption key (stored somewhere safe) and run a Grunt task. First-time setup shouldn't involve more manual labor than getting your environment configuration in place; it should be that easy.

Okay, you've taken care of all the environments, distributions, configuring, and automating, including the tedious first-time set up. It's time for the fun I promised at the beginning of the chapter! Continuous development is up next!

3.4   Working in continuous development

Continuous development is the ability to work uninterruptedly in your code base, and by interruptions I don't mean pesky project managers asking what you're up to or coworkers asking for help with a bug they can't seem to track down. When I say interruptions, I mean the repetitive stuff that slowly pecks away at your work day, such as re-executing node every time your application changes. Even now, with your fancy new build process in place, do you have to run it yourself every time files change? No way! You don't have time for all that. You'll use yet another task to do that.

Then there's the smaller stuff, like saving your changes and refreshing your browser. You'll get rid of that too, by letting the tools do that. Repetitive routines don't carry much prestige in Build First systems. Let's see how much you can automate away from your workflow. This isn't to prove you can automate anything; the benefit instead lies in that you can spend more time doing what matters: thinking and tinkering with code.

The first step you're going to take in this direction is investing in a good watch (in the figurative sense—using a watch task in your favorite task runner), which will allow you to have the build process restart itself whenever you save changes to your files.

3.4.1   Waste no time, use a watch!

If you're like me, you hit save or change tabs every few seconds. You can't afford to run a full build every time you change a comment or a comma; that would be a tremendous waste of your time. Yet many people do this, because they haven't found a better way to go about it yet. You're reading this, so you're one step ahead. Kudos.

One of Grunt's most useful plugins is, undoubtedly, grunt-contrib-watch. This plugin will watch your file system for changes to your code and run the tasks affected by those code changes. Whenever a file change affects one of your build tasks, you should execute that task again. This is one of the pillars of continuous development, because you won't have to do anything; the build process will run itself as needed. Let's look at a quick example:

```
watch: {
  rebuild: {
    tasks: ['build:debug'],
    files: ['public/**/*']
  }
}
```

With this example, called 04_watch-task, and found under ch03 in the code samples, you can run the build process again entirely whenever any file changes or is created in your `public` folder. Now you won't ever have to worry about constantly running the build; it can run itself!

But even this approach isn't the most efficient way to do it, because this will run all your build tasks, even the ones unaffected by the changed file. For example, it won't matter if you edit a LESS file; any JavaScript-related tasks such as `jshint` will also run, because they're part of the build, too. To correct that behavior, you should break down `watch` into many targets: one for each build task that can be affected by file changes. The following listing is a brief demonstration of what I'm talking about.

Listing 3.2 Breaking down `watch` into multiple targets

```
watch: {
  less: {
    tasks: ['less:debug'],
    files: ['public/css/**/*.less']
  },
  lint_client: {
    tasks: ['jshint:client'],
    files: ['public/js/**/*.js']
  },
  lint_server: {
    tasks: ['jshint:server'],
    files: ['srv/**/*.js']
  }
}
```

Breaking down your watch like this might seem tedious, but it will be well worth it. It will speed up your continuous development flow, because you're getting into a mode where what you build is what changed, rather than blindly rebuilding everything, every time. You can find the fully working sample in the code listings, labeled as ch03/05_better-watch-closely.[4]

Watching for such changes in your build is great, but what if you could expand on that, watching for changes to your Node application? Well, it turns out you can and should do that. Gather round, and let's talk about `nodemon`.

3.4.2 *Monitoring for changes to the Node app*

In the continuous development field, you try as hard as possible not to repeat anything incessantly, and to stay DRY instead of WET. You just saw how beneficial that could be—not having to run the build every time something changes. Now you'll take the same shortcut for Node.

Think of the `nodemon` command as using the `node` command, except it will monitor for changes and restart your application, running `node` again so you don't have to.

---

[4] You can find the code sample online at http://bevacqua.io/bf/watch-out.

To install it, use `npm`, with the `-g` modifier, so that it's installed globally, making it readily accessible from the command line:

```
npm install -g nodemon
```

Now you can run `nodemon app.js`, instead of `node app.js`. By default, `nodemon` monitors `*.js` files, but you might want to restrict that even further. In these cases, you can provide it with a `.nodemonignore` file, which works much like `.gitignore`, and lets you ignore files you don't want `nodemon` to monitor. Here's an example

```
# package control
./node_modules/*

# build artifacts
./bin/*

# ignore client-side js
./src/client/*

# ignore tests
./test/*
```

Running `grunt watch` and using another terminal to run `nodemon app.js` is admittedly a tad faster than running both together through Grunt, due to the overhead Grunt adds. However, it's convenient enough to run a single command, not having to spin up two terminal windows, that it might cancel out the extra overhead introduced. Generally speaking, there's a tradeoff of speed (running them separately) versus convenience (running them both under Grunt). Personally, I prefer the convenience of not having to execute an additional command separately.

Next, we'll examine how to integrate `nodemon` into Grunt.

COMBINING WATCH AND NODEMON

There's a problem you need to resolve before you can integrate `nodemon` into Grunt, and that is that both `nodemon` and `watch` are *blocking tasks*: these tasks never end; they sit and watch for changes to your code. Grunt runs tasks sequentially, waiting for a task to end before you can run another one. But if neither of them end, the other one can't start!

To get around this you could use `grunt-concurrent`, which will spawn a new process for each task you provide, and turn you into a happier nerd. Running `nodemon` through Grunt can be easily achieved using `grunt-nodemon`. The following listing is an example.

Listing 3.3 Using `nodemon` from Grunt

```
nodemon: {
  dev: {
    script: 'app.js'
  }
},
concurrent: {
  dev: {
    tasks: ['nodemon', 'watch']
  }
}
```

This example is also in the accompanying source code listings, named 06_nodemon (under chapter 3.) In this chapter, you've improved the sequence of events because your changes get saved, but you're still doing the saving!

Let's have a quick word about saving changes.

3.4.3 *A text editor that cares*

Picking the right editor is key to your day-to-day work productivity, and productivity translates into happiness. Take your time to learn the ins and outs of your editor of choice. You might feel nerdy the first time you find yourself watching a YouTube video about a text editor's shortcuts, but it will be time well spent. You spend most of the day using code editing tools, so you might as well learn how to exploit the features those editors provide.

Luckily, most editors now provide a mechanism to get them to auto-save your changes. It feels kind of weird at first, but as you get used to it, you'll fall in love and never look back. Personally, I like Sublime Text, the editor I typed these words with, and the one I use for most of my writing. If you're on a Mac, TextMate seems like a viable option. Other options include WebStorm, which is an IDE specifically tailored for web development, and then there's vim, for those who dare learn to use its complex, shortcut-intensive user interface.

All the editors I mentioned are capable of auto-saving; if the editor you're using isn't, I strongly suggest you switch to one that is. You'll be uncomfortable at first, but you'll quickly start writing me thank-you notes after using your new text editor.

Let's wrap up with talk about the LiveReload technology for browser reloading, and how you can benefit from it.

3.4.4 *Browser refresh is so Y2K*

LiveReload is a technology that understands you can't waste precious time refreshing your browser whenever something changes. It exploits web sockets, a real-time communication technology that's available in browsers (and which is awesome). Through its use of web sockets, LiveReload can decide whether it needs to apply small changes to your CSS, for example, or perform a full page reload when the HTML changes.

Enabling it is fairly easy, enough so that we don't have any excuse not to do it at this point. It comes bundled with `grunt-contrib-watch`, so setting it up is as easy as adding a `watch` target, as shown in the following listing.

Listing 3.4   Enabling LiveReload

```
watch: {
  livereload: {
    options: {
      livereload: true
    },
    files: [
      'public/**/*.{css,js}',
```

```
        'views/**/*.html'
    ]
  }
}
```

Next, you'll need to install the browser extension and enable it. Now you won't ever again need to refresh your browser by yourself while debugging your applications. There's also a readily available example[5] for you to look at (labeled ch03/ 07_livereload in the code samples), filled with all the necessary setup instructions, but it's straightforward to get up and running.

3.5 Summary

You made it through the environments and development workflow crash course! Here's a quick recap of the teachings in this chapter:

- The debug and release distributions affect your build flow in different ways; debug aims for bug catching and continuous development, while release aims for monitoring and speed optimizations, as you'll see in the next chapter.
- Your application should be configured so that secrets don't make their way to the source code, and also provide enough flexibility to configure it based on the environment you're running.
- We've covered continuous development and how you can benefit from using a watch task that rebuilds your application and nodemon to restart it after changes, as well as the importance of picking the right tool for text editing.

In the following chapter we'll cover in more detail the performance optimizations that you can consider for release builds, what continuous integration is and how to use it to your advantage, how you should monitor analytics in your application, and finally, how to deploy your application to hosted environments such as staging and production.

---

[5] See LiveReload in action using this code sample at http://bevacqua.io/bf/livereload.

Release, deployment, and monitoring

We've covered the build process, common build tasks you can perform (and how to do that using Grunt), and, at a high level, environments and configuration. We discussed the development environment extensively, but that's only half the story. The development environment is where you'll spend most of your time working, because you'll have a system in place, so you can prepare your application for a release, deploy it to a platform that humans can access, and then monitor the application state. Thanks to the Build First mentality, you'll be automating the workflows I've just mentioned, avoiding repetition, human error, and running tests, all while saving time, as I promised in chapter 1.

A continuous integration (CI) platform will help deploy more robust builds to production by ensuring your tests pass in a hosted environment. As you'll see later

71

in the chapter, CI helps test your code base remotely every time you push to your version control system (VCS). Build automation (and continuous development) is crucial for keeping your day-to-day development efforts productive and efficient. Comparably, having a workflow that's easy to execute ensures you can deploy your application as often as needed, without worrying about an embarrassing manual set of tasks that take half an hour to perform.

By the end of this chapter, you'll be ready to perform safe, continuous deployments, which are similar to continuous development in spirit. They're both intended to cut down the repetitive work and reduce human mistakes. The release flow has a few stages we're going to follow in this book:

- The first step is the build process, under the release distribution.
- Once the build is compiled, you'll run tests to make sure recent changes didn't break the build. Minor syntax issues should be constantly resolved during development by using lint programs.
- If the tests succeed, you might get into predeployment operations such as updating the version number and the release changelog.
- After that, you'll investigate deployment options, such as cloud hosting options and CI platforms.

Figure 4.1 describes this proposed release and deployment flow. As you look at the figure, keep a mental note of my proposal to deploy to staging first, to make sure everything works as expected in a hosted environment, before going live to production.

You have a long road ahead; let's commence by discussing the release and deployment flow. You'll visit predeployment operations in detail in section 4.2. Then in section 4.3, I'll tell you all about deployments, and you'll learn how to deploy an application to Heroku. Section 4.4 covers continuous integration and the tools you can use to get CI to do the heavy lifting on your behalf.

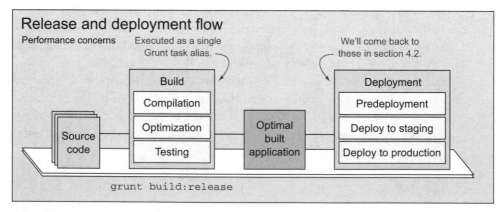

Figure 4.1   Proposed release and deployment flow

4.1   *Releasing your application*

When preparing your application for release, you'll want to place the web's best practices on your plate. In chapter 2, we discussed *minification*, shrinking your assets for better performance, and *concatenation*, joining files together to reduce the number of HTTP requests, which you'll definitely want to include in your release builds. These improve the web application's user experience by bundling your developer-readable source code into single files containing everything in the source code, but in a compressed form to hasten downloads. In that chapter we also covered *sprite maps and sprites*, large files containing many images. These would be used for debug distributions, too, for the sole reason that they enable you to keep debug and release more tightly bound together and less dissimilar. Otherwise you'd need to reference the individual icons in your debug CSS, and then somehow reference the spritemap and each icon's position in release, defeating the purpose of uniting both build flows and repeating yourself, breaking the DRY principle.

Minification, concatenation, spriting—what else is there to a release flow? In this section we'll go over image optimization and asset caching; then we'll move on to the deployment flow, semantic versioning, and keeping changelogs up-to-date effortlessly.

4.1.1   *Image optimization*

Concatenated and minified JavaScript and CSS files don't tell the whole story. Images represent, more often than not, the bulk of a web page's download footprint, meaning they are even more important to optimize than any other static assets. You already did a good chunk of optimization in chapter 2, when you examined how to generate a spritesheet using different images, which is comparable to how concatenation works for text files, merging many files into a single one. The other optimization, minification, reduces the contents of script and stylesheet files by shortening variable names and other micro-optimizations that minifiers perform. In the world of images, you have various ways to compress files, resulting in gains somewhere between 9% and 80%, typically above 50%. Luckily for us, certain Grunt packages, much like we're becoming accustomed to, do the heavy lifting for us in this regard.

One such package is `grunt-contrib-imagemin,` which does exactly what you want: image compression for different formats such as PNG, GIF, and JPG. Before plunging into it, I'll briefly cover the two aspects of image optimization it can help you with: lossless compression and interlacing.

LOSSLESS IMAGE COMPRESSION

Lossless image compression is, much like JavaScript minification, tasked with the removal of unimportant bits of data from your image's raw binary data. The important thing to notice is that lossless compression doesn't alter the image's appearance, but solely its binary representation. The only result of lossless compression is a smaller image that looks identical to the larger image. Lucky for us, smarter people have spent time working on tools that do advanced image compression work for us. You can specify the path to your image and have their algorithms work at it. Furthermore, `grunt-contrib-imagemin` configures these low-level programs with the right parameters, so you don't have to. Note that lossless compression produces modest byte savings compared to lossy compression; it's great, however, when you can't afford to lose any image quality. When you can afford to lose image quality (and most of the time the losses are almost unnoticeable), you should use lossy image compression.

LOSSY IMAGE COMPRESSION

Lossy compression is an image compression technique where inexact approximation is applied (also known as partial data discarding) when re-encoding the image, resulting in far greater byte savings than those gained through lossless compression (up to 90% savings), where the removed information is usually only metadata such as geolocation, camera type, and so on. The `grunt-contrib-imagemin` package uses lossy compression by default, in addition to lossless compression, to remove unnecessary metadata. If you only want to use lossless compression, you should consider using the `imagemin` package directly.

INTERLACING IMAGES

The other image optimizing task you're going to study is *interlacing*.[1] Interlaced images have a larger size than regular images, but these added bytes are usually well worth it, because they improve perceived performance. Even though the image might take a little longer to complete downloading, it will start rendering faster than normal images do. Progressive images work exactly as they sound. They render a minimum view of the pixels in the image, which roughly looks like your complete image, and then they're progressively enhanced (as more data gets streamed to the browser), until the full-quality image is available.

Traditionally, images load top-down, in full quality, which translates into a faster download time but slower perceived rendering. The time to view the entire image equals the completion time. In progressive rendering mode, humans perceive a faster experience because they don't have to wait as long to see a (garbled) view of the entire image.

SETTING UP GRUNT-CONTRIB-IMAGEMIN

Setting up `grunt-contrib-imagemin` is, happily, as easy as the rest of the tasks we've gone over. Keep in mind that the important bits are in learning what the tasks do and how and when to apply them. The following listing configuration optimizes `*.jpg` images during release builds.

Listing 4.1 Optimizing images during release builds

```
imagemin: {
  release: {
    files: [{
      expand: true,
      src: 'build/img/**/*.jpg'
```

---

[1] Learn more about how interlacing improves perceived performance by visiting http://bevacqua.io/bf/interlacing. There's also an animated GIF that better explains how an interlaced image works.

```
    }],
    options: {
      progressive: true // progressive jpgs
    }
  }
}
```

Listing 4.1 doesn't need any extra configuration to compress the images; that's done by default. A fully working example can be found in the accompanying source for this chapter, labeled ch04/01_image-optimization, with a complete build workflow for both the `debug` and `release` distributions. Now that you've made the web a slightly better place for humans to drift around aimlessly, you can turn your attention to static asset caching.

4.1.2 Static asset caching

In case you're unfamiliar with the term, think of *caching* as photocopying history books from the library. Rather than going to the library every time you want to read them, you might prefer to print copies of a few pages, take those home, and read them whenever you please without having to hit the library again.

Caching in the web is more complicated than photocopying books borrowed from a library, but that should give you the gist of it.

EXPIRES HEADERS

A best practice you should definitely follow is using `Expires` headers for your static assets. This header, according to the HTTP protocol, tells the browser not to request the resource again if it was requested at least once (and therefore cached), and the cached version hasn't become stale. The expiration date in the `Expires` header determines when the cached version is no longer considered valid, and the asset has to be redownloaded. An example `Expires` header might be `Expires: Tue, 25 Dec 2012 16:00:00 GMT`.

This is both an awesome and a terrible practice. It's awesome for humans, because after their first visit to one of your pages, they don't need to redownload resources their browser stored in its cache, saving them requests and time. It's terrible for us, the developers, because it won't matter if you deploy changes to your assets, humans won't download them anymore.

To solve that inconvenience, and make `Expires` headers useful, you can rename your assets every time you deploy changes to them, appending a hash to their names, which forces browsers to download the file again, because for all intents and purposes, it's a different file from what they used to have in their cache.

> HASHING A *hash* is a function that returns a fixed-length value that's an encoded representation of data. In your situation, the hash could be computed from the asset contents and its last modified date. One such hash might be `a38cbf9e`. Although seemingly arbitrary, there's no randomness involved. That would defeat the purpose of using an `Expires` header, because files would always have different names and be requested again every time.

Once you've computed a hash, you can use it as a query string parameter in your page, /all.js?_=a38cbf9e, or you can append it to the filename, such as /a38cbf9e .all.js. Alternatively, you can add the hash to an ETag header. Choosing the right approach is a matter of identifying your needs. If you're dealing with static assets such as JavaScript resources, then you're probably better off hashing the filename (or its query string) and using an Expires header. If you're dealing with dynamic content, setting the hash in an ETag is preferred.

USING LAST-MODIFIED OR AN ETAG HEADER

An ETag header uniquely identifies one version of a resource. Similarly, Last-Modified identifies the last modification date of the resource. If you use either of these headers, then you should use the max-age modifier in the cache-control header, instead of the Expires header. This combination allows for softer caching, as the user agent can determine whether the cached copy should be used, or if the resource should be requested again. The following example shows how to combine the ETag and the cache-control headers:

```
ETag: a38cbf9e
Cache-Control: public, max-age=3600
```

The Last-Modified header behaves as an alternative to the ETag header, for convenience. Here we don't specify a uniquely identifying ETag, but achieve the same uniqueness by setting a modification date:

```
Last-Modified: Tue, 25 Dec 2012 16:00:00 GMT
Cache-Control: public, max-age=3600
```

Let's find out how you can use Grunt to create hashes for your file names that can then be used to set far-futures Expires headers safely.

CACHE BUSTING WITH GRUNT

Within your build process, you can do little to set HTTP headers, as those must go out with each response, rather than be statically determined. But what you can do is assign hashes to your assets using grunt-rev. This package will compute the hash for each of your assets and then rename them, appending the corresponding hash to their original names. For example, public/js/all.js would be changed to something such as public/js/1be2cd73.all.js, where 1be2cd73 would be the computed hash for the contents of all.js. One issue emerges from this task, and it's that now your views won't reference the correct assets, because they've been renamed with a hash in front of them. To remedy that, you can use the grunt-usemin package, which looks for static asset references in your HTML and CSS and refreshes them with the updated filenames. That's exactly what you need. The relevant Grunt configuration then looks like the following listing (labeled ch04/02_asset-hashing in the samples).

Listing 4.2   Updating filenames

```
rev: {
  release: {
    files: {
```

```
        src: ['build/**/*.{css,js,png}']
    }
  }
},

usemin: {
  html: ['build/**/*.html'],
  css: ['build/**/*.css']
}
```

Keep in mind you don't have any use for either of these tasks in the `debug` flow, because these are optimizations that do nothing to benefit you during development, so it might be appropriate to name their targets `release` to make that distinction more explicit. The `usemin` task, however, is written in such a way that Grunt targets have a special meaning. The `css` and `html` targets are respectively used to configure which CSS and HTML files you want to update with the hashed filenames, but targets such as `release` would be ignored by `usemin`.

The next technique we'll cover involves inlining CSS in a style tag to avoid the render-blocking request for CSS, resulting in faster page loads.

4.1.3 *Inlining critical above-the-fold CSS*

Browsers block rendering whenever they encounter a CSS resource they need to download. Yet, we've taught each other for years to place CSS at the top of our pages (in the <head>), so users won't see a flash of unstyled content (abbreviated as FOUC). The inlining technique aims to improve page load time speed without damaging user experience by avoiding FOUC. This technique only works effectively if you're rendering your views on the server side as well as the client side, as we explore in chapter 7.

To implement this feature, you have to do a number of different things:

- First, you need to identify the "above-the-fold" CSS; these are the styles that are required to correctly render the visible elements on the page, on first load.
- Once we've identified the styles that are effectively used above the fold (those that the browser needs to render the page properly and avoid the FOUC), you need to inline them in a <style> tag on the <head> of your pages.
- Last, now that the required styles are inlined in a <style> tag, you can eliminate the render-blocking request for the CSS style sheet by deferring the request until after the `onload` event has triggered, using JavaScript.
- Naturally, you wouldn't want to leave users with JavaScript turned off stranded, and because we're good citizens of the web, you'll also use a fallback <noscript> tag to make the render-blocking request anyway.

As you've probably noticed, this is a complicated and error-prone process, much like the case study in chapter 1, where Knight's Capital lost half a billion dollars due to human error. It's probably not going to be that catastrophic for you if something goes wrong, but automating this process is almost mandatory: there's too much work involved to be done every time your styles change, or whenever your markup changes!

Let's learn how we can use Grunt to automate this process, using `grunt-critical`.

HAVING GRUNT DO THE HEAVY LIFTING

Using `grunt-critical` for this purpose is incredibly easy, although it does provide a wealth of configuration options. In the following code, you'll find the configuration for a simple use case. In this case, you're extracting critical CSS from a page and inlining those styles after the build, inside a `<style>` tag. `critical` goes the extra mile of deferring the rest of the styles so as not to block rendering, and it also adds the `<noscript>` fallback tag for those that have JavaScript disabled:

```
critical: {
  example: {
    options: {
      base: './',
      css: [
        'page.css'
      ]
    },
    src: 'views/page.html',
    dest: 'build/page.html'
  }
}
```

You probably are already familiar with all of the provided options, which are file paths. The base option indicates the root directory that should be used when finding absolute resource paths such as `/page.css`. Once you set up Grunt to perform inlining on your behalf, remember to serve the upgraded HTML files, rather than the prebuilt ones.

Before switching gears and soaking in the thermal spring waters of automated deployments, you need to reflect upon the importance of testing a release build ahead of each deployment to mitigate the possibility of the spring being in an active volcanic area.

4.1.4   *Testing before a deployment*

Before you get into the deployment stage, or even the predeployment stage as we'll explore soon, you need to test your release build. Testing a release build becomes important when there's a deployment in your future, because you want to make sure your application behaves as you expect, or at the least, behaves as the tests you've written expect it to behave.

In the next part of the book, we'll delve into the underworld of application testing and examine two types of testing (though many, many more exist) in detail. These are unit testing and integration testing:

- Unit testing: Here you test individual components of your application by isolating them, making sure the components work fine on their own.
- Integration (or end-to-end) testing: This takes a series of unit-tested components and tests the interactions between them, making sure they communicate appropriately.

It'll be a while before you embark on testing practices and examples. We'll discuss testing practices and see examples in chapter 8. Keep in mind that before deployments, you need to test your application, reducing the odds of shipping a faulty build to one of your hosted environments, particularly if said environment is production. Let's discuss a few more tasks you can perform after a release is tested but before it's deployed.

4.2 Predeployment operations

Once you've prepared a build for release and had it carefully tested, you're ready to deploy. But I have a couple of important predeployment tasks I want to mention before taking a swim in the deployment hot springs.

Figure 4.2 is an overview of the deployment flow, as well as the operations that come before a build can be considered deploy-ready. It also shows how you're going to progressively roll out your update to different environments, ensuring maximum predictability.

PREDEPLOYMENT OPERATIONS

- *Semantic versioning*: This helps keep track of meaningful application versions. Semantic versions are formatted similarly to `MAJOR.MINOR.PATCH-BUILD`. This standard helps avoid confusion when managing dependencies. Keeping your application versioned is important if you want any control over what code is currently deployed on hosted environments, such as production. It enables you to roll back to an older version when things go awry. Considering this is fairly easy to set up, and taking into account how costly it is to be unprepared for deployments not panning out, versioning becomes a no-brainer.

- *Change logging*: A *changelog* is a list of changes that were made throughout the history of your project, divided by which version they were introduced in (partly why keeping versions is important) and further segmented as bug fixes, breaking changes, and new features. By convention, changelogs in `git` repositories are often placed at the project root, and named something along the lines of

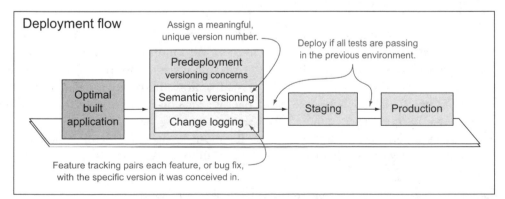

Figure 4.2 Versioning before a deployment and progressive deployment rollout. Testing by QA team in staging ensures robustness before deployment to production.

CHANGELOG.txt, or using whatever extension you prefer (such as md for Markdown,[2] a text-to-HTML conversion tool).

We'll delve into how you can better allocate your changelog upkeep time in a bit, but first let's explore the details of semantic versioning.

4.2.1 *Semantic versioning*

Because you're using Node, you might be familiar with the term semantic versioning. npm uses semantic versioning[3] for all packages, because it's a powerful specification to manage dependency resolution among different Node modules. Because every Node application you produce already has a package.json, and considering those contain a semantic version in them, you'll use these to tag your releases before deployments.

When I talk about versioning, I mean updating the package version and then creating a tag (a moment in your version history you can refer to) in your VCS. You can set up any scheme you want when it comes to numbering your releases, but the important part is that you don't overwrite a release; you shouldn't make two releases using the same version number. To ensure this uniqueness, I've settled for increasing the build number after every build (regardless of distribution) automatically with Grunt, and I also increase the patch number when I perform a deploy. Major version changes are intentionally manual, as those are probably introducing breaking changes. The same applies for minor version changes, as new features are usually introduced in new minors.

With Grunt, you could perform these version increments (from now on referred to as bumps) using the grunt-bump package. It's easy to configure, it does the version tagging for you, and it even commits the changes to the package.json file for you. Here's an example:

```
bump: {
  options: {
    commit: true,
    createTag: true,
    push: true
  }
}
```

These are, in fact, the defaults provided by this task. They're sensible enough that you don't have to configure it at all. The task will bump the version found in package.json, commit exactly that file with a relevant message, and then create a tag in git to finally push those changes to the origin remote. If you turn off all three of those options, the task only updates your package version. Sample ch04/03_version-bump shows this behavior in action.

Once versioning is sorted out, you'll want to set up a changelog, enumerating what changed since the previous release. Let's mull that over.

---

[2]   The Markdown format is a plain-text representation of HTML that's easy to read, write, and convert into HTML. Read the original article introducing Markdown in 2004 at http://bevacqua.io/bf/markdown.

[3]   You can read more about semantic versioning at http://bevacqua.io/bf/semver.

4.2.2 Using changelogs

You're probably used to reading changelogs from products that interest you when new releases come out (games, in particular, have a strong presence of changelogs in their culture), but have you ever maintained one yourself? It's not as hard as you might think.

Setting up a changelog—as an internal document that helps track changes made over time—could be a positive addition to your project even if you're not showing it to consumers.

If you have any sort of transparency policy, or you don't like keeping humans in the dark, then a changelog becomes almost mandatory to maintain. You shouldn't update the changelog every time you build for release, because you might want to produce a release build for debugging purposes. You shouldn't update them before testing, either. If testing fails, then the changelog would be out of sync with the last release-ready build. Then you're left with the need to update the changelog after you produce a build that passes all of the tests. Then and only then can you update the changelog to reflect the changes made since the last deployment.

Putting changelogs together is often hard because you forget what changed since the previous release, and you don't want to go through the git version history figuring out which changes deserve a spot in the changelog. Similarly, updating it by hand every time you make a change is tedious, and you might forget to do that if you're in the zone. A better alternative might be to set up grunt-conventional-changelog and have it build a changelog for you. All you'd have to do then is commit messages that, by convention, start with fix for bug fixes, feat when new features are introduced, or BREAKING when you break backwards compatibility. Furthermore, this package will allow you to edit the changelog by hand once it's done with its own parsing and updates.

As far as configuration goes, this task doesn't need any. Here are a few sample commit messages:

```
git commit -m "fix: buffer overflows, closes #17"
git commit -m "feat: reticulate splines for geodesic cape, closes #23"
git commit -m "feat: added product detail view"
git commit -m "BREAKING: removed POST /api/v1/users/:id/kill endpoint"
```

4.2.3 Bumping changelogs

The bump-only and bump-commit tasks allow you to bump the version without committing any changes, so that you can then update your changelog (as you'll see in a minute). Last, you should bump-commit to check in both package.json and CHANGELOG.txt at once in the same commit. Once you configure the bump task to also commit the changelog, you can now use the following alias to update your build version and changelog in one fell swoop. You can find an example using grunt-conventional-changelog in the samples, listed as ch04/04_conventional-changelog.

```
grunt.registerTask('notes', ['bump-only', 'changelog', 'bump-commit']);
```

Now you're done building for release, your tests are passing, and you've updated your changelog. You're ready to deploy to a hosted environment from which you can serve your application. In the past, it was fairly commonplace to deploy applications merely by means of uploading your built packages by hand to your production servers. You've come a long way from those good old days, and deployment tools, as well as application hosting platforms, have gotten better.

Let's next dive into Heroku, a Platform as a Service (PaaS) provider that enables you to deploy your application easily from the command line.

4.3   *Deploying to Heroku*

Setting up a deployment flow can be as hard as preparing sushi or as easy as ordering take-out; it all depends on how much control you want over the deployment. At one end of the spectrum you have services such as Amazon's Infrastructure as a Service (IaaS) platform, where you have full control over your hosted environment. You can pick your preferred operating system, choose how much processing power you'd like, configure it at will, install things on it, and then deal with the whole SysOps heavy lifting, such as securing the application against attacks, setting up proxies, picking a deployment strategy that guarantees uptime, and configuring most everything from the ground up.

On the other end of the spectrum are services where you don't have to do anything, such as those solutions often offered by domain name registrars such as GoDaddy. In these solutions you generally pick a theme, flesh out a few pages of static content, and you're done; everything else is done for you.

For the purposes of this book, I looked into the possibility of explaining how to host an application on Amazon, but I concluded that it'd be going too far off-scope. That being said, I'll be mentioning near the end of this section a way in which you can explore this alternative on your own.

I decided to go with Heroku (although there are similar alternatives, such as DigitalOcean), which isn't as complicated as setting up an instance on Amazon Web Services (AWS), but is fairly nontrivial, as opposed to using a website generator. Heroku simplifies your life by easily enabling you to configure and deploy your application to a hosted environment on their platform, straight from the command line. As I mentioned previously, Heroku is a Platform as a Service (PaaS) provider where you can host your application regardless of language or lack of server administration knowledge. In this section we'll go over the deployment of a simple application to Heroku, step by step.

At the time of this writing, Heroku offers a tier that allows you to host your applications with them for free. Let's get started there. You can find these instructions[4] in the accompanying source code as well.

---

[4]   Find the Heroku deployment example online at http://bevacqua.io/bf/heroku.

1 Go to https://id.heroku.com/signup/devcenter, and enter your email.
2 The next manual step you need to follow is installing their toolbelt, a series of command-line programs that help you manage your applications hosted on Heroku. You can find it at https://toolbelt.heroku.com, and then follow the instructions to run `heroku login`, which you can find on that same website.
3 You'll then need a `Procfile`, which is a fancy file to describe the OS processes your application runs on.

Heroku's definition of a Procfile can be found below. Note that there are also a few more steps to this process that can be found a few paragraphs later.

PROCFILE A `Procfile` is a text file named Procfile placed in the root of your application that lists the process types in an application. Each process type is a declaration of a command that's executed when an instance (called `dyno` in Heroku's jargon) of that process type is started. You can use a Procfile to declare various process types, such as multiple types of workers, a singleton process like a clock, or a consumer of the Twitter streaming API.

Long story short, for most well-designed Node applications out there, the Procfile will look similar to the following code:

```
web: node app.js
```

As far as the application goes, you're going for the bare minimum, because this is a taste of what deploying to Heroku feels like. `app.js` could be as small as the following snippet of JavaScript (ch04/05_heroku-deployments):

```
var http = require('http');
var app = http.createServer(handler);

app.listen(process.env.PORT || 3000);

function handler (req, res) {
  res.writeHead(200, { 'Content-Type': 'text/plain' });
  res.end('It\'s alive!');
}
```

Note that you use `process.env.PORT || 3000`, because Heroku will provide your application with a port it should listen on that will be exposed on the environment variable named `PORT`.

Then you use `3000` for local development. Now, here are a few more steps to take:

1 Once you're sitting on your project root, execute the following in terminal, to initialize a `git` repository:

```
git init
git add .
git commit -m "init"
```

2 Next create the app on Heroku with `heroku create`. This is a one-time thing.

At this point, your terminal should look similar to figure 4.3.

Figure 4.3   Creating an app on Heroku using their CLI

On every deploy you want to make, you can push to the `heroku` remote using `git push heroku master`. This will trigger a deploy, which looks something like figure 4.4.

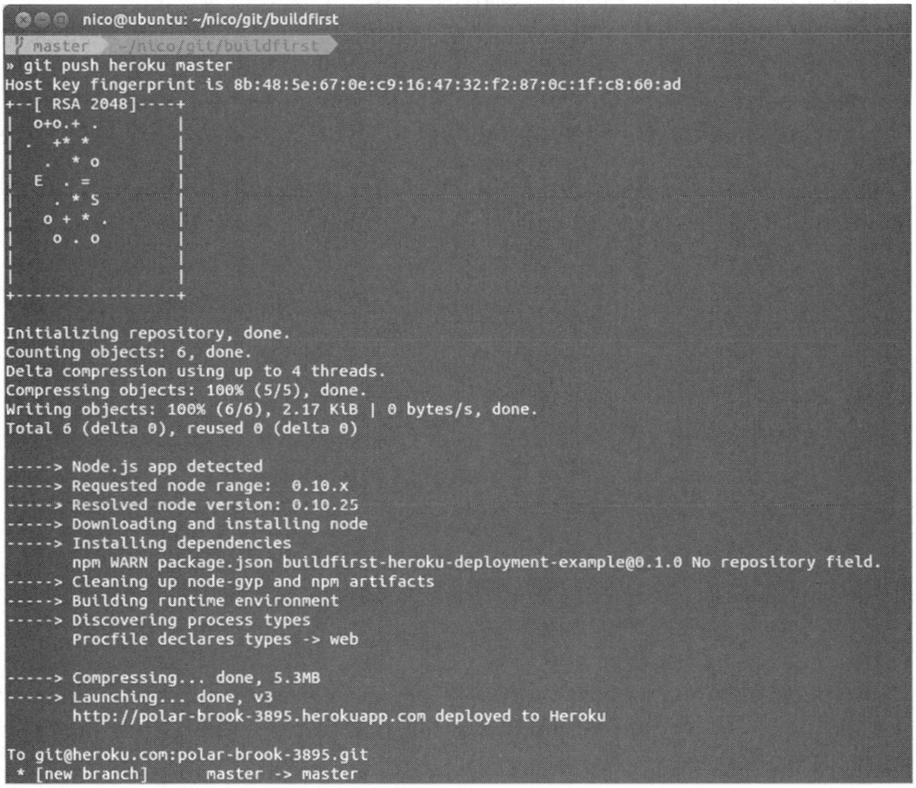

Figure 4.4   Deploying to Heroku—as simple as `git push`

If you want to pull up the application in the browser, use the following command:

```
heroku open
```

There's one caveat about Heroku and PaaS providers. When it comes to deploying build results, there's no simple solution. You shouldn't include build artifacts in your repository, as that may cause undesirable results such as forgetting to rebuild after changing something. You shouldn't get too comfortable building on their platforms, either, because building is something that should be done locally or on an integration platform, but not on the application server itself, because that would put a dent in your application's performance.

4.3.1 Deploying builds

The problem is you shouldn't put build results in version control, because those are the output of your source. Instead you should build before deployments, and deploy the build results along with the rest of your code. Most PaaS providers don't offer many alternatives. Platforms such as Heroku take deployments from Git when you push to their remote, but you don't want to include the build artifacts in revision control, so that becomes an issue. The solution: treat Heroku as you would any continuous integration platform (more on that in section 4.4), and allow Heroku to build your application in its servers.

Heroku doesn't usually install devDependencies for Node projects, because it uses npm install --production, and you need to use a custom buildpack to get around that. *Buildpacks* are interfaces between the language you use and the Heroku platform, and they're collections of shell scripts. Creating an application with the custom Grunt-enabled buildpack is easy using the following command, where thing is the name of your app on Heroku:

```
heroku create thing --buildpack https://github.com/mbuchetics/heroku-
    buildpack-nodejs-grunt.git
```

Once you've created an application using the custom buildpack, you could push the way you usually do, and that would trigger a build on Heroku servers. The last thing you need to set up is a heroku task:

```
grunt.registerTask('heroku', ['jshint']);
```

Heroku will terminate deployments if the build fails, keeping the previously deployed application unaffected by failed builds. There's a detailed explanation in the accompanying samples, listed as ch04/06_heroku-grunt, which will walk you through setting this up.

Let's take a look at how you can fit multiple environments in a single Heroku application.

4.3.2 Managing environments

If you want to set yourself up so you can host multiple environments[5] on Heroku, such as staging and production, use different git remote endpoints to achieve this. Create a remote other than heroku with the CLI:

```
heroku create --remote staging
```

---

[5] Heroku has advice on managing multiple environments. Go to http://bevacqua.io/bf/heroku-environments.

Instead of `git push heroku master`, you should now do `git push staging master`. Similarly, instead of doing `heroku config:set FOO=bar`, you now need to explicitly tell `heroku` to use a particular remote, such as `heroku config:set FOO=bar --remote staging`. Remember environment configuration is environment-specific, and should be treated as such, so environments shouldn't share API keys to third-party services, database credentials, or any authentication data in general.

Now that you can configure and deploy to specific environments directly from your command line, it's time to learn about a practice known as continuous integration, which will help tighten the leash on overall code quality. If you want to look into deployments to Amazon Web Services, there's a small guide[6] you can follow in the accompanying source code (labeled ch04/07_aws-deployments in the samples).

4.4   Continuous integration

Martin Fowler is one of the most renowned proponents of continuous integration. In his own words,[7] Fowler describes CI as follows.

> **CONTINUOUS INTEGRATION**   is a software development practice where members of a team integrate their work frequently; usually each person integrates at least daily, leading to multiple integrations per day. Each integration is verified by an automated build (including test) to detect integration errors as quickly as possible. Many teams find that this approach leads to significantly reduced integration problems and allows a team to develop cohesive software more rapidly.

Furthermore, he entices us to run the test suite in an environment that's as close to our production environment as possible. The implication is that your best bet, when it comes to testing your application, is doing it in the cloud, the way you do your hosting. CI platforms such as Travis-CI provide features like build error notifications and access to the full build logs, detailing everything that happened during the build (and its testing).

I mentioned Travis-CI; let's see how we can set ourselves up in such a way that we can remotely add builds to a queue on its platform on every commit made to our repository. Then Travis-CI build servers will process this queue one item at a time, running our builds and letting us know about the results.

4.4.1   Hosted CI using Travis

Continuous integration means to run tests on a remote server (which is as similar as possible to the production environment) in hopes of catching bugs that would otherwise make their way to the general population. Travis-CI is one CI platform (Circle-CI is another) where you can get feedback remotely on the result of a build once you've properly configured it. If the build is successful, you won't even notice. If the build

---

[6] Walk through the deployment process to AWS with this code sample at http://bevacqua.io/bf/aws.

[7] Read Fowler's full article on continuous integration at http://bevacqua.io/bf/integration.

Figure 4.5 A typical Travis notification for a build fix

fails, you'll get an email notification telling you someone broke your build (oops!). Later, when a subsequent push fixes the build, you'll get another notification letting you know about the fix. Additionally, you can also access full build logs on the Travis website, which always comes in handy when figuring out why a build failed. Figure 4.5 shows one such email notification.

Setting up CI is almost too easy in this day and age. The first thing you'll need to do is create a `.travis.yml` file at the project root. In the file, you'll need to declare the language you're using, which in your case is identified as `node_js`, the runtime version you're testing your builds against, and a series of scripts to execute before, during, and after the integration test. For the purposes of illustration, such a file might look like the following code:

```
language: node_js

node_js:
  - "0.10"

before_install:
  - npm install -g grunt-cli  script:   - grunt ci --verbose --stack
```

CONFIGURING TRAVIS AND GRUNT

Before executing your tests, you need to install the command-line interface for Grunt, `grunt-cli`, through `npm`. You'll need it in the integration test server the way you need it in your development environments so you can run Grunt tasks. You can use the `before_install` section to install the CLI.

All that's left then is to set up a `ci` task for Grunt. The ci task could run `jshint` to mitigate syntax errors, just like you're already doing locally every time something changes, thanks to your newfangled continuous development workflow. You should configure the `ci` task to run unit and integration tests as well, on top of linting your code with `jshint`.

The real value in CI comes from having the remote server build your entire application and apply your tests (lint included) against the code base, ensuring you don't depend on files not checked into version control or dependencies you might have installed locally but not made available in your code base at large.

You'll probably want to try out this example yourself, and I recommend you do so, because it's a good exercise for deployment-craving minds. You can follow the detailed instruction set I laid out in the accompanying sample repository,[8] named 08_ci-by-example, under ch04. Once you're done with that, you might as well learn about continuous deployments, a practice that may or may not fit into your workflow, but one that you should be fully aware of, regardless.

4.4.2 *Continuous deployments*

The Travis platform supports continuous deployments to Heroku.[9] *Continuous deployments* are a fancy way of saying that every single time you push to version control, you also trigger a build job in the CI server (which you're already doing as of last section, when you turned on Travis CI integration). When those builds succeed, the CI server deploys on your behalf to the release environments of your choosing.

In my experience, continuous deployments are a two-edged sword. When they work, you are cutting into a world of joy and less tedious deployments where passing the build and test integration cycle is validation enough to push to production. But you have to be confident that you've got enough tests in place to catch errors sensibly. A safe bet might be to enable continuous deployment to your staging environment rather than directly to production. Then, you'd make sure there are no issues in staging, and perform a deploy to production. This workflow looks like figure 4.6.

There's work involved in enabling continuous deployments to Heroku. You need an API key from Heroku, and you need to encrypt it and then configure .travis.yml with the encrypted data. I'll leave that up to you, now that I've voiced my concerns about deploying to production directly. If you choose to do that, visit http://bevacqua.io/bf/travis-heroku for instructions.

We've spent the majority of this chapter addressing deployments, which is a good thing. Now you can finally turn your attention to the options you have when it comes

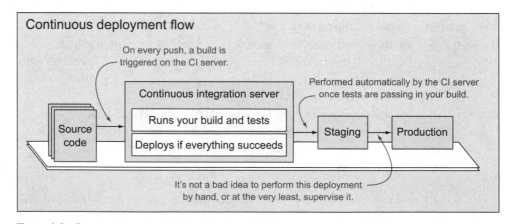

Figure 4.6 Proposed continuous deployment flow

---

[8] Find the fully documented code sample online at http://bevacqua.io/bf/travis.
[9] Read the article on Travis continuous deployments to Heroku at http://docs.travis-ci.com/user/deployment/heroku/.

to monitoring the state of your application as a whole, and individual requests in particular, when live in production. You'll also examine approaches to logging, debugging, and catastrophe tracing.

4.5 Monitoring and diagnostics

Production application monitoring is as important as having loyal customers. If you don't appreciate application uptime, your customers won't appreciate you. This is to say that you can't afford not to monitor your production servers. By monitoring I mean keeping access logs (who's visited what, when, and where from), as well as error logs (what went wrong), and perhaps even more importantly, setting up alerts so that you are immediately notified when things go *expectedly* wrong. "Expectedly" wasn't a typo; you should expect things to go wrong, and be as prepared as you can for those situations. Your enterprise probably doesn't warrant a simian army roaming around and randomly terminating off instances and services like Netflix advocates[10] to ensure their servers can reliably and consistently endure faults, such as hardware failure, without it affecting the end users consuming their services. But their advice, quoted as follows, still applies to most every software development effort.

> **QUOTE FROM NETFLIX BLOG** If we aren't constantly testing our ability to succeed despite failure, then it isn't likely to work when it matters most—in the event of an unexpected outage.

How do you plan for failure, though? Well, that's the sad part; nothing you do will prevent failure. Everyone has downtime, even giants such as Microsoft, Google, Facebook, and Twitter. You can plan all you want, but your application is going to fail regardless of what you do. What you can do is develop a modular architecture that's capable of dealing with services going boom and instances going bust. If you can achieve that modularity, it shouldn't be as damaging when a single module stops working, because the rest would still be perfectly functional. We'll develop notions of modularity, and the single responsibility principle (SRP) in chapter 5, dedicated to modular design and a crash-course introduction to the Node.js platform.

The first rule about Fight Club is you do not talk about Fight Club. Sorry, wrong movie. The first rule about application monitoring is you log things and set up notifications when bad things happen. Let's go over a possible implementation for that.

4.5.1 Logging and notifications

I'm sure you're more than used to `console.log` on the front end to inspect variables, and maybe even as a debugging mechanism, using it to figure out which code paths are being followed, and helping you nail down bugs. On the server side you have the standard output and standard error streams, both logging to your terminal window. These transports (`stdout` and `stderr`; more on transports in a minute!) are useful for

---

[10] Learn about Chaos Monkey, a chaos mongering service at Netflix, at http://bevacqua.io/bf/netflix.

development, but they are near useless to you if you can't capture what's being transmitted to them in a hosted environment, where you can't monitor the process in your own terminal.

Heroku has a mechanism where it captures the standard output of your processes, so you can access it down the road. It also has add-ons to further extend that behavior. Heroku add-ons provide much-needed companion services such as databases, emailing, caching, monitoring, and other resources. Most logging add-ons would allow you to set up filtering and notifications; however, I'd advise against leveraging Heroku's logging capabilities, as that would be too platform-specific, and it can severely limit your ability to migrate to another PaaS provider. Dealing with logging on your own isn't that hard, and you'll soon see the upside of doing so.

WINSTON FOR LOGGING

I'm not a huge fan of taking advantage of the Heroku logging facilities, because it binds your code base to their infrastructure by assuming writing to standard output will suffice in your log tracking efforts. A more durable and versatile approach would be to use a multitransport logger rather than writing to `stdout`. Transports dictate what happens with the information you're trying to log. A transport might log to a file, write a database record, send an email, or send push notifications to your phone. In multitransport loggers, you can use many of these at the same time, but you'd still use the same API to perform the logging. Adding or removing transports doesn't affect the way you write log statements.

Node has a few popular logging libraries, and I've picked `winston` because it has every feature you're looking for in a logger: logging levels, contexts, multiple transports, an easy API, and community support. Plus, it's easily extensible, and people have written transports for nearly everything you'll ever need.

By default, `winston` uses the `Console` transport, which is the same as using `stdout` directly. But you can set it up to use other transports, such as logging to a database or to a log management service. The latter are notably flexible in that they provide a platform where you can choose to get notified on important events without changing anything in your application.

Using a logging solution such as `winston` is platform agnostic. Your code won't depend on the hosting platform to capture standard output to work. To get started using `winston`, you have to install the package by the same name:

```
npm install --save winston
```

USING –SAVE VS USING –SAVE-DEV

In this case, you'll use the `--save` flag rather than `--save-dev`, because `winston` isn't a build-only package like the Grunt packages you've toyed with so far. When providing the `--save` flag to `npm`, the package will be added to your `package.json` file under `dependencies`.

Once you've installed `winston`, you can use it right away by putting `logger` where you used to put `console`:

```
var logger = require('winston');

logger.info('east coast clear as day');
logger.error('west coast not looking so hot.');
```

You might have gotten used to the idea of `console` being a global variable. In my experience, it's not wrong to use globals in this kind of scenario, and it's one of the two cases where I allow myself to use globals (the other one being `nconf`, as I mentioned in chapter 3). I like setting all the globals in a single file (even if there are only two), so that I can quickly scan it and figure out what's going on when I call something that's not otherwise defined in a module, or a part of Node. An illustrative `globals.js` might be as follows:

```
var nconf = require('nconf');

global.conf = nconf.get.bind(nconf);
global.logger = require('./logger.js');
```

I also propose keeping a single file where you can define the transports for your logger. Let's kick things off by using a `File` transport, as well as the default `Console` one. This would be the `logger.js` file referenced in the previous snippet:

```
var logger = require('winston');
var api = module.exports = {};
var levels = ['debug', 'info', 'warn', 'error'];

levels.forEach(function(level){
    api[level] = logger[level].bind(logger);
});

logger.add(logger.transports.File, { filename: 'persistent.log' });
```

Now, whenever you do `logger.debug`, you'll be logging a debug message to both the terminal and to a file. Although convenient, other transports offer more flexibility and reliability, and such is the case of a few transports we'll be covering in the accompanying samples: `winston-mail` will enable you to send out emails whenever something happens (at a level that warrants an email), `winston-pushover` sends notifications directly in your phone, and `winston-mongodb` is one of many traditional logging transports where you write a record in your database.

Once you've made sure to check out the sample listings, you'll have a better idea of how configuration, logging, and globals are tied together according to what I suggested. In case you're religiously against globals, don't panic. I've also included a sample where they aren't used. I like globals (in the two cases I mentioned previously) only because I find it convenient not having to `require` the same things in every module.

Now that you've spent time dealing with logging, we might as well talk about debugging Node applications.

4.5.2 Debugging Node applications

You'll want all the help you can get when it comes to tracing down a bug, and in my experience the best approach to debugging is increased logging, which is one of the reasons we've talked about it. That being said, you have more than a few ways to debug Node apps. You might use node-inspector[11] inside of Chrome's DevTools, you could use the features provided by an integrated IDE such as WebStorm, and then there's good old `console.log`. You could also use the native debugger[12] in V8 (the JavaScript engine Node runs on) directly.

Depending on which kind of bug you're tracing, you'll pick the right tool for the job. For example, if you're tracing a memory leak, you might use a package such as `memwatch`, which emits events when it's likely that a memory leak occurred. A more common use case, such as pinning down a rounding bug, or finding out what's wrong with your API calls, can be satisfied by adding log statements (temporarily with `console.log`, or in a more permanent fashion with `logger.debug`), or using the node-inspector package.

USING NODE INSPECTOR

The `node-inspector` package hooks onto the native debugger in V8, but it lets you debug using the full-featured debugging tools found in Chrome as an alternative to the terminal-based debugger provided by Node. To use it, the first thing you'll need to do is install it globally:

```
npm install -g node-inspector
```

To enable debugging on your Node process, you can pass the `--debug` flag to `node` when you launch the process, like so:

```
node --debug app.js
```

As an alternative, you can enable it on a running process. To do this, you'll need to find the process ID (PID). The following command, `pgrep`, takes care of that:

```
pgrep node
```

The output will be the PID for your running Node process. For example, it might be as follows:

```
89297
```

Sending a `USR1` signal to the process will enable debugging. This is done using the `kill -s` command (note I'm using the process ID from the results of the previous command):

```
kill -s USR1 89297
```

---

[11] Find the open source repository for node-inspector at GitHub at http://bevacqua.io/bf/node-inspector.

[12] Read the Node.js API documentation on debugging at http://bevacqua.io/bf/node-debugger.

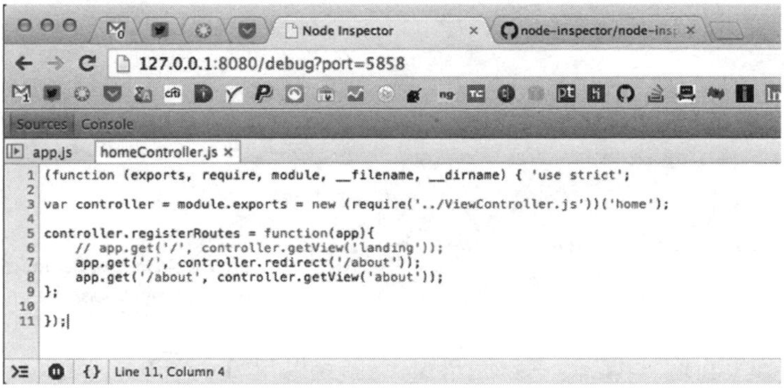

Figure 4.7 Debugging Node.js code in Chrome using Node Inspector

If everything worked correctly, Node will notify you where the debugger is listening through its standard output:

```
Hit SIGUSR1 - starting debugger agent.
debugger listening on port 5858
```

Now you need to execute `node-inspector` and then open Chrome, pointing it at the link provided by the inspector:

```
node-inspector
```

If all goes well, you should see something similar to figure 4.7 and have a full-blown debugger in your Chrome browser ready to use, which will behave (for the most part) exactly like the debugger for client-side JavaScript applications. This debugger will allow you to watch expressions, set breakpoints, step through the code, and inspect the call stack, among other useful features.

On a higher level than debugging, there's performance analysis, which will help detect potential problems in your code, such as memory leaks causing a spike in memory consumption that could cripple your servers.

4.5.3 Adding performance analytics

You have a few options when it comes to performance profiling, depending on how specific (we must track down a memory leak!) or generic (how could we detect a spike in memory consumption?) your needs are. Let's look into a third-party service, which can relieve you of the burden of doing the profiling on your own.

Nodetime is a service you can literally set up in seconds, which tracks analytics such as server load, free memory, CPU usage, and the like. You can sign up at http://bevacqua.io/bf/nodetime-register with your email, and once you do you'll be provided with an API key you can use to set up `nodetime`, which takes a few lines of JavaScript to configure:

```
require('nodetime').profile({
  accountKey: 'your_account_key',
  appName: 'your_application_name'
});
```

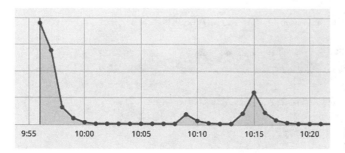

Figure 4.8   Server load over time, tracked by Nodetime

That's it, and you'll now have access to metrics, as well as the ability to take snapshots of CPU load, like the one presented in figure 4.8.

To conclude, we'll analyze a useful process scaling technique available to Node applications, known as `cluster`.

4.5.4   *Uptime and process management*

When it comes to release environments, production in particular, you can't afford to have your process roll over and die with any particular exception. This can be mitigated using a native Node API called `cluster` that allows you to execute your application in multiple processes, dividing the load among them, and create new processes as needed. `cluster` takes advantage of multicore processors and the fact that Node is single-threaded, allowing you to easily spawn an array of processes that run the same web application. This has the benefit of making your app more fault tolerant; you can spawn a new process! For example, in a few lines of code, you could configure `cluster` to spawn a worker every time another one dies, effectively replacing it:

```
var cluster = require('cluster');

// triggered whenever a worker dies
cluster.on('exit', function () {
  console.log('workers are expendable, bring me another vassal!');
  cluster.fork(); // spawn a new worker
});
```

This doesn't mean you should be careless about what happens inside your processes, as starting new ones can be expensive. Forking has a cost, tied to the amount of load your servers are under (requests / time), and also tied to the *startup time* for your process (wait period between spawning it and when it can handle HTTP requests). What `cluster` gives us is a way to transparently keep serving responses even if your workers die: others will come in his name.

In chapter 3 we introduced nodemon as a way to reload your application whenever a file changed during active development. This time you'll review pm2, which is similar to nodemon in spirit, but geared toward release environments.

ARRANGING A CLUSTER

Configuring `cluster` can be tricky, and it's also an experimental API at this time, so it might change in the future. But the upsides brought forth by the `cluster` module are undeniable and definitely appealing. The `pm2` module allows you to use fully configured `cluster` functionality in your application without writing a single line of code, making it a no-brainer to use. `pm2` is a command-line utility, and you need to install it using the `-g` flag:

```
npm install -g pm2
```

Once installed, you can now run your application through it, and `pm2` will take care of setting up `cluster` for you. Think of the following command as a drop-in replacement for `node app`:

```
pm2 start app.js -i 2
```

The main difference is that your application will use `cluster` with two workers (due to the `-i 2` option). The workers will handle requests to your app, and if one of them crashes, another one will spawn so that the show can go on. Another useful perk of `pm2` is the ability to do *hot code reloads*, which will allow you to replace running apps with their newly deployed counterpart without any downtime. You'll find related examples in the accompanying source code, listed as ch04/11_cluster-by-pm2, as well as one on how to use `cluster` directly, listed as ch04/10_a-node-cluster.

While clustering across a single computer is immediately beneficial and cheap, you should also consider clustering across multiple servers, mitigating the possibility of your site going down when your server crashes.

4.6   Summary

Phew, that was intense! We worked hard in this chapter:

- You became more intimate friends with release flow optimizations such as image compression and static asset caching.
- You learned about the importance of testing a release before calling it a day, bumping your package version, and putting together a changelog.
- Then you went through the motions of deploying to Heroku, and I mentioned `grunt-ec2`, which is one of many alternative deployment methods.
- Attaining knowledge on continuous integration was a good thing, as you've learned the importance of validating your build process and the quality of the code base you released.
- Continuous deploys are something you can perform, but you understand the implications of doing that, so you'll be careful about it.
- You also took a quick look at logging, debugging, managing, and monitoring release environments, which will prove fundamental when troubleshooting production applications.

All this talk about monitoring and debugging calls for a deeper analysis of architecture design, code quality, maintainability, and testability, which are conveniently at the core of part 2 in the book. Chapter 5 is all about modularity and dependency management, different approaches to JavaScript modules, and part of what's coming in ES6 (a long awaited ECMAScript standard update). In chapter 6, you'll uncover different ways you can properly organize the asynchronous code that's the backbone of Node applications, while playing it safe when it comes to exception handling. Chapter 7 will help you model, write, and refactor your code effectively. We'll also analyze small code examples together. Chapter 8 is dedicated to testing principles, automation, techniques, and examples. Chapter 9 teaches you how to design REST API interfaces and also explains how they can be consumed on the client side.

You'll leave part 2 with a deep understanding of how to design a coherent application architecture using JavaScript code. Pairing that with everything you've learned in part 1 about build processes and workflows, you'll be ready to design a JavaScript application using a Build First approach, the ultimate goal of this book.

Part 2

Managing complexity

The second part of the book is more interactive than the first, as it contains even more practical code samples. You'll get to explore different little angles at which we can attack complexity in our application designs, such as modularity, asynchronous programming patterns, testing suites, keeping your code concise, and API design principles.

Chapter 5 is a detailed examination of modularity in JavaScript. We start with the basics, learning about encapsulation, closures, and a few quirks of the language. Then we delve into the different formats that allow us to build modular code, such as CommonJS, AMD, and ES6 modules. We'll also go over different package managers, comparing what they bring to the table.

Chapter 6 teaches you to think about asynchronous code. We'll go through tons of practical code samples, following a few different styles and conventions. You'll learn all about Promises, the `async` control flow library, ES6 generators, and event-based programming.

Chapter 7 aims to expand your JavaScript horizons by teaching you about MVC. You'll take a fresh look at jQuery and learn how you could be writing more modular code instead. Later on, you'll leverage the Backbone.js MVC framework to componentize your front-end efforts even further. Backbone.js can even be used to render views on the server side, and we'll leverage the Node.js platform to do exactly that.

In chapter 8 you'll learn how to automate testing right off the bat, using Grunt tasks. Then you'll learn how to write tests for the browser, and how to run them using either Chrome or the PhantomJS headless browser. You won't only learn to do unit testing, but also visual testing and even performance testing as well.

Chapter 9 is dedicated to REST API design principles. In this chapter you're exposed to the best practices you should follow when laying out the foundations for an API service, as well as how you could design a layered architecture to complement the API. Last, you'll learn how to easily consume the API, using the conventions set forth by following a RESTful design approach.

Embracing modularity and dependency management

Now that we're done with the Build First crash course, you'll notice a decline in Grunt tasks, though you'll definitely continue to improve your build. In contrast, you'll see more examples discussing the tradeoffs between different ways you can work with the JavaScript code underlying your apps. This chapter focuses on *modular design*, driving down the code complexity of applications by separating concerns into different modules of interconnected, small pieces of code that do one thing well and are easily testable. You'll manage complexity in asynchronous code flows, client-side JavaScript patterns and practices, and various kinds of testing in chapters 6, 7, and 8, respectively.

Part 2 boils down to increasing the quality in your application designs through separation of concerns. To improve your ability to separate concerns, I'll teach you

99

all about modularity, shared rendering, and asynchronous JavaScript development. To increase the resiliency of your applications, you should test your JavaScript, as well, which is the focus of chapter 8. While this is a JavaScript-focused book, it's crucial that you understand REST API design principles to improve communication across pieces of your application stack, and that's exactly the focus of chapter 9.

Figure 5.1 shows how these bits and pieces of the second half of the book relate to each other.

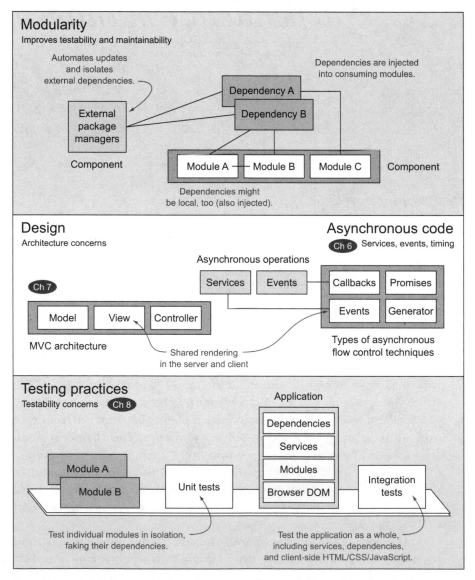

Figure 5.1   Modularity, good architecture, and testing are fundamentals of designing maintainable applications.

Applications typically depend on external libraries (such as jQuery, Underscore, or AngularJS), which should be handled and updated by using package managers, rather than manually downloaded. Similarly, your application can also be broken down into smaller pieces that interact with each other, and that's another focus of this chapter.

You'll learn the art of code encapsulation, treating your code as self-contained components; designing great interfaces and arranging them precisely; and information hiding to reveal everything the consumer needs, but nothing else. I'll spend a good number of words explaining elusive concepts such as *scoping*, which determines where variables belong; the `this` keyword, which you must understand; and *closures,* which help you hide information.

Then we'll look at dependency resolution as an alternative to maintaining a sorted list of script tags by hand. Afterward, we'll jump to package management, which is how you'll install and upgrade third-party libraries and frameworks. Last, we'll look at the upcoming ECMAScript 6 specification, which has a few nice new tricks in store for building modular applications.

5.1 *Working with code encapsulation*

Encapsulation means keeping functionality self-contained and hiding implementation details from consumers of a given piece of code (those who access it). Each piece, whether a function or an entire module, should have a clearly defined responsibility, hide implementation details, and expose a succinct API to satisfy its consumers' needs. Self-contained functionality is easier to understand and change than code that has many responsibilities.

5.1.1 *Understanding the Single Responsibility Principle*

In the Node.js community, inspired by the UNIX philosophy of keeping programs concise and self-contained, packages are well known for having a specific purpose. The high availability of coherent packages that don't go overboard with features plays a big role in making the `npm` package manager great. For the most part, package authors accomplish this by following the Single Responsibility Principle (SRP): build packages that do one thing, and do it well. SRP doesn't apply only to packages as a whole; you should follow SRP at the module and method levels, as well. SRP helps your code stay readable and maintainable by keeping it simple and concise.

Consider the following use case. You need to build a component that takes a string and returns a hyphenated representation. It will be helpful when generating semantic links in web applications such as blogging platforms. This component might take blog post titles such as `'Some Piece Of Text'`, and convert them to `'some-piece-of-text'`. This is called *slugging*.

Suppose you start with the following listing (available as ch05/01_single-responsibility-principle in the samples). It uses a two-step process in which it first normalizes all nonalphanumeric character sequences into single dashes and then removes leading and trailing dashes. Then it lowercases the string. Exactly what you need but nothing else.

Listing 5.1   Converting text using slugging

```
function getSlug (text) {
    var separator = /[^a-z0-9]+/ig;
    var drop = /^-|-$/g;
    return text
        .replace(separator, '-')
        .replace(drop, '')
        .toLowerCase();
}
var slug = getSlug('Some Piece Of Text');
// <- 'some-piece-of-text'
```

The first expression, `/[^a-z0-9]+/ig` is used to find sequences of one or more characters that aren't alphanumerical, such as spaces, dashes, or exclamation points. These expressions are replaced by dashes. The second expression looks for dashes at either end of the string. Combining these two, you can build a URL-safe version of blog post titles.

> **Understanding regular expressions**
>
> Although you don't need to know regular expressions to understand this example, I encourage you learn the basics. Regular expressions are used to find patterns in strings, and they can also be used to replace those occurrences with something else. These expressions are supported in virtually all major languages.
>
> Expressions such as `/[^a-z0-9]+/ig` can be confusing to look at, but they aren't that hard to write! My blog has an entry-level article you can read if the subject interests you.[a]
>
> ---
> [a]   You can find the article on my blog at http://bevacqua.io/bf/regex.

In the previous example, the `separator` variable is a simple regular expression that will match sequences of non-letter, non-numeric characters. For example, in the `'Cats, Dogs and Zebras!'` string, it will match the first comma and space as a single occurrence, both spaces around `'and'`, and the `'!'` at the end. The second regular expression matches dashes at either end of the string, so that the resulting slug begins and ends with words, especially because you're converting any nonalphanumeric characters into dashes in the previous step. Combining these two steps is enough to produce a decent slugging function for your component.

Imagine a feature request for which you need to add a timestamp of the publication date to the slug. An optional argument in the slugging method to turn on this functionality might be tempting, but it would also be wrong: your API would become more confusing to use, harder to refactor (change its code without breaking other components, detailed in chapter 8 when we discuss testing), and even more difficult to document. It would be more sensible to build your component by following the SRP principle using a composition pattern instead. *Composition* only means applying functions in sequence, rather than mashing their functionality together. So first you'd apply slugging and then you could add a timestamp to the slugs, as shown in the following code snippet:

```
function stamp (date) {
    return date.valueOf();
}
var article = {
  title: 'Some Piece Of Text',
  date: new Date()
};
var slug = getSlug(article.title);
var time = stamp(article.date);
var url = '/' + time + '/' + slug;
// <- '/1385757733922/some-piece-of-text'
```

Now, imagine that your Search Engine Optimization (SEO) expert comes along, and he wants you to exclude irrelevant words from your URL slugs so you get better representation in search results. You might be tempted to do that right in the getSlug function, but here are a few reasons why that would be wrong in this case, too:

- It would become harder to test the slugging functionality on its own, because you'd have logic that doesn't have anything to do with the slugging.
- The exclusion code might become more advanced as time goes on, but it'd still be contained in getSlug.

If you're cautious, you'll code a function aimed at the expert's requirements, which looks like the following code snippet:

```
function filter (text) {
    return text.replace(keywords, '');
}
var keywords = /\bsome|the|by|for|of\b/ig; // match stopwords
var filtered = filter(article.title);
var slug = getSlug(filtered);
var time = stamp(article.date);
var url = '/' + time + '/' + slug;
// <- '/1385757733922/piece-text'
```

That looks fairly clean! By giving each method a clear responsibility, you extended your functionality without complicating matters too much. In addition, you uncovered the possibility of reuse. You might use the SEO expert's filtering functionality all over an application, and that would be easy to extract from your slugging module, because it doesn't depend on that. Similarly, testing each of these three methods will be easy. For now, it should be enough to say that keeping code succinct and to the point and doing exactly what the function name implies is one of the fundamental aspects of maintainable, testable code. In chapter 8 you'll learn more about unit testing.

Splitting functionality in a modular way is important, but it's not enough. If you're building a typical component, which has a few methods but shouldn't expose its variables, you need to hide this information from the public interface. I'll discuss the importance of information hiding next.

5.1.2   *Information hiding and interfaces*

As you're building out an application, code will invariably grow in both volume and complexity. This can eventually turn your code base into an unapproachable tangle, but you can help it by writing more straightforward code and making it easier to follow the flow of code. One way to drive down the complexity creep is to hide away unnecessary information, keeping it inaccessible on the interface. This way only what matters gets exposed; the rest is considered to be irrelevant to the consumer, and it's often referred to as *implementation details.* You don't want to expose elements such as state variables you use while computing a result or the seed for a random number generator. This has to be done at every level; each function in every module should attempt to hide everything that isn't relevant to its consumers. In doing this, you'll do fellow developers and your future self a favor by reducing the amount of guesswork involved in figuring out how a particular method or module works.

As an example, consider the following listing illustrating how you might build an object to calculate a simple average sum. The listing (found as ch05/02_information-hiding in the samples) uses a constructor function and augments the prototype so `Average` objects have an `add` method and a `calc` method.

Listing 5.2   Calculating an average sum

```
function Average () {
    this.sum = 0;
    this.count = 0;
}

Average.prototype.add = function (value) {
    this.sum += value;
    this.count++;
};

Average.prototype.calc = function () {
    return this.sum / this.count;
};
```

All that's left to do is create an `Average` object, add values to it, and calculate the average. The problem in this approach is that you might not want people directly accessing your private data, such as `Average.count`. Maybe you'd rather hide those values from the API consumers using the techniques we'll cover soon. An even simpler approach might be to ditch the object entirely and use a function instead. You could use the `.reduce` method (found on the Array prototype, new in ES5) to apply an accumulator function on an array of values to calculate the average:

```
function average (values) {
    var sum = values.reduce(function (accumulator, value) {
        return accumulator + value;
    }, 0);

    return sum / values.length;
}
```

The upside of this function is that it does exactly what you want. It takes an array of values, and it returns the average, as its name indicates. In addition, it doesn't keep any state variables the way your prototypical implementation did, effectively hiding any information about its inner workings. This is what's called a *pure function*: the result can only depend on the arguments passed to it, and it can't depend on state variables, services, or objects that aren't part of the argument body. Pure functions have another property: they don't produce any side effects other than the result they provide. These two properties combined make pure functions good interfaces; they are self-contained and easily testable. Because they have no side effects or external dependencies, you can refactor their contents as long as the relationship between input and output doesn't change.

FUNCTIONAL FACTORIES

An alternative implementation might use a *functional factory*. That's a function that, when executed, returns a function that does what you want. As you'll better understand in the next section, anything you declare in the factory function is private to the factory, and the function that resides within. This is easier to understand after reading the following code:

```
function averageFactory () {
    var sum = 0;
    var count = 0;
    return function (value) {
        sum += value;
        count++;
        return sum / count;
    };
}
```

The sum and count variables are only available to instances of the function returned by averageFactory; furthermore, each instance has access only to its own context, those variables that were declared within that instance, but not to the context of other instances. Think of it like a cookie cutter. The averageFactory is the cookie cutter, and it cuts cookies (your function) that take a value and return the cumulative average (so far). As an example, here's how its use might look:

```
var avg = averageFactory();
// <- function
avg(1);
// <- 1
avg(3);
// <- 2
```

Much like using your cookie cutter to cut out new cookies won't affect existing cookies, creating more instances won't have any effect on existing ones. This coding style is similar to what you did previously using a prototype, with the difference that sum and count can't be accessed from anywhere other than the implementation. Consumers can't access these variables, effectively making them an implementation detail of the API. Implementation details don't only introduce noise; they can also potentially present security concerns: you wouldn't want to grant the outside world the ability to modify the inner state of your components.

Understanding *variable scopes,* which define where variables are accessible, and `this` keyword, which provides context about the caller of a function, is essential in building solid structures that can hide information properly. Properly scoping variables enables you to hide the information that consumers of an interface aren't supposed to know about.

5.1.3   *Scoping and this keyword*

In his undisputed classic, *JavaScript: The Good Parts* (O'Reilly Media, 2008),[1] Douglas Crockford explains many of the quirks of the language, and encourages us to avoid the "bad parts," such as `with` blocks, `eval` statements, and type-coercing equality operators (`==` and `!=`). If you've never read his book, I recommend you do so sooner rather than later. Crockford says that `new` and `this` are tricky to understand, and he suggests avoiding them entirely. I say you need to understand them. I'll describe what `this` represents, and then I'll explain how it can be manipulated and assigned. In any given piece of JavaScript code, the context is made up of the current function scope, and `this`.

If you're used to server-side languages, such as Java or C#, then you're used to thinking of a scope: the bag where variables are contained, which starts and ends whenever a curly brace is opened and closed, respectively. In JavaScript, scoping happens at the function level (called *lexical scoping*), rather than at the block level.

```
Scoping in C#
Block scoping

    public void NullGuard (thing)                          Message is unavailable
    {                                                       outside of the block it
      if (thing == null)                                    was defined in.
      {
        var message = "Reference must be non-null!";
        throw new ArgumentNullException(message);
      }
    }
```

```
Scoping in JavaScript
Lexical scoping                                    Message is hoisted to the top
                                                   of the lexical scope, becoming
    function NullGuard (thing) {                   available to the entire function.
      if (thing == null) {
        var message = "Reference must be non-null!";
        throw new Error(message);
      }
    }
```

Figure 5.2   Discrepancies in scoping across languages

---

[1]   You can find *JavaScript: The Good Parts* at Amazon following this link: http://bevacqua.io/bf/goodparts.

Figure 5.2 disambiguates lexical scoping from block scoping by comparing C#, which has block scoping (other examples include Java, Perl, C, and C++) with JavaScript, which has lexical scoping (R is another example).

In the figure, a message variable is used in both examples. In the first example, message is only available inside the if statement block, while in the second example message is available to the entire function, thanks to lexical scoping. As you'll learn, this has both benefits and drawbacks.

VARIABLE SCOPING IN JAVASCRIPT

An understanding of how scopes work will set you up to understand the module pattern, which we'll visit in section 5.2 as a way of componentizing your code base. In JavaScript, function is a first-class citizen, and it's treated like any other object. Nested functions each come with their own scope, and inner functions have access to the parent scope up until the global space. Consider the getCounter function in the following code:

```
function getCounter () {
    var counter = 0;
    return function () {
        return counter++;
    };
}
```

In this example, the counter variable is context-bound to the getCounter function. The returned function can access counter, because it's part of the parent scope. But nothing outside getCounter can create a reference to counter; access to it has been shut down and only the privileged children of getCounter can manipulate it. If you introduce a console.log(this) statement at either scoping level, you'll see in both cases the global Window object instance is referenced. This is the true "bad part;" by default, the this keyword will be a reference to the global object, as demonstrated in the following listing.

Listing 5.3 Understanding the this keyword

```
function scoping () {
    console.log(this);

    return function () {
        console.log(this);
    };
}
scoping()();
// <- Window
// <- Window
```

There are different ways we can manipulate the this keyword. The most common way to assign a this context is to invoke methods on an object. For example, when doing 'Hello'.toLowerCase(), 'Hello' will be used as the this context for the function call.

GETTING TO THE CALL SITE

When functions are invoked directly as properties on an object, the object will become the `this` reference. If the method is in the object's prototype—for example `Object.prototype.toString`—this will also be the object the method has been invoked on. Note that this is a fragile behavior; if you get a direct reference to a method and invoke that, then `this` won't be the `parent` anymore but rather the global object once again. To illustrate, let me show you another listing.

Listing 5.4 Scoping the `this` keyword

```
var parent = {
    method: function () {
        console.log(this);
    }
};
parent.method();
// <- parent
var parentless = parent.method;
parentless();
// <- Window
```

> When the method's call site is on a parent object, then that object is used.

> If there's no parent object, then we fall back to the default context.

Under strict mode, `this` will default to `undefined`, instead of `Window`. Outside strict mode, `this` is always an object; it's the provided object if it's called with an object reference; it's a boxed representation if it's called with a primitive boolean, string, or numeric value; or it's the global object (again, `undefined` under strict mode) if it's called with either `undefined` or `null`, either by getting a direct reference to the method or by using any one of these: `.apply`, `.call`, or `.bind`. The value passed as `this` to a function in strict mode isn't boxed into an object. We'll get to what else strict mode does shortly.

Other than what happens out of the box when invoking functions, you can use different methods to assign a value to `this`; it's not entirely out of your control. In fact, you could use `.bind` to create a function that will always have the `this` value provided to it. Alternative ways of executing a method include `.apply`, `.call`, and the `new` operator. Here's a cheat sheet so you can see the methods in action:

```
Array.prototype.slice.call([9, 5, 7], 1, 2)
// <- [5]

String.prototype.split.apply('13.12.02', ['.'])// <- ['13', '12', '02']

var data = [1, 2];
var add = Array.prototype.push.bind(data, 3);

add(); // effectively the same as data.push(3)
add(4); // effectively the same as data.push(3, 4)

console.log(data);
// <- [1, 2, 3, 3, 4]
```

In JavaScript, variables fill a scope in the following order:

- Scope context variables: this and arguments
- Named function parameters: function (these, variable, names)
- Function expressions: function something () {}
- Local scope variables: var foo

If you're not experimenting or following along with a JavaScript interpreter by your side, make sure to look at the code sample (ch05/03_context-scoping); I've included these examples in the source code provided with the book, and they have a few inline comments if you have trouble understanding. Let's now discuss what the strict mode entails.

5.1.4 *Strict mode*

When enabled, strict mode modifies semantics in the way your code works, reducing the leniency toward missing var statements and similarly error-prone practices, sort of complementary to using a linter.[2] Strict mode can be enabled on individual functions or on an entire script.

For client-side code, the function form is preferred. To turn on strict mode, put the 'use strict'; statement (double quotes work, too) at the top of a file or function:

```
function () {
    'use strict';
    // here lies strict mode
}
```

Aside from this defaulting to undefined, rather than the global object, strict is less tolerant of mistakes, turning them into errors rather than correcting them. Restrictions also include banning the with statement, octal notation, and preventing keywords such as eval and arguments to be assigned.

```
'use strict';
foo = 'bar' // ReferenceError foo is not defined
```

Under strict mode, the engine also throws an exception if you attempt to write on read-only properties, delete undeletable properties, instantiate an object with duplicate property keys, or declare a function with duplicate argument names. This kind of intolerance helps catch issues due to sloppy coding.

The last quirk I want to cover while we're on the topic of scoping is something that's commonly referred to as hoisting. Understanding hoisting is important if you're to write complex JavaScript applications sensibly.

---

[2] Get a detailed explanation of strict mode in Mozilla Developer Network at http://bevacqua.io/bf/strict.

5.1.5   *Variable hoisting*

A large number of JavaScript interview questions can be answered with an understanding of scoping, how `this` works, and hoisting. We've covered the first two, but what exactly is hoisting? In JavaScript, *hoisting* means that variable declarations are pulled to the beginning of a scope. This explains the unexpected behavior you can observe in certain situations.

Function expressions are hoisted entirely: the function body is also hoisted, not only their declaration. If I had a single thing to take away from *The Good Parts*, it would be learning about hoisting; it changed the way I write code, and reason about it.

Hoisting is the reason invoking function expressions before declaring them works as expected. Assigning functions to a variable won't do the trick, because the variable won't be assigned by the time you want to invoke the function. The following code is one example; you'll find more examples in the accompanying source code, listed as ch05/04_hoisting:

```
var value = 2;

test();

function test () {
  console.log(typeof value);
  console.log(value);
  var value = 3;
}
```

You might expect the method to print `'number'` first, and 2 afterward, or maybe 3. Try running it! Why does it print `'undefined'` and then `undefined`? Well, hello hoisting! It'll be easier to picture if you rearrange the code the way it ends up after hoisting takes place. Let's look at the following listing.

Listing 5.5   Using hoisting

```
var value;

function test () {
  var value;
  console.log(typeof value);
  console.log(value);
  value = 3;
}

value = 2;
test();
```

The `value` declaration at the end of the `test` function got hoisted to the top of the scope, and it's also why `test` didn't give a `TypeError` exception, warning that `undefined` isn't a function. Keep in mind that if you used the variable form of declaring the `test` function, you would, in fact, have gotten that error, because although `var test` would be hoisted, the assignment wouldn't be, effectively becoming the code in the following listing.

Listing 5.6   Hoisting `var` test

```
var value;
var test;

value = 2;
test();

test = function () {
  var value;
  console.log(typeof value);
  console.log(value);
  value = 3;
};
```

The code in listing 5.6 won't work as expected, because `test` won't be defined by the time you want to invoke it. It's important to learn what gets hoisted and what doesn't. If you make a habit of writing code as if it were already hoisted, pulling variable declarations and functions to the top of their scope, you'll run into fewer problems than you might run into otherwise. At this point you should feel comfortable with scoping and the `this` keyword. It's time to talk about closures and modular patterns in JavaScript.

5.2 JavaScript modules

Up to this point, you've looked at the single responsibility principle, information hiding, and how to apply those in JavaScript. You also have a decent idea of how variables are scoped and hoisted. Let's move on to closures. These will help you create new scopes and prevent variables from leaking information.

5.2.1 Closures and the module pattern

Functions are also referred to as closures, particularly when focusing on the fact that functions create new scopes. An IIFE is a function that you execute immediately. The term IIFE stands for Immediately-Invoked Function Expression. Using an IIFE is useful when all you want is a closure. The following code is an example IIFE:

```
(function () {
    // a new scope
})();
```

Note the parentheses wrapping the function. These tell the interpreter you're not only declaring an anonymous function, but also using it as a value. These expressions can also be used in assignments, which are useful if you need variables accessible by the exported return value. This is commonly referred to as the module pattern, as shown in the following code (labeled ch05/05_closures in the samples):

```
var api = (function () {
    var local = 0; // private and in-place!
    var publicInterface = {
        counter: function () {
            return ++local;
        }
```

```
    };
    return publicInterface;
})();
api.counter();
// <- 1
```

A common variant to the previous code doesn't rely on anything outside of the closure, but instead imports the variables it's going to use. If it wants to expose a public API, then it imports the global object. I tend to favor this approach because everything is nicely wrapped by a closure, and you can instruct JSHint to blow up on issues due to undeclared variables. Without a closure and JSHint, these would inadvertently become globals. To illustrate, look at the following code:

```
(function (window) {
    var privateThing;

    function privateMethod () {
    }

    window.api = {
        // public interface
    };
})(window);
```

Let's consider *prototypal modularity*, which augments a prototype rather than using closures, as a complementary alternative to IIFE expressions. Using prototypes provides performance gains, as many objects can share the same prototype and adding functions on the prototype provides the functionality to all the objects that inherit from it.

5.2.2 *Prototypal modularity*

Depending on your use case, prototypes might be exactly what you need. Think of prototypes as JavaScript's way of declaring classes, even though it's an entirely different model, because prototypes are simply links, and you can't override properties unless you replace them entirely (and do the overriding by hand). In short, don't try to treat prototypes as classes, because it will assuredly result in maintainability issues. Prototypes are most useful when you expect to have multiple instances of your module. For example, all JavaScript strings share the `String` prototype. A good use for prototypes is when interacting with DOM nodes. Sometimes I find myself declaring prototypal modules inside a closure and then keeping private state in the closure, outside the prototype. The following listing shows pseudo-code, but please look at the accompanying code sample listed as ch05/06_prototypal-modularity for a fully working example and to get a better understanding of the pattern.

> **Listing 5.7 Using pseudo-code for prototypes**

```
var lastId = 0;
var data = {};

function Lib () {
    this.id = ++lastId;
    data[this.id] = {
```

```
        thing: 'secret'
    };
}

Lib.prototype.getPrivateThing = function () {
    return data[this.id].thing;
};
```

This is one way to keep data safe from consumers; many scenarios exist when data privatization isn't necessary and where allowing consumers to manipulate your instance data might be a good thing. You should wrap all of this in a closure so your private data doesn't leak out. I believe prototypes in JavaScript are most useful when dealing with DOM interaction, as we'll investigate in chapter 7. That's because when dealing with DOM objects, you usually have to work with many elements at the same time; prototypes improve performance because their methods aren't replicated on each instance, saving resources.

Now that you have a clearer understanding of how scoping, hoisting, and closures work, we can move on to how modules are meant to interact with one another. First, let's look at CommonJS modules: a way to keep code well-organized and deal with dependency injection (DI) at once.

5.2.3 *CommonJS modules*

CommonJS (CJS) is a specification adopted by Node.js, among others, which allows you to write modular JavaScript files. Each module is defined by a single file, and if you assign a value to `module.exports`, it becomes that module's public interface. To consume a module, you call `require` with the relative path from the consumer to the dependency.

Let's look at a quick example, labeled ch05/07_commonjs-modules in the samples:

```
// file at './lib/simple.js'
module.exports = 'this is a really simple module';

// file at './app.js'
var simple = require('./lib/simple.js');

console.log(simple);
// <- 'this is a really simple module'
```

One of the most useful advantages of these modules is that variables don't leak to the global object: you have no need to wrap your code in a closure. The variables that are declared on the top-most scope (such as the `simple` variable in the previous snippet) are merely available in that module. If you want to expose something, you need to make that intent explicit by adding it to `module.exports`.

At this point you might think I went off the trail with CJS, given that it's not supported natively in browsers any more than are CoffeeScript and TypeScript. You'll soon learn how to compile these modules using Browserify, a popular library designed to compile CJS modules to something browsers can deal with. CJS has the following benefits over the way browsers behave:

- No global variables, less cognitive load
- Straightforward process to expose an API and consume a module

- Easier to test modules by mocking dependencies
- Access to packages on npm, thanks to Browserify
- Modularity, which translates into testability
- Easy to share code between client and server, if you're using Node.js

You'll learn more about package management solutions (npm, Bower, and Component) in section 5.4. Before we get there, we'll look at *dependency management*, or how to deal with the components needed by your application, and how different libraries can help manage them.

5.3   *Using dependency management*

We'll discuss two kinds of dependency management here: internal and external. When talking about internal dependencies, I'm referring to those that are part of the program you're writing. Most frequently, these are a one-to-one mapping to physical files, but you might also have multiple modules in a single file. By modules I mean pieces of code that have a single responsibility, regardless of them being services, factories, models, controllers, or something else. External dependencies are, in contrast, those in which the code isn't governed by your application itself. You may own or have authored the package, but the code belongs to a different repository altogether, regardless.

I'll explain what dependency graphs are, and then we'll investigate ways of working through them, such as the caveats with resorting to the RequireJS module loader, the innocent straightforwardness made available by CommonJS, and the elegant way AngularJS (a Model-View-Controller framework built by Google) resolves dependencies while keeping everything modular and testable.

5.3.1   *Dependency graphs*

When writing out a module which depends on something else, the most common approach is to have your module create an instance of the object you depend on. To illustrate the point, bear with me through a little Java code; it should be easy to wrap your head around. The following listing displays a `UserService` class, which has the purpose of serving any data requests from a domain logic layer. It could consume any `IUserRepository` implementation which is tasked with retrieving the data from a repository such as a MySQL database or a Redis store. This listing is labeled ch05/08_ dependency-graphs in the samples.

Listing 5.8   Using a module to create an object

```
public class UserService {
    private IUserRepository _userRepository;

    public UserService () {
        _userRepository = new UserMySqlRepository();
    }

    public User getUserById (int id) {
        return _userRepository.getById(id);
    }
}
```

But that doesn't cut it; if your service is supposed to use any repository that conforms to the interface, why are you hard-coding UserMySqlRepository that way? Hard-coded dependencies make it more difficult to test a module, because you wouldn't merely test against the interface, but rather against a concrete implementation. A better approach, which is coincidentally more testable, might be passing that dependency through the constructor, as shown in the following listing. This pattern is often referred to as dependency injection, which is a smart-sounding alternative to giving an object its instance variables.

Listing 5.9   Using dependency injection

```
public class UserService {
    private IUserRepository _userRepository;

    public UserService (IUserRepository userRepository) {
        if (userRepository == null) {
            throw new IllegalArgumentException();
        }
        _userRepository = userRepository;
    }

    public User getUserById (int id) {
        return _userRepository.getById(id);
    }
}
```

This way, you can build out your service the way it was intended, as a consumer of any repository conforming to the IUserRepository interface without any knowledge of implementation specifics. Creating a UserService might not sound like such a great deal, but it gets harder as soon as you take into consideration its dependencies, and its dependencies' dependencies. This is called a *dependency tree*. The following snippet is certainly unappealing:

```
String connectionString = "SOME_CONNECTION_STRING";
SqlConnectionString connString = new SqlConnectionString(connectionString);
SqlDbConnection conn = new SqlDbConnection(connString);
IUserRepository repo = new UserMySqlRepository(conn);
UserService service = new UserService(repo);
```

The code shows *inversion of control* (IoC),[3] which is a wordy definition for something rather simple. IoC means that instead of making an object responsible for the instantiation of its dependencies, or getting references to them, the object is given the dependencies through its constructor or through public properties. Figure 5.3 examines the benefits of using an IoC pattern.

---

[3] Read a primer on inversion of control and dependency injection by Martine Fowler at http://bevacqua.io/bf/ioc.

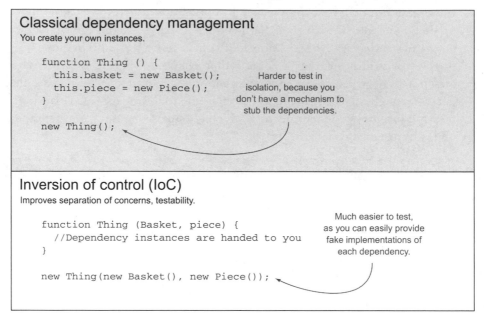

Figure 5.3   Classical dependencies compared with using IoC to improve testability

The IOC code (at the bottom of the figure) is easier to test, more loosely coupled, and easier to maintain as a result, than the classic dependency management code shown at the top of the figure.

IoC frameworks are used to address dependency resolution and mitigate dependency hell. The basic gist of these frameworks is that you ditch the new keyword and rely on an IoC container. The *IoC container* is a registry that has knowledge about how to instantiate your services, repositories, and any other modules. Learning how to configure a traditional IoC container (such as Spring in the case of Java, or Castle Windsor for C#) is outside of the scope of this book, but a top-level view of the issue is required to pave the road ahead.

IS IOC IMPORTANT FOR TESTABILITY?

Ultimately, the importance of avoiding hard-coded dependencies lies in the ability to easily mock them when unit testing, as you'll see in chapter 8.

Unit testing is about asserting whether interfaces work as expected, regardless of how they're implemented. *Mocks* are stubs that implement the interface, but don't do anything other than the bare minimum to conform to them. For example, a mocked user repository might always return the same hard-coded User object. This is useful in the context of unit testing, where you might want to test the UserService class on its own, but don't need details about its inner workings, much less how its dependencies are implemented!

Great! Enough Java for now, though. What does any of this have to do with JavaScript Application Design? Understanding testability principles is required if you hope to write testable code. Although you may not agree with the Test-Driven Development movement, it's undeniable that code that isn't written with testability in mind is much harder to write tests for. When speaking about client-side JavaScript, you have an additional layer of complexity: networking. Modules aren't immediately available unless your code is bundled together the way you learned to do it in chapter 2.

Next, I'll introduce you to RequireJS, an asynchronous module loader, which is a better option than the classical approach of having an unmanaged dependency soup.

5.3.2   *Introducing RequireJS*

RequireJS is a JavaScript asynchronous module loader (AMD) that allows you to define modules and have them depend on one another. The following code (found as ch05/ 09_requirejs-usage in the samples) is an example usage of AMD, depicting a module that depends on something else:

```
require(['lib/text'], function(text) {
    var result = text('foo bar');
    console.log(result);
    // <- 'FOO BAR'
});
```

By convention, `'lib/text'` looks for the file that can be found at the `./lib/text.js` path, relative to the JavaScript directory root. That resource will be requested, interpreted, and once all dependencies have been loaded, the module's function will be invoked, getting its dependencies as arguments to the module's function, much like the Java code I talked about in section 5.3.1. The sample `'lib/text'` module is defined as follows:

```
define([], function () {
    return function (input) {
        return input.toUpperCase();
    };
});
```

Next, let's analyze where RequireJS is better than the alternatives, and where it falls short.

BENEFITS AND DRAWBACKS OF REQUIREJS

In this case, the definition uses an empty array because it has no dependencies. The returned function is the public interface provided by the `'lib/text'` module. The use of RequireJS has a few benefits:

- Dependency graph is automatically resolved. No more worrying about ordering script tags!
- Asynchronous module loading is included.
- A compile step isn't required during development.
- It's unit testable, so you only load the module that needs to be tested.
- Closures are enforced, because your module is defined in a function.

These are all true and nice to have, but drawbacks exist. If a package your code depends on isn't wrapped in AMD magic, you have no option other than adding a compile step to bundle everything together. Unless you bundle your modules together, RequireJS will create an HTTP request cascade to fetch each dependency, which would be too slow in production systems. Many of the benefits of AMD came from the lack of a compile step, so you're left with a glorified dependency graph resolver packed with the following drawbacks:

- Asynchronous loading functionality is unavailable if you use the bundler.
- It requires vendors to conform to the AMD model.
- It clutters your code with AMD wrappers.
- Production needs compilation.
- Code in release environments diverges from local development.

It's been a while since we spoke of Grunt in chapter 4, and you wouldn't want to release a bunch of unoptimized scripts! Grunt will help compile AMD modules during your builds so they don't need to be fetched asynchronously.

To compile[4] AMD modules through r.js, the RequireJS optimizer, using Grunt, you can use the grunt-contrib-requirejs package. That package allows you to pass options through to r.js. The following listing is the pertinent task configuration. You'll set default options that apply to every target in Grunt and tweak the debug target. This is useful when you'd otherwise have to repeat parts of the configuration, breaking the DRY principle.

Listing 5.10   Using Grunt to configure a module

```
requirejs: {
  options: {
    name: 'app',
    baseUrl: 'js/amd',
    out: 'build/js/app.min.js'
  },
  debug: {
    options: {
      preserveLicenseComments: false,
      generateSourceMaps: true,
      optimize: 'none'
    }
  },
  release: {}
}
```

In the debug distribution you generate a source map,[5] which helps browsers map what they're executing to the source code you used to compile it. This is useful when

---

[4] Check out the accompanying code sample that shows how to compile RJS modules at http://bevacqua.io/bf/requirejs.

[5] For more information on source maps, refer to this introductory article on HTML5Rocks at http://bevacqua.io/bf/sourcemap.

Figure 5.4   Typical file structure when using RequireJS during Grunt builds

debugging, as you'll get stack traces that point to the source code rather than hard-to-debug compilation results. The `release` target doesn't have any additional configuration, because it merely uses the defaults provided previously. It'll be easier for you to visualize the configuration if you take a look at the directory structure in the accompanying samples, which looks like the one in figure 5.4.

> **NOTE** A sample that integrates RequireJS with Grunt can be found in the book's source code at ch05/10_requirejs-grunt. It contains detailed information about the meaning of each option used to configure the RequireJS build task.

Not having to add script tags in a specific order is a nice feature to have, and you have a few ways to accomplish that. If you're not entirely sold on the AMD solution, or if you're curious, read on for an explanation of how you could bring CommonJS modules to the browser, as an alternative.

5.3.3 *Browserify: CJS in the browser*

In section 5.2.3 I explained the benefits of CJS, the module system used in Node.js packages. These modules also have a place in the browser, thanks to Browserify. This option is frequently pitched as an alternative to AMD, although opinions vary. As you're following a Build First approach, compiling CJS modules for the browser won't be a big deal; it's another step in your build process!

In addition to the advantages described in section 5.2.3, such as no implicit globals, CJS offers a terse alternative to AMD in that you don't need all the clutter and boilerplate needed by AMD to define a module. A continuously improving trait in favor of CJS modules is immediate access to any package in the npm registry out of the box. In 2013, the npm registry grew by an order of magnitude (or 10x), and at the time of this writing, it boasts well more than 100,000 registered packages.

Browserify will recursively analyze all the `require()` calls in your app to build a bundle that you can serve up to the browser in a single `<script>` tag. As you might expect, Grunt has numerous plugins eager to compile your CJS modules into a Browserify bundle, and one such plugin is `grunt-browserify`. Configuring it is more akin to what you saw in chapter 2, where you provided a filename declaring the entry point of your CJS module and an output filename as well:

```
browserify: {
  debug: {
    files: { 'build/js/app.js': 'js/app.js' },
    options: { debug: true }
  },
  release: {
    files: { 'build/js/app.js': 'js/app.js' }
  }
}
```

I think most of the mental load in taking this approach won't come from Browserify, but rather learning about `require` and modularity in CJS modules. Luckily, you already used CJS modules when configuring Grunt tasks throughout part 1, and that should give you insight into CJS, as well as a bunch of code samples to look at! A fully working example of how to compile CJS modules, using `grunt-browserify`, can be found at ch05/11_browserify-cjs in the accompanying code samples. Next up, we'll look at how AngularJS deals with dependency resolution, as a third (and last) way to deal with dependency management.

5.3.4   *The Angular way*

Angular is an innovative client-side Model-View-Controller (MVC) framework developed at Google. In chapter 7 you'll use another popular JavaScript MVC framework called Backbone. But Angular's dependency resolver deserved a mention in this section.[6]

LEVERAGING DEPENDENCY INJECTION IN ANGULAR

Angular has a fairly elaborate dependency injection solution in place, so we won't get into the details. Luckily for us, it's abstracted well enough that it's easy to use. I've personally used many different DI frameworks, and Angular makes it feel natural: you don't even realize you're doing DI, similarly to Java and RequireJS. Let's walk together through a contrived example, which can be found at ch05/12_angularjs-dependencies in the samples. It's convenient to keep the module declaration in its own file, something like this:

```
angular.module('buildfirst', []);
```

---

[6]   Angular's documentation has an extensive guide explaining how DI works in Angular at http://bevacqua.io/bf/angular-di.

Then each of the different pieces of a module, such as services or controllers, are registered as extensions to that module, which you previously declared. Note that you're passing an empty array to the `angular.module` function so your module doesn't depend on any other modules:

```
var app = angular.module('buildfirst');

app.factory('textService', [
  function () {
    return function (input) {
      return input.toUpperCase();
    };
  }
]);
```

Registering controllers is also similar; in the following example you'll use the `text-Service` service you created. This works in a similar way to RequireJS, because you need to use the name you gave to the service:

```
var app = angular.module('buildfirst');
app.controller('testController', [
  'textService',
  function (text) {
    var result = text('foo bar');
    console.log(result);
    // <- 'FOO BAR'
  }
]);
```

Next up, let's compare Angular to RJS in a nutshell.

COMPARING ANGULAR AND REQUIREJS

Angular is different from RequireJS in that, rather than acting as a module loader, Angular worries about the dependency graph. You need to add a script tag for each file you're using, unlike with AMD, which dealt with that for you.

In the case of Angular you see an interesting behavior where script order isn't all that relevant. As long as you have Angular on top and then the script that declares your module, the rest of the scripts can be in whatever order you want, and Angular will deal with that for you. You need code such as the following on top of your script tag list, which is why the module declaration needs its own file:

```
<script src='js/vendor/angular.js'></script>
<script src='js/app.js'></script>
```

The rest of the scripts, which are part of the `app` module (or whatever name you give it), can be loaded in any order, as long as they come after the module declaration:

```
<!--
    These could actually be in any order!
-->
<script src='js/app/testController.js'></script>
<script src='js/app/textService.js'></script>
```

Let's draw a few quick conclusions on the current state of module systems in JavaScript.

BUNDLING ANGULAR COMPONENTS USING GRUNT

As a side note, when preparing a build, you can explicitly add Angular and the module to the top, and then glob for the rest of the pieces of the puzzle. Here's how you might configure the `files` array passed to a bundling task, such as the ones in the `grunt-contrib-concat` or `grunt-contrib-uglify` packages:

```
files: [
    'src/public/js/vendor/angular.js',
    'src/public/js/app.js',
    'src/public/js/app/**/*.js'
]
```

You might not want to commit to the full-featured framework that is AngularJS, and you're not about to include it in your project for its dependency resolution capabilities! As a closing thought, I'd like to add that there's no right choice, which is why I presented these three methods:

- RequireJS modules, using AMD definitions
- CommonJS modules, and then compiling them with Browserify
- AngularJS, where modules will resolve the dependency graph for you

If your project uses Angular, that's good enough that you wouldn't need either AMD or CJS, because Angular provides a sufficiently modular structure. If you're not using Angular, then I'd probably go for CommonJS, mostly because of the abundance of npm packages you can potentially take advantage of.

The next section sheds light on other package managers, and as you did for npm, teaches you how to leverage them in your client-side projects.

5.4   *Understanding package management*

One of the drawbacks of using package managers is that they tend to organize dependencies using a certain structure. For example, npm uses `node_modules` to store installed packages, and Bower uses `bower_components`. One of the great advantages to Build First is that's not a problem, because you can add references to those files in your builds and that's that! The original location of the packages won't matter at all. That's a huge reason to use a Build First approach.

I want to discuss two popular front-end package managers in this section: Bower and Component. We'll consider the tradeoffs in each and compare them to npm.

5.4.1   *Introducing Bower*

Although npm is an extraordinary package manager, it isn't fit for all package management needs: virtually all of the packages published to it are CJS modules, because it's ingrained into the Node ecosystem. Although I chose to use Browserify so that I could write modular front-end code under the CJS format, this might not be the choice for every project you work on.

Bower is a package manager for the web, created at Twitter, and it's *content agnostic*, meaning it doesn't matter whether authors pack up images, style sheets, or JavaScript code. By now you should be accustomed to the way npm tracks packages and version numbers, using the `package.json` manifest. Bower has a `bower.json` manifest that's similar to `package.json`. Bower is installed through npm:

```
npm install -g bower
```

Installing packages with `bower` is fast and straightforward; all you need to do is specify the name or a git remote endpoint. The first thing you'll need to do on a given project is run `bower init`. Bower will ask you a few questions (you can press Enter because the defaults are fine), and then it'll create a `bower.json` manifest for you, as in figure 5.5.

```
 latest    ~/nico/git/buildfirst
» bower init
[?] name: buildfirst
[?] version: 0.0.1
[?] description:
[?] main file:
[?] keywords:
[?] authors: Nicolas Bevacqua <nicolasbevacqua@gmail.com>
[?] license: MIT
[?] homepage: https://github.com/bevacqua/buildfirst
[?] set currently installed components as dependencies? Yes
[?] add commonly ignored files to ignore list? Yes
[?] would you like to mark this package as private which prevents it from being accidentally published
[?] would you like to mark this package as private which prevents it from being accidentally published
to the registry? No

{
  name: 'buildfirst',
  version: '0.0.1',
  homepage: 'https://github.com/bevacqua/buildfirst',
  authors: [
    'Nicolas Bevacqua <nicolasbevacqua@gmail.com>'
  ],
  license: 'MIT',
  ignore: [
    '**/.*',
    'node_modules',
    'bower_components',
    'test',
    'tests'
  ]
}

[?] Looks good? Yes
```

Figure 5.5 Using `bower init` to create a `bower.json` manifest file

Once that's out of the way, installing packages is a breeze. The following example installs Lo-Dash, a utility library similar to Underscore, but more actively maintained. It will download the scripts and place them in a `bower_components` directory, as shown in figure 5.6.

```
bower install --save lodash
```

```
 latest    ~/nico/git/buildfirst
» bower install --save angular
bower cached       git://github.com/angular/bower-angular.git#1.2.5
bower validate     1.2.5 against git://github.com/angular/bower-angular.git#~1.2.5
bower cached       git://github.com/angular/bower-angular.git#1.2.5
bower validate     1.2.5 against git://github.com/angular/bower-angular.git#*
bower new          version for git://github.com/angular/bower-angular.git#~1.2.5
bower resolve      git://github.com/angular/bower-angular.git#~1.2.5
bower download     https://github.com/angular/bower-angular/archive/v1.2.6-build.2000+sha.73c6671.tar.gz
bower extract      angular#~1.2.5 archive.tar.gz
bower resolved     git://github.com/angular/bower-angular.git#1.2.6-build.2000+sha.73c6671
bower install      angular#1.2.6-build.2000+sha.73c6671

angular#1.2.6-build.2000+sha.73c6671 bower_components/angular
```

Figure 5.6 Using bower `install --save` to fetch a dependency and add it to the manifest

That's it! You should have scripts in the `bower_components/lodash` directory. Including them in your builds is a matter of adding the file to your distribution configuration. As usual, this example can be found in the accompanying source code; look for `ch05/13_bower-packages`.

Bower is arguably the second-largest package manager, with close to 20,000 packages in its registry, and behind npm, which has more than 100,000. Component, another package management solution, lags behind with nearly 3,000 packages under its belt, but it offers a more modular alternative and a more comprehensive solution to client-side package management. Let's take a look!

5.4.2 *Big libraries, small components*

Huge libraries such as jQuery do everything you need, as well as things you don't need. For instance, you might not need the animations or the AJAX that come with it. In this sense, struggling to keep pieces out of jQuery using custom builds is an uphill battle; automating the process isn't trivial, and you're doing more to get less, which I guess is what the "write less, do more" slogan refers to.

Component is a tool that's all about small components that do one thing only but do it well. Rather than using a big library for all your needs, TJ Holowaychuk,[7] prolific open source author, advocates using multiple small blocks to build exactly what you need in a modular way and without any added bloat.

The first thing you'll need to do, as usual, is install the CLI tool from npm:

```
npm install -g component
```

If you're consuming components, you can get away with a manifest with the bare minimum valid JSON. Let's create that, too:

```
echo "{}" > component.json
```

Installing components such as Lo-Dash works similarly to what you did previously with Bower. The main difference is that rather than using a registry whose sole purpose is tracking packages, like Bower does, Component uses GitHub as its default registry. Specifying the username and repository, as shown in the following command, is enough to fetch a component:

```
component install lodash/lodash
```

In contrast with what other libraries do, Component will always update the manifest, adding the packages you install. You must also add the entry point to the scripts field in the component manifest.

```
"scripts": ["js/app/app.js"]
```

Another difference you can find in Component is that it has an additional build step, which will bundle any components you've installed into a single `build.js` concate-

---

[7] Read an introduction to Component on Holowaychuk's blog at http://bevacqua.io/bf/component.

nated file. Given that components use CommonJS-style `require` calls, the necessary `require` function will also be provided.

```
component build
```

I encourage you to look at a pair of accompanying samples, which might help you learn how to use Component. The first one, ch05/14_adopting-component, is a fully working example of what has been described here.

The second, ch05/15_automate-component-build, explains how to automate the build step with Grunt, using the `grunt-component-build` package. Such a build step is particularly useful if your code is also treated as components.

To wrap things up, I'll give you an overview of each of the systems we've discussed, which might help you decide on a package manager or module system.

5.4.3 *Choosing the right module system*

Component has the right idea behind it—modular pieces of code that do one thing well—but it has subtle drawbacks, as well. For instance, it has an unnecessary build step in `component install`. Executing `component install` should build everything you need for the components to work, the way npm does. It's also kind of mystical to configure, and the documentation is hard to find. Poor naming is a huge drawback in this regard, as you can't do a web search for Component and not get unrelated results, making it hard to find the documentation you want.

Bower is fine if you don't buy into the CJS concept, and it's certainly better than downloading code and placing it into directories by yourself and dealing with version upgrades on your own. Bower is fine for fetching packages, but it does little to help you with modularity, and that's where it falls short.

As far as Browserify goes, at the moment it's the best option that's available to us, if you're willing to concede that CJS is the simplest module format available today. The lack of a package manager embedded into Browserify is a good thing, because it doesn't matter which source you pick for modules you consume. They can come from npm, Bower, GitHub, or somewhere else.

Browserify provides mechanisms for both bringing vendor code into the CJS format and exporting a CJS formatted application into a single file. As we discussed in 5.3.3, Browserify can produce source maps that help debug during development, and using it gives you access to any CJS modules originally written for Node development.

Last, AMD modules might be a good fit for using Bower, because they don't interfere with each other. The benefit here is that you don't have to learn the CJS approach, although I would argue that there isn't all that much to learn about it.

Before discussing the changes coming to the JavaScript language in ECMAScript 6, there's one more topic we need to tend to. That's the topic of circular dependencies, such as a chicken depending on an egg that depends on a chicken.

5.4.4   *Learning about circular dependencies*

Circular dependencies, explained previously as a chicken depending on an egg that depends on a chicken, are a tough nut to crack, and they're straight up unsupported by many module systems. In this brief section I aim to dispel any issues you have by answering the following questions:

- Is there a good reason to use circular dependencies?
- What patterns can you use to avoid them?
- How do the solutions we've talked about handle circular dependencies?

Components that depend on each other represent a code smell, meaning there might be a deeper problem in your code. The best approach to circular dependencies is to avoid them altogether. You can use a few patterns to avoid them. If two components are talking to each other, it might be a sign that they need to communicate through a service they both consume, for example. That way, it'll be easier to reason about (and write code for) the affected components. In chapter 7, you'll look at the ways you can avoid these chicken-and-egg type of situations when using AngularJS in client-side applications.

Using a service as a middleman is one of many ways to solve circular dependencies. You might have your chicken module depend on egg and talk to it directly, but if egg wants to talk to chicken, then it should use the callbacks chicken gives to it. An even simpler approach is to have instances of your modules depend on each other. Have a chicken and an egg depending on each other, rather than the entire families, and the problem is circumvented.

You also need to take into account that different systems deal with circular dependencies differently. If you try to resolve a circular dependency in Angular, it will throw an error. Angular doesn't provide any mechanisms to deal with circular dependencies at the module level. You can get around this by using their dependency resolver. Once an egg module that depends on the chicken module is resolved, then the chicken module can fetch the egg module when it's used.

In the case of AMD modules, if you define a circular dependency such that chicken needs egg and egg needs chicken, then when egg's module function is called, it will get an undefined value for chicken. egg can fetch chicken later, after modules have been defined by using the require method.

CommonJS allows circular dependencies by pausing module resolution whenever a require call is made. If a chicken module requires an egg module, then interpretation of the chicken module is halted. When the egg module requires chicken, it will get the partial representation of the chicken module, until the require call is made. Then the chicken module will finish being interpreted. The code sample labeled ch05/16_circular-dependencies illustrates this point.

The bottom line is that you should avoid circular dependencies like the plague. Circular dependencies introduce unnecessary complexity into your programs, module systems don't have a standard way of dealing with them, and they can always be avoided by writing code in a more organized way.

To wrap up this chapter, we'll go through a few changes coming to the language in ECMAScript 6, and what they bring to the table when it comes to modular component design.

5.5 Harmony: a glimpse of ECMAScript 6

As you might know, ECMAScript (ES) is the spec that defines the behavior of JavaScript code. ES6, also known as Harmony, is the (long-awaited) upcoming version of the spec. Once ES6 lands, you'll benefit from hundreds of small and large improvements to the language, part of which I'll cover in this section. At the time of this writing, parts of Harmony are in Chrome Canary, the edge version of Google Chrome, and also in the Firefox Nightly build. In Node, you can use the `--harmony` flag when invoking the `node` process to enable ES6 language features.

Please note that ES6 features are highly experimental and subject to change; the spec is constantly in flux. Take what's discussed in this section with a pinch of salt. I'll introduce you to concepts and syntax in the upcoming language release; features proposed as part of ES6 at this point are unlikely to change, but specific syntax is more likely to be tweaked.

Google has made an interesting effort in popularizing ES6 learning through their Traceur project, which compiles ES6 down to ES3 (a generally available spec version), allowing you to write code in ES6 and then execute the resulting ES3. Although Traceur doesn't support every feature in Harmony, it's one of the most featured compilers available.

5.5.1 Traceur as a Grunt task

Traceur is available as a Grunt task, thanks to a package called `grunt-traceur`. You can use the following configuration to set it up. It will compile each file individually and place the results in a `build` directory:

```
traceur: {
  build: {
    src: 'js/**/*.js',
    dest: 'build/'
  }
}
```

With the help of this task, you can compile a few of the ES6 Harmony examples I'll show you along the way. Naturally, the accompanying code samples have a working example of this Grunt task, as well as a few different snippets of what you can do with Harmony, so be sure to check out `ch05/17_harmony-traceur` and skim through those samples. Chapters 6 and 7 also contain more pieces of ES6 code, to give you a better picture of what features are coming to the language.

Now that you know of a few ways to turn ES6 features on, let's dive into Harmony's way of doing modules.

5.5.2 *Modules in Harmony*

Throughout this chapter, you've navigated different module systems and learned about modular design patterns. Input from both AMD and CJS have influenced the design decisions behind Harmony modules, in a way that aims to please proponents of either system. These modules have their own scope; they export public API members using the `export` keyword, which can later be imported individually using the `import` keyword. An optional explicit `module` declaration allows for file concatenation.

What follows is an example of how these mechanics work. I'm using the latest syntax available[8] at the time of this writing. The syntax comes from a meeting held in March 2013 by TC39, the technical committee in charge of moving the language forward. If I were you, I wouldn't focus too much on the specifics, only the general idea.

To begin with, you'll define a basic module with a couple of exported methods:

```
// math.js

export var pi = 3.141592;

export function circumference (radius) {
    return  2 * pi * radius;
}
```

Consuming these methods is a matter of referencing them in an `import` statement, as shown in the following code snippet. These statements can choose to import one, many, or all the exports found in a module. The following statement imports the `circumference` export into the local module:

```
import { circumference } from "math";
```

If you want to import multiple exports, you comma-separate them:

```
import { circumference, pi } from "math";
```

Importing every export from a module in an object, rather than directly on the local context, can be done using the as syntax:

```
import "math" as math;
```

If you want to define modules explicitly, rather than having them be defined implicitly, for release scenarios where you're going to bundle your scripts in a single file, there's a literal way in which you can define a module:

```
module "math" {
    export // etc...
};
```

If you're interested in the module system in ES6, you should read an article[9] that encompasses what you've learned so far about ES6, and sheds light on the module

---

[8] Find the ES6 article at http://bevacqua.io/bf/es6-modules.
[9] Find this ES6 article at http://bevacqua.io/bf/es6-modules.

system's extensibility. Always keep in mind that the syntax is subject to change. Before heading to chapter 6, I have one last little ES6 feature to touch on with regard to modularity. That's the `let` keyword.

5.5.3 *Let there be block scope*

The ES6 `let` keyword is an alternative to `var` statements. You may remember that `var` is function scoped, as you analyzed in section 5.1.3. With `let`, you get block scoping instead, which is more akin to the scoping rules found in traditional languages. Hoisting plays an important role when it comes to variable declaration, and `let` is a great way to get around the limitations of function scoping in certain cases.

Consider, for instance, the scenario below, a typical situation where you conditionally want to declare a variable. Hoisting makes it awkward to declare the variable inside the `if`, because you know it'll get hoisted to the top of the scope, and keeping it inside the `if` block might cause trouble if someday you decide to use the same variable name in the `else` block.

```
function processImage (image, generateThumbnail) {
    var thumbnailService;
    if (generateThumbnail) {
        thumbnailService = getThumbnailService();
        thumbnailService.generate(image);
    }

    return process(image);
}
```

Using the `let` keyword you could get away with declaring it in the `if` block, not worrying about it leaking outside of that block, and without the need to split the variable declaration from its assignment:

```
function processImage (image, generateThumbnail) {
    if (generateThumbnail) {
        let thumbnailService = getThumbnailService();
        thumbnailService.generate(image);
    }

    return process(image);
}
```

The difference is subtle in this case, but getting away from having a long list of variables listed on the top of a function scope, which might only be used in one of the code paths, is a code smell in current JavaScript implementations using `var`. It's a code smell that could easily be avoided by using the `let` keyword, keeping variables in the block scope they belong to.

5.6 Summary

At long last, you're done with scoping, module systems, and so on!

- You learned that keeping code self-contained that has a clear purpose, as well as information hiding, can greatly improve your interface designs.

- Scoping, `this`, and hoisting are much clearer now, which will help you design code that fits the JavaScript paradigm better, without even realizing it.
- Using closures and the module pattern taught you how module systems work.
- You compared how CommonJS, RequireJS, and Angular deal with module loading, and how they handle circular dependencies.
- You learned about the importance of testability, which we'll expand on in chapter 8, and how the Inversion of Control pattern can make your code more testable.
- We discussed how to leverage npm packages in the browser thanks to Browserify, downloading dependencies with Bower, and the UNIX philosophy of writing modular code with Component.
- You saw what's coming in ES6, such as the module system and the `let` keyword, and you learned how to play around with ES6 using the Traceur compiler.

In chapter 6 you'll learn about asynchronous JavaScript development. You'll learn your way around common pitfalls, and you'll work through examples that will help you understand how to effectively debug these functions. You'll look at various patterns for writing asynchronous functions, such as callbacks, events, Promises, and the upcoming generators API in Harmony.

6

Understanding asynchronous flow control methods in JavaScript

Chapter 5 taught the importance of building your components in a modular fashion, and you learned a great deal about scoping, hoisting, and closures, all of which are necessary to understand asynchronous JavaScript code effectively. Without a modest understanding of asynchronous development in JavaScript, it becomes harder to write quality code that's easy to read, refactor, and maintain.

One of the most frequently recurring issues for JavaScript development beginners is dealing with "callback hell," where many functions are nested inside each other, making it hard to debug or even understand a piece of code. This chapter aims to demystify asynchronous JavaScript.

Asynchronous execution is when code isn't executed immediately, but rather in the future; such code isn't synchronous because it doesn't run sequentially. Even though JavaScript is single-threaded, user-triggered events such as clicks, timeouts, or AJAX responses can still create new execution paths. This chapter will cover different ways you can handle asynchronous flow in a tolerable and painless way, by applying a consistent style to asynchronous code flows. Much like chapter 5, this chapter has many practical code examples for you to follow!

To kick things off, we'll look at one of the oldest patterns available: passing a callback as an argument so the caller of a function can determine what happens in the future when the callback is invoked. This pattern is referred to as continuation-passing style, and it's the bread and butter of asynchronous callbacks.

6.1 Using callbacks

A prime example of using callbacks is found in the `addEventListener` API, which allows us to bind event listeners on DOM (Document Object Model) nodes. When those events are triggered, our callback function gets called. In the following trivial example, when we click anywhere in the document, a log statement will be printed to the console:

```
document.body.addEventListener('click', function () {
  console.log('Clicks are important.');
});
```

Click event handling isn't always that trivial. Sometimes you end up looking at something that resembles the following listing.

Listing 6.1   Callback soup using logic noodles

```
(function () {
  var loaded;
  function init () {
    document.body.addEventListener('click', function handler () {
      console.log('Clicks are important.');
      handleClick(function handled (data) {
        if (data) {
          return processData(data, function processed (copy) {
            copy.append = true;
            done(copy);
          };
        } else {
          reportError(function reported () {
            console.log('data processing failed.', err);
          });
        }
      });
    });
    function done(data) {
      loaded = true;
      console.log('finished', data);
    }
  }
  init();
})();
```

Procedural code mixed with nested callbacks negatively impacts code readability.

What's going on? My thoughts exactly. You've been dragged through callback hell, that friendly name that describes deeply nested and indented callbacks on top of more callbacks, which make it pretty difficult to follow the flow and understand what's going on. If you can't make sense of the code presented in listing 6.1, that's good. You shouldn't have to. Let's dig deeper into the subject.

6.1.1 Avoiding callback hell

You should understand how a piece of code flows at a glance, even if it's asynchronous. If you need to spend more than a few seconds to understand how it flows, then there's probably something wrong with that piece of code. Each nested callback means more nested scopes, as observed in chapter 5, and indentation one level deeper, which consumes a little more real estate in your display, making it harder to follow the code.

Callback hell doesn't happen overnight, and you can prevent it from ever happening. Using an example (named ch06/01_callback-hell in the samples), let's see how it might slowly creep through the cracks of your code base over time. Suppose you have to make an AJAX request to fetch data, and then show that to a human. You'll use an imaginary http object to simplify the AJAX-foo. Let's also assume you have a record variable holding a reference to a particular DOM element.

```
record.addEventListener('click', function () {
  var id = record.dataset.id;
  var endpoint = '/api/v1/records/' + id;

  http.get(endpoint, function (res) {
    record.innerHTML = res.data.view;
  });
});
```

That's still easy to follow! What if you need to update another component after the GET request succeeded? Consider the following listing. Let's assume there's a DOM element in the status variable.

> **Listing 6.2 Callback creep**

```
function attach (node, status, done) {
  node.addEventListener('click', function () {
    var id = node.dataset.id;
    var endpoint = '/api/v1/records/' + id;

    http.get(endpoint, function (res) {
      node.innerHTML = res.data.view;
      reportStatus(res.status, function () {
        done(res);
      });
    });

    function reportStatus (status, then) {
      status.innerHTML = 'Status: ' + status;
```

```
      then();
    }
  });
}

attach(record, status, function (res) {
  console.log(res);
});
```

Okay, that's starting to get bad! Nested callbacks add complexity every time you add a nesting level into the piece of code, because now you have to keep track of the context of the existing function as well as the context of the deeper callback. Take into account that in a real application each of these methods would probably have more lines in them, making it even harder to keep all of that state in your memory.

How do you fight the callback creep? All that complexity can be avoided by reducing the callback nesting depth.

6.1.2   *Untangling the callback jumble*

You have ways to untangle these innocent pieces of code. Here's a list of things you should take into account and fix:

- *Name anonymous functions,* to improve their readability, and give hints as to what they're doing. Named anonymous callbacks provide two-fold value. Their names can be used to convey intent, and it also helps when tracking down exceptions, as the stack trace will show the function name, instead of showing up as "anonymous function." A named function will be easier to identify and save you headaches when debugging.

- *Remove unnecessary callbacks,* such as the one after reporting the status in the example. If a callback is only executed at the end of the function, and not asynchronously, you can get rid of it. The code that used to be in the callback could come right after the function call.

- *Be careful about mixing conditionals with flow control code.* Conditionals hinder your ability to follow a piece of code, because new possibilities are introduced, and you need to think of all the possible ways in which the code might be followed. Flow control presents a similar problem. It makes it harder to read through the code, because the next instruction isn't always the following line. Anonymous callbacks containing conditionals make it particularly hard to follow the flow, and they should be avoided. The first example in section 6.1 is a good demonstration of how this mixture is a recipe for disaster. You can mitigate this problem by separating the conditionals from the flow control. Provide a reference to the function, instead of an anonymous callback, and you can keep the conditionals as they were.

After making the changes suggested in the previous list, the code ends up like the following listing.

Listing 6.3   Cleaning up the jumble

```
function attach (node, status, done) {
  node.addEventListener('click', function handler () {      ⟵   Named functions are
    var id = node.dataset.id;                                     easier to debug.
    var endpoint = '/api/v1/records/' + id;

    http.get(endpoint, function ajax (res) {
      node.innerHTML = res.data.view;
      reportStatus(res.status);
      done(res);
    });

    function reportStatus (code) {              ⟵   Since the method is synchronous,
      status.innerHTML = 'Status: ' + code;          using a callback was unnecessary.
    }
  });
}

attach(record, status, function (res) {
  console.log(res);
});
```

That's not that bad; what else?

- The `reportStatus` function now seems pointless; you could inline its contents, move them to the only call site, and reduce the mental overhead. Simple methods that aren't going to be reused can be replaced with their contents, reducing cognitive load.
- Sometimes it makes sense to do the opposite, too. Instead of declaring the click handler inline, you could pull it into a named function, making the `addEventListener` line shorter. This one is mostly a matter of preference, but it can help when lines of code get longer than the 80 character mark.

The next listing shows the resulting code after applying these changes. Although the code is functionally equivalent, it's gotten much easier to read. Compare it with listing 6.2 to get a clearer picture.

Listing 6.4   Pulling functions

```
function attach (node, status, done) {

  function handler () {
    var id = node.dataset.id;
    var endpoint = '/api/v1/records/' + id;

    http.get(endpoint, updateView);
  }

  function updateView (res) {
    node.innerHTML = res.data.view;
    status.innerHTML = 'Status: ' + res.status;
```

```
        done(res);
    }

    node.addEventListener('click', handler);
}

attach(record, status, function done (res) {
    console.log(res);
});
```

What you did was make your code read as it flows. The trick is to keep each function as small and focused as you can get away with, as covered in chapter 5. Then it's a matter of giving the functions proper, descriptive names that clearly state the purpose of the method. Learning when to inline unnecessary callbacks, as you did with report-Status, is a matter of practice.

In general, it won't matter if the code itself becomes a bit longer, as long as its readability improves. Readability is the single most important aspect of the code you write, because that's how you'll spend most of your time: reading code. Let's go over one more example before moving on.

6.1.3   *Requests upon requests*

In web applications, it's not uncommon to have web requests that depend on other AJAX requests; the back end might not be suited to give you all the data you need in a single AJAX call. For example, you might need to access a list of your customer's clients, but to do that you must first get the customer ID, using their email address, and then you need to get the regions associated with that customer before finally getting the clients associated with that region and that customer.

Let's look at the following listing (found as ch06/02_requests-upon-requests in the samples) to see how this AJAX-fest might look.

Listing 6.5   Using AJAX for callback nesting

```
http.get('/userByEmail', { email: input.email }, function (err, res) {
    if (err) { done(err); return; }

    http.get('/regions', { regionId: res.id }, function (err, res) {
        if (err) { done(err); return; }

        http.get('/clients', { regions: res.regions }, function (err, res) {
            done(err, res);
        });
    });
});

function done (err, res) {
    if (err) { throw err; }
    console.log(res.clients);
}
```

As you'll learn in chapter 9 while analyzing REST API service design, having to jump through so many hoops to get to the data you need is usually a symptom of client-side code conforming to whatever API the back-end server offers, rather than having a dedicated API that's specifically built for the front end. In the case I described, it would be best if the server did all that work based off a customer email, rather than making that many round-trips to the server.

Figure 6.1 shows the repeated round-trips to the server, compared with an API dedicated to the front end. As you can see in the figure, with a preexisting API, chances are it won't fit the needs of your front end, and you'll have to massage inputs in your browser before handing them off to the API. In the worst-case scenario, you might even have to make multiple requests to get the desired result, meaning extra round-trips. If you had a dedicated API, it would be up for whatever task you ask of it, allowing you to optimize and reduce the number of requests made against the server, reducing server load and eliminating unnecessary round-trips.

If you take into account that this code might be inside a closure and also inside an event handler, the indentation becomes unbearable: it's too hard to follow code through all of those nesting levels, particularly if the methods are long. Naming the

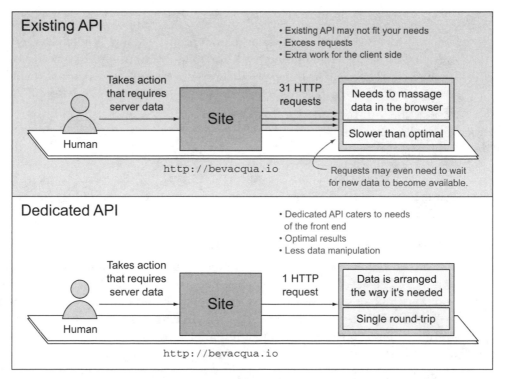

Figure 6.1   The trade-offs between resorting to an existing API or using one dedicated to the front end

callback functions and extracting them, rather than using anonymous functions, is good enough to start refactoring the functionality so it's easier to understand.

The following listing shows the refactored code as an example of how you might break down nesting.

Listing 6.6   Nesting no more

```
function getUser (input) {
  http.get('/userByEmail', { email: input.email }, getRegions);
}

function getRegions (err, res) {
  if (err) { done(err); return; }
  http.get('/regions', { regionId: res.id }, getClients);
}

function getClients (err, res) {
  if (err) { done(err); return; }
  http.get('/clients', { regions: res.regions }, done);
}

function done (err, res) {
  if (err) { throw err; }
  console.log(res.clients);
}
```

Error checking in every callback

You can already see how this is easier to understand; the flow is much clearer now that everything is at the same nesting level. You might've noticed the pattern where every method checks for errors to ensure the next step isn't met with any surprises. In the next few sections we'll look at different ways to handle asynchronous flow in JavaScript:

- Using callback libraries
- Promises
- Generators
- Event emitters

You'll learn how each of those solutions simplifies error handling. For now, you'll build on the current sample, figuring out how to get rid of those error checks.

6.1.4   *Asynchronous error handling*

You should plan for errors, rather than ignore them. You should never let errors go unnoticed. That being said, when using either the callback hell or the named functions approach, it's tedious to do any sort of error handling. Surely there's a better way to go about it than adding an error handling line to each of your functions.

In chapter 5 you learned about different ways you can manipulate function invocation, such as using `.apply`, `.call`, and `.bind`. Imagine you could get away with writing a line such as the following code and have that get rid of repeated error-checking statements, while still checking for them, but in one place. Wouldn't that be great?

```
flow([getUser, getRegions, getClients], done);
```

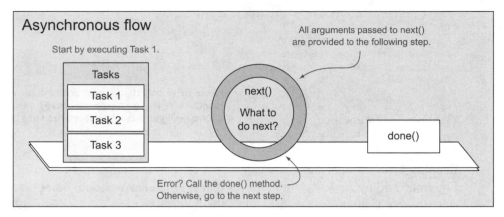

Figure 6.2 Understanding an asynchronous flow method

In the previous statement, the `flow` method takes an array of functions and executes each one in turn. Each function is passed a `next` argument that it should invoke when it's done. If the first argument passed to `next` is "truthy" (JavaScript slang for any value that's not `false`, `0`, `''`, `null`, or `undefined`), then `done` gets called immediately, interrupting the flow.

The first argument is reserved for errors. If that argument is truthy, then you'll short-circuit and call done directly. Otherwise, the next function in the array is called, and it gets passed all the arguments provided to `next`, except for the error, plus a new `next` callback function that allows the following method to continue chaining. Pulling that off does seem difficult.

First, you'll ask consumers of the `flow` method to call a `next` callback when the method is done working. That'll help with the flow part. You'll have to provide that callback method and have it call the next function in the list, passing it all the arguments that were used to call `next`. You'll append a new `next` callback, which will call the following method, and so on.

Figure 6.2 explains the `flow` function you're going to implement.

Before you implement your `flow` method, let's look at a full usage example. This is what you were doing previously, finding clients for a particular customer, but you're not doing the error checking in every step anymore; the `flow` method will take care of that. The following listing shows what using `flow` would look like.

Listing 6.7 Using the flow method

```
flow([getUser, getRegions, getClients], done);

function getUser (next) {
  http.get('/userByEmail', { email: input.email }, next);
}

function getRegions (res, next) {
```

The flow() method takes in an array of steps and a done() callback.

Steps are completed by calling next() with an optional error and a result.

```
  http.get('/regions', { regionId: res.id }, next);
}

function getClients (res, next) {
  http.get('/clients', { regions: res.regions }, next);
}

function done (err, res) {
  if (err) { throw err; }
  console.log(res.clients);
}
```

Note we're only checking for errors in the done() method. Whenever a step calls next() with an error, done() will get that error, short-circuiting the flow.

Keeping in mind what we've discussed, let's look at the implementation of the `flow` function. Adding a *guard* clause ensures that calling `next` multiple times on any given step doesn't have a negative effect. Only the first call to `next` will be taken into consideration. A `flow` implementation can be found in the following listing.

Listing 6.8   Implementing the asynchronous series `flow` method

```
function flow (steps, done) {
  function factory () {
    var used;
    return function next () {
      if (used) { return; }
      used = true;
      var step = steps.shift();
      if (step) {
        var args = Array.prototype.slice.call(arguments);
        var err = args.shift();
        if (err) { done(err); return; }
        args.push(factory());
        step.apply(null, args);
      } else {
        done.apply(null, arguments);
      }
    };
  }
  var start = factory();
  start();
}
```

Uses a factory so that used is local to each step.

Stores whether the callback has already been used.

After one use, next becomes a no-op.

Gets the next step, and removes it from the list.

Are there more steps?

Casts arguments to an array.

Gets the error argument, and removes it from the arguments.

Short-circuits if an error was provided.

Invokes the step passing in the needed arguments.

Adds a completion callback to the argument list.

Call done; no need to manipulate arguments.

Creates the first step function.

Executes the step; doesn't provide additional arguments.

Experiment and follow the flow on your own, and if you get lost, keep in mind that the `next()` method merely returns a function that has an effect once. If you didn't want to include that safeguard, you could reuse that same function every step of the way. This approach, however, accounts for programming mistakes by the consumers where they might call `next` twice during the same step.

Maintaining methods such as `flow` to keep them up-to-date and bug-free can be cumbersome if all you want is to avoid the nesting hell of a callback-based asynchronous flow and get error handling to go with that. Luckily, smart people have implemented this and many other asynchronous flow patterns into a JavaScript library called `async`, and also baked it into popular web frameworks such as Express, too. We'll go over control flow paradigms in this chapter, such as callbacks, Promises, events, and generators. Next up, you'll get acquainted with `async`.

6.2 Using the async library

In the world of Node, many developers find it hard not to use the `async` control flow library. *Native modules,* those that are part of the Node platform itself, follow the pattern where the last argument taken by a function is a callback that receives an error as its first argument. The following code snippet illustrates the case in point, using Node's file system API to read a file asynchronously:

```
require('fs').readFile('path/to/file', function (err, data) {
  // handle the error, use data
});
```

The `async` library provides many asynchronous control flow methods, much like the one in section 6.1.3, when you built the `flow` utility method. Your `flow` method is much the same as `async.waterfall`. The difference is that `async` provides tens of these methods that can simplify your asynchronous code if applied correctly.

You can get `async` from either `npm` or `Bower`, or from GitHub.[1] While you're on GitHub, you might want to check the excellent piece of documentation that Caolan McMahon (`async`'s author) has written.

In the following subsections we'll go into detail about the `async` control flow library, discussing problems you might run into and how `async` can solve those for you, making it easier for you, and everyone else, to read the code. To get started, you'll look at three slightly different flow control methods: `waterfall`, `series`, and `parallel`.

6.2.1 Waterfall, series, or parallel?

One of the most important aspects of mastering asynchronous JavaScript is learning about all the different tools at your disposal, and you certainly will in this chapter. One such tool is common control flow techniques:

- Do you want to run tasks asynchronously so they don't depend on each other to do their thing? Run them *concurrently* using `.parallel`.
- Do your tasks depend on the previous ones? Run them in *series,* one after the other, but still asynchronously.
- Are your tasks tightly coupled? Use a waterfall mechanism that lets you *pass* arguments to the next task in the list. The HTTP cascade we discussed earlier is a perfect use case for waterfall.

Figure 6.3 compares the three alternatives in greater detail.

---

[1] You can download async from GitHub at https://github.com/caolan/async.

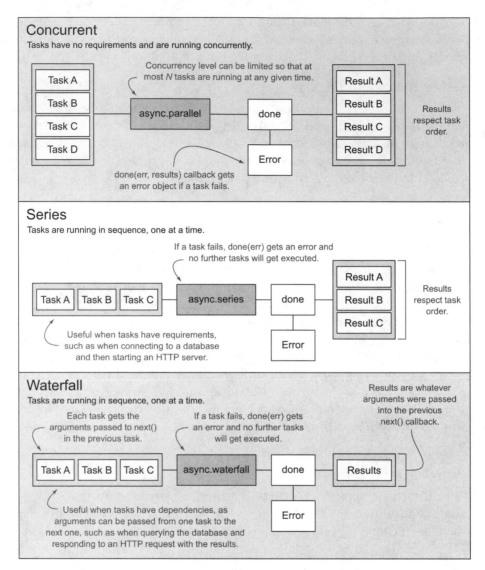

Figure 6.3   Comparison of parallel, series, and waterfall in the async library.

As you can see in the figure, subtle differences exist between these three strategies. Let's break them down.

CONCURRENT

Concurrent task execution is most helpful when you have a few different asynchronous tasks that have no interdependencies, but where you still need to do something when all of them finish; for example, when fetching different pieces of data to render a view. You can define a concurrency level, or how many tasks can be busy while the rest are queued up:

- Once a task finishes, another one is grabbed from the queue until the queue is emptied.
- Each task is passed a special `next` method that should be invoked when processing completes.
- The first argument passed to `next` is reserved for errors; if you pass in an error, no further tasks will be executed (although the ones already executing will run to completion).
- The second argument is where you'll pass in the results for your task.
- Once all tasks end, the `done` callback is invoked. Its first argument will be the error (if any), and the second one will have the results sorted by the tasks, regardless of how long they took to finish.

SERIES

Sequential execution helps you connect correlative tasks, meant to be executed one by one, even if the code execution happens asynchronously, outside of the main loop. Think of the series flow as the concurrent flow with its concurrency level set to 1. In fact, that's exactly what it is! The same conventions of `next(err, results)` and `done(err, results)` apply.

WATERFALL

The waterfall variant is similar to sequential execution, but it allows you to easily roll the arguments from one task to the next in a cascade. This type of flow is most useful when tasks can only be initiated using the data provided by the response of other tasks. In the case of waterfall the flow is different in that `next` takes in an error followed by any number of result arguments: `next(err, result1, result2, result...n)`. The `done` callback behaves in this exact same way, giving you all of the arguments that were passed to the last `next` callback.

Next, let's get more insight into how `series` and `parallel` work.

FLOW CONTROL IN SERIES

You've already seen `waterfall` in action, in the `flow` method you implemented. Let's talk about `series`, which is a slightly different approach from what `waterfall` does. It executes the steps in series, one at a time the way `waterfall` does, but it doesn't fiddle with the arguments of each step function. Instead, each step only receives a `next` callback argument, expecting the `(err, data)` signature. You might wonder, "How does that help me?" The answer to that is sometimes the consistency of having a single argument, and having that argument be a callback, is useful. Consider the following listing as an illustrative example of how `async.series` works.

Listing 6.9 Using `async.series`

```
async.series([
  function createUser (next) {
    http.put('/users', user, next);
  },
  function listUsers (next) {
```

```
      http.get('/users/list', next);
    },
    function updateView (next) {
      view.update(next);
    }
], done);

function done (err, results) {
  // handle error
  updateProfile(results[0]);
  synchronizeFollowers(results[1]);
}
```

Sometimes the results need to be manipulated individually, the way you did in the previous listing. In those cases, it makes more sense to use an object to describe the tasks rather than an array. If you do that, the done callback will get a results object, mapping results to the property name for each task. This sounds complicated, but it isn't, so let's modify the code in the following listing to illustrate the point.

Listing 6.10   Using the done callback

```
async.series({
  user: function createUser (next) {
    http.put('/users', user, next);
  },
  list: function listUsers (next) {
    http.get('/users/list', next);
  },
  view: function updateView (next) {
    view.update(next);
  }
}, done);

function done (err, results) {
  // handle error
  updateProfile(results.user);
  synchronizeFollowers(results.list);
}
```

If a task merely involves calling a function that takes arguments and the next callback, you could use async.apply to shorten your code; that'll make it easier to read. The apply helper will take the method you want to call and the arguments you want to use and return a function that takes a next callback and appends that to your argument list. The two approaches shown in the following code snippets are functionally equivalent:

```
function (next) {
  http.put('/users', user, next);
}

async.apply(http.put, '/users', user)
// <- [Function]
```

The following code is a simplified version of the task flow you put together previously, using `async.apply`:

```
async.series({
  user: async.apply(http.put, '/users', user),
  list: async.apply(http.get, '/users/list'),
  view: async.apply(view.update)
}, done);
```

If you used `waterfall`, this kind of optimization wouldn't have been possible. The function created by `async.apply` expects only a `next` argument but nothing else. In `waterfall` flows, tasks can get passed an arbitrary number of arguments. In contrast, in a `series`, tasks always receive exactly one argument, the `next` callback.

CONCURRENT FLOW CONTROL

Then there's `async.parallel`. Running tasks concurrently works exactly like running tasks in series does, except you don't chip away at tasks one at a time, but rather run them all at the same time. Concurrent flows result in faster execution time, making `parallel` the favorite when you don't have any specific requirements for your workflow other than asynchronicity.

The `async` library also provides functional methods, allowing you to loop through lists, map objects to something else, or sort them. Next we'll look at these functional methods and an interesting task queue functionality built into `async`.

6.2.2 *Asynchronous functional tasks*

Suppose you need to go through a list of product identifiers and fetch their object representations over HTTP. That's an excellent use case for a map. Maps transform input into output using a function that modifies the input. The following listing (available as ch06/05_async-functional in the samples) shows how it's done using `async.map`.

Listing 6.11 Transforming input into output with maps

```
var ids = [23, 33, 118];

async.map(ids, transform, done);

function transform (id, complete) {
  http.get('/products/' + id, complete);
}

function done (err, results) {
  // handle the error
  // results[0] is the response for ids[0],
  // results[1] is the response for ids[1],
  // and so on
}
```

At the point `done` is called, it will either have an error argument as the first argument, which you should handle, or an array of results as the second argument, which will be in the same order as the list you provided when calling `async.map`. A few methods behave similarly to `map` in `async`. They'll take in an array and a function, apply the function to every item in the array, and then call `done` with the results.

For instance, `async.sortBy` allows you to sort an array in place (meaning it won't create a copy), and all you need to do is pass in a value as the sort criteria for the `done` callback of the function. You could use it as shown in the following listing.

Listing 6.12 Sorting an array

```
async.sortBy([1, 23, 54], sort, done);

function sort (id, complete) {
  http.get('/products/' + id, function (err, product) {
    complete(err, product ? product.name : null);
  });
}

function done (err, result) {
  // handle the error
  // result contains ids sorted by name
}
```

Both `map` and `sortBy` are based on `each`, which you can think of as `parallel`, or `series` if you use the `eachSeries` version. `each` merely loops through an array and applies a function to each element; then an optional `done` callback is invoked that has an error argument telling you if something went wrong. The following listing shows an example of using `async.each`.

Listing 6.13 Using `async.each`

```
async.each([2, 5, 6], iterator, done);

function iterator (item, done) {
  setTimeout(function  () {
    if (item % 2 === 0) {
      done();
    } else {
      done(new Error('expected divisible by 2'));
    }
  }, 1000 * item);
}

function done (err) {
  // handle the error
}
```

More methods in the `async` library deal with functional situations, all of which revolve around asynchronously transforming an array into an alternative representation of its data. We won't cover the rest of them, but I encourage you to look at the extensive documentation on GitHub.[2]

---

[2] You can find the flow control library `async` on GitHub at https://github.com/caolan/async.

6.2.3 *Asynchronous task queues*

Moving on to the last method, `async.queue`, this method will create a queue object that can be used to run tasks in series or concurrently. It takes two arguments: the worker function, which will take a task object and a callback to signal that the work is complete, and the concurrency level, which determines how many tasks can run at any given moment.

If the concurrency level is 1, you're effectively turning the queue into a series, executing tasks as the previous one ends. Let's create a simple queue in the following listing (labeled ch06/06_async-queue in the samples).

Listing 6.14 Creating a simple queue

```
var q = async.queue(worker, 1);

function worker (id, done) {
  http.get('/users/' + id, function gotResponse (err, user) {
    if (err) { done(err); return; }

    console.log('Fetched user ' + id);
    done();
  });
}
```

You can use the `q` object to put your queue to work. To add a new job to the queue, use `q.push`. You'll need to pass a task object, which is what gets passed to the worker; in our case the task is a numeric literal, but it could be an object or even a function; and an optional callback, which gets called when this particular job is done. Let's see how to do that in code:

```
var id = 24;
q.push(id, function (err) {
  if (err) {
    console.error('Error processing user 23', err);
  }
});
```

That's it. The nicety is that you can push more tasks at different points in time, and it'll still work. In contrast, `parallel` or `series` are one-shot operations where you can't add tasks to the list at a later time. That being said, our last topic regarding the async control flow library is about composing flows and creating task lists dynamically—both of which may bring further flexibility to your approach.

6.2.4 *Flow composition and dynamic flows*

At times, you'll need to craft more advanced flows where

- Task b depends on task a
- While task c needs to be performed afterward
- And task d can be executed in parallel to all of that

When all of it is done, you'll run a last task: task e.

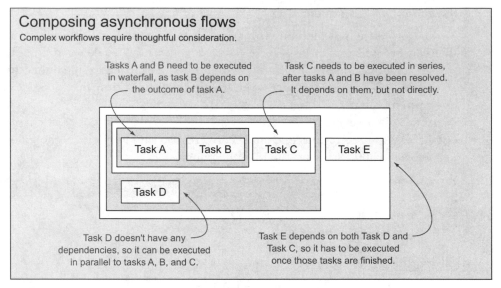

Figure 6.4   Dissection of a complex asynchronous flow. Hint: always group tasks, in your brain, according to their requirements.

Figure 6.4 shows what that flow might look like:

- Tasks A (getting on a bus) and B (paying the bus fare) need to be executed in waterfall, as task B depends on the outcome of task A.
- Task C (getting to your workplace) needs to be executed in series, after tasks A and B have been resolved. It depends on both of them, but not directly.
- Task D (reading a book) doesn't have any dependencies, so it can be executed in parallel to tasks A, B, and C.
- Task E (working) depends on both task C and task D, so it has to be executed once those tasks are finished.

This sounds, and looks, more complicated than it is. All you need to do, provided you're using a control flow library such as async, is write a few functions on top of each other. That could look like the pseudo-code shown in the following example. Here I'm using async.apply, introduced in section 6.2.1, to make the code shorter. A fully documented sample can be found at ch06/07_async-composition in the samples:

```
async.parallel([
    async.apply(async.series, [
        async.apply(async.waterfall, [getOnBus, payFare]),
        getToWork
    ]),
    readBook
], doWork);
```

Composing flows in this way is most useful if you're writing Node.js applications, which involve many async operations, such as querying a database, reading files, or connecting to an external API, all of which can often result in highly complex, asynchronous operation trees.

COMPOSING FLOWS DYNAMICALLY

Creating flows dynamically, by adding tasks to an object, allows you to put together task lists that would've been much harder to organize without using a control flow library. This is a nod to the fact that you're writing code in JavaScript, a dynamic language. You can exploit that by coding up dynamic functions, so do so! The following listing takes a list of items and maps each of them to a function, which then queries something with that item.

Listing 6.15   Mapping and querying a list of items

```
var tasks = {};

items.forEach(function queryItem (item) {
    tasks[item.name] = function (done) {
        item.query(function queried (res) {
            done(null, res);
        });
    };
});
function done (err, results) {
  // results will be organized by name
}
async.series(tasks, done);
```

A lightweight alternative to async

There's something I'd like to mention about `async` regarding client-side usage. `async` was originally developed mostly for the Node.js community, and, as such, it isn't as rigorously tested for the browser.

I built my own version, `contra`, which has an extensive suite of unit tests that get executed before every release. I kept the code in `contra` to a minimum; it's 10 times smaller than `async`, making it ideal for the browser. It provides methods that can be found on `async`, as well as a simple way to implement event emitters, which are explained in section 6.4. You can find it on GitHub,[a] and it's available on both npm and Bower.

---

[a] Get `contra`, my flow control library at https://github.com/bevacqua/contra, on GitHub.

Let's move on to Promises, a way to deal with asynchronous programming by chaining functions together, and dealing in contracts. Have you used jQuery's AJAX functionality? Then you've worked with a flavor of Promises called Deferred, which is slightly different than the official ES6 Promises implementation, but fundamentally similar.

6.3   *Making Promises*

Promises are an up-and-coming standard, and are in fact part of the official ECMA-Script 6 draft specification. Currently you can use Promises by including a library, such as Q, RSVP.js, or when. You could also use Promises by adding the ES6 Promises poly-fill.[3] A *polyfill* is a piece of code that enables technology that you'd expect the language runtime to provide natively. In this case, a polyfill for Promises would provide Promises, as they're natively supposed to work in ES6, made available to previous implementations of the ES standard.

In this section, I'll describe Promises per ES6, which you can use today, provided you include the polyfill. The syntax varies slightly if you're using something other than the polyfill for Promises, but these variations are subtle enough, and the core concepts remain the same.

6.3.1   *Promise fundamentals*

Creating a Promise involves a callback function that takes fulfill and reject functions as its arguments. Calling fulfill will change the state of the Promise to fulfilled; you'll see what that means in a minute. Calling reject will change the state to rejected. The following code is a brief and self-explaining Promise declaration where your Promise will be fulfilled half of the time and rejected the other half:

```
var promise = new Promise(function logic (fulfill, reject) {
  if (Math.random() < 0.5) {
    fulfill('Good enough.');
  } else {
    reject(new Error('Dice roll failed!'));
  }
});
```

As you might've noticed, Promises don't have any inherent properties that make them exclusively asynchronous, and you can also use them for synchronous operations. This comes in handy when mixing synchronous and asynchronous code, because Promises don't care about that. Promises start out in pending, and once they fail or succeed, they're resolved and can't change state anymore. Promises can be in one of three mutually exclusive states:

- Pending: Hasn't fulfilled or rejected yet.
- Fulfilled: The action relating to the Promise succeeded.
- Rejected: The action relating to the Promise failed.

PROMISE CONTINUATION

Once you create a Promise object, you can add callbacks to it via the then(success, failure) method. These callbacks will be executed accordingly when the Promise is resolved. When the Promise is fulfilled, or if it's already fulfilled, the success callback will be called, and if it's rejected or if it's already rejected, failure will be invoked.

---

[3]   Find the ES6 Promises polyfill at http://bevacqua.io/bf/promises.

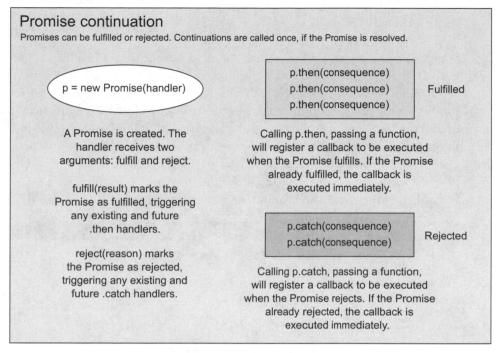

Figure 6.5   Promise continuation basics

Figure 6.5 illustrates how Promises can be rejected or fulfilled and how Promise continuation works.

There are a few takeaways from figure 6.5. First, remember that when creating a Promise object you'll take both fulfill and reject callbacks, which you can then use to resolve the Promise. Calling p.then(success, fail) will execute success when and if the Promise is fulfilled, and fail when and if the Promise is rejected. Note that both callbacks are optional, and you could also use p.catch(fail) as syntactic sugar for p.then(null, fail).

The following expanded listing shows the then continuation calls added to our previous example. You can find it under ch06/08_promise-basics in the code samples.

Listing 6.16   Promise with continuation calls

```
var promise = new Promise(function logic (fulfill, reject) {
  if (Math.random() < 0.5) {
    fulfill('Good enough.');
  } else {
    reject(new Error('Dice roll failed!'));
  }
});

promise.then(function success (result) {
  console.log('Succeeded', result);
```

Similarly the reject callback is used to reject it, with an error.

When defining a Promise, fulfill is used to resolve it to any value passed to it.

You can then chain success callbacks by using .then.

```
}, function fail (reason) {
  console.log('Rejected', reason);
});
```

> Optional failure callbacks can be passed as the second argument to .then.

You can invoke `promise.then` as many times as you please, and all the callbacks in the correct branch (either success or rejection) will be invoked when the Promise is resolved, in the same order in which they were added. If the code was asynchronous, maybe if a `setTimeout` or an `XMLHttpRequest` was involved, the callbacks that depend on the outcome of the Promise won't be executed until the Promise resolves, as shown in the following listing. Once the Promise is resolved, callbacks passed to `p.then(success, fail)` or `p.catch(fail)` will be executed immediately, where appropriate: success callbacks will only be executed if the Promise was fulfilled, and `fail` callbacks will only be executed if the Promise was rejected.

Listing 6.17   Executing Promises

```
var promise = new Promise(function logic (fulfill, reject) {
  console.log('Pending...');

  setTimeout(function later () {
    if (Math.random() < 0.5) {
      fulfill('Good enough.');
    } else {
      reject(new Error('Dice roll failed!'));
    }
  }, 1000);
});

promise.then(function success (result) {
  console.log('Succeeded', result);
}, function fail (reason) {
  console.log('Rejected', reason);
});
```

Besides creating different branches by invoking `.then` multiple times on a Promise object, you could also chain those callbacks together, altering the result each time. Let's look into Promise chaining.

PROMISE TRANSFORMATION CHAINS

This is where things get harder to understand, but let's go step by step. When you chain callbacks, they get whatever the previous one returned. Consider the following listing, where the first callback will parse the JSON value resolved by the Promise into an object, and the following callback prints whether `buildfirst` is `true` on that object.

Listing 6.18   Using a transformation chain

```
var promise = new Promise(function logic (fulfill) {
  fulfill('{"buildfirst": true}');
});
```

> In this case, our Promise always resolves with a JSON string.

```
promise
  .then(function parse (value) {
    return JSON.parse(value);
  })
  .then(function print (value) {
    console.log(value.buildfirst);
    // <- true
  });
```

⤺ **This method takes the resolved JSON string and parses it into an object.**

⤺ **The print callback gets the JSON object as transformed by the parse callback.**

Chaining callbacks to transform previous values is useful, but it won't do you any good if what you need is to chain asynchronous callbacks. How can you chain Promises that perform asynchronous tasks? We'll look at that next.

6.3.2 Chaining Promises

Instead of returning values in your callbacks, you could also return other Promises. Returning a Promise has an interesting effect, where the next callback in the chain will wait until the returned Promise is completed. In preparation for your next example, where you'll query the GitHub API for a list of users and then get the name of one of their repositories, let's sketch out a `Promise` wrapper of the `XMLHttpRequest` object, the native browser API uses to make AJAX calls.

A BARE AJAX CALL

The specifics of how the `XMLHttpRequest` works are outside of the scope of this book, but the code should be self-explanatory. The following listing shows how you could make an AJAX call using minimal code.

Listing 6.19 Making an AJAX call

```
var xhr = new XMLHttpRequest();
xhr.open('GET', endpoint);
xhr.onload = function loaded () {
  if (xhr.status >= 200 && xhr.status < 300) {
    // get me the response
  } else {
    // report error
  }
};
xhr.onerror = function errored () {
  // report error
};
xhr.send();
```

It's a matter of passing in an endpoint, setting an HTTP method—GET, in this case—and doing something with the results asynchronously. That's a perfect opportunity to turn AJAX into a Promise.

PROMISING AJAX DATA

You don't have to change the code at all, other than appropriately wrapping the AJAX call in a Promise and calling `resolve` and `reject` as necessary. The following listing depicts a possible `get` implementation, which provides access to the XHR object through the use of Promises.

Listing 6.20   Promising AJAX

```
function get (endpoint) {
  function handler (fulfill, reject) {
    var xhr = new XMLHttpRequest();
    xhr.open('GET', endpoint);
    xhr.onload = function loaded () {
      if (xhr.status >= 200 && xhr.status < 300) {
        fulfill(xhr.response);
      } else {
        reject(new Error(xhr.responseText));
      }
    };
    xhr.onerror = function errored () {
      reject(new Error('Network Error'));
    };
    xhr.send();
  }

  return new Promise(handler);
}
```

If status code is in the 200-299 range, then fulfill using the response.

If not, reject the Promise, using Error object.

Reject on network errors as well (such as a request timeout).

Once that's out of the way, putting together the sequence of calls leading up to the name of a repository looks bafflingly easy. Notice how you're mixing asynchronous calls thanks to Promises, and synchronous calls by using `then` transformations. Here's what the code looks like, taking into account the `get` method you implemented:

```
get('https://api.github.com/users')
  .catch(function errored () {
    console.log('Too bad. That failed.');
  })
  .then(JSON.parse)
  .then(function getRepos (res) {
    var url = 'https://api.github.com/users/' + res[0].login + '/repos';
    return get(url).catch(function errored () {
      console.log('Oops! That one failed.');
    });
  })
  .then(JSON.parse)
  .then(function print (res) {
    console.log(res[0].name);
  });
```

You could've packed the `JSON.parse` method in the `get` method, but it felt like a good opportunity to display how you might mix and match asynchronous and synchronous operations using Promises.

This is great if you want to do operations similar to what you did with `async.waterfall` in section 6.2.1, where each task was fed the results from the previous one. What about using another flow control mechanism you got from `async`? Read on!

6.3.3 *Controlling the flow*

Flow control with Promises is arguably as easy as flow control using a library such as async. If you want to wait on a collection of Promises before doing another task, the way you did with async.parallel, you could wrap the Promises in a Promise.all call, as shown in the following listing.

Listing 6.21 Promising to pause

```
function delay (t) {
  function wait (fulfill) {
    setTimeout(function delayedPrint () {
      console.log('Resolving after', t);
      fulfill(t);
    }, t);
  }
  return new Promise(wait);
}

Promise
  .all([delay(700), delay(300), delay(500)])
  .then(function complete (results) {
    return delay(Math.min.apply(Math, results));
  });
```

Promise.all will wait for each Promise to fulfill. Then it allows continuation.

The results of the Promises are passed to Promise.all in an array.

The delay(Math.min.apply(Math, results)) Promise will be run only after all the previous Promises have resolved successfully; also note how then(results) gets passed an array of results containing the result of each Promise. As you might've inferred from the .then call, Promise.all(array) returns a Promise which will be fulfilled when all the items in array are fulfilled.

Using Promise.all is particularly useful when executing long-running operations, such as a series of AJAX calls, because you wouldn't want to make them in series if you could make them all at once. If you know all of the request endpoints, make the requests concurrently rather than serially. Then, once those requests are done, you can finally compute whatever depended on performing those asynchronous requests.

FUNCTIONAL PROGRAMMING USING PROMISES

To perform functional tasks such as the ones provided by methods such as async.map or async.filter, you're better off using the native Array methods when using Promises. Rather than resorting to a Promise-specific implementation, you can use a .then call to transform the results into what you need. Consider the following listing, using the same delay function as above, which takes results above 400 and then sorts them.

Listing 6.22 Using the delay function to sort results

```
Promise
  .all([delay(700), delay(300), delay(500)])
  .then(function filterTransform (results) {
    return results.filter(function greaterThan (result) {
      return result > 400;
    });
```

We wait until all of the delayed methods are resolved.

Then we filter them by applying a transform callback.

```
  })
  .then(function sortTransform (results) {
    return results.sort(function ascending (a, b) {
      return a - b;
    });
  })
  .then(function print (results) {
    console.log(results);
    // <- [500, 700]
  });
```

You can use as many transforms as you'd like!

At every step of the chain you'll get the transformed results back.

As you can see, mixing synchronous and asynchronous operations using Promises couldn't be easier, even when functional operations or AJAX requests are involved. You've been looking at the happy path so far, where everything works fine, but how exactly should you approach sensible error handling when using Promises?

6.3.4 *Handling rejected Promises*

You can provide rejection handlers by passing a callback function as the second argument to a .then(success, failure) call, as you examined in section 6.3.1. Similarly, using .catch(failure) makes it easier to convey intent, and it's an alias for .then(undefined, failure).

Until now we've talked in terms of explicit rejections, as in rejections when you explicitly call reject in the callback passed to the Promise constructor, but that's not your only option.

Let's examine the example below, which includes error throwing and handling. Note that I'm using throw in the Promise, although you should use the more semantic reject argument to display that you can throw exceptions from the original Promise as well as in then calls.

Listing 6.23 Catching and throwing

```
function delay (t) {
  function wait (fulfill, reject) {
    if (t < 1) {
      throw new Error('Delay must be greater than zero.');
    }
    setTimeout(function later () {
      console.log('Resolving after', t);
      fulfill(t);
    }, t);
  }
  return new Promise(wait);
}

Promise
  .all([delay(0), delay(400)])
  .then(function resolved (result) {
    throw new Error('I dislike the result!');
  })
  .catch(function errored (err) {
    console.log(err.message);
  });
```

If you execute this example, you'll notice how the error thrown by the `delay(0)` Promise will prevent the success branch from firing, therefore never showing the `'I dislike the result!'` message. But if `delay(0)` wasn't there, then the success branch would throw another error, which would prevent further progress in the success branch.

At this point, you've looked at callback hell and how to avert it. You've looked at asynchronous flow control using the `async` library, and you've also dealt with flow control using Promises, which is coming in ES6, but is already widely available through other libraries and polyfills.

Next up we'll discuss *events*, which are a form of asynchronous JavaScript that I'm sure you've come across when dealing with JavaScript development at one point or another. Later, you'll check out what else is coming in ES6 in terms of asynchronous flow. Namely, you'll look at ES6 generators, which are a novel feature to deal with iterators lazily, similar to what you can find in languages such as C# in their enumerable implementation.

6.4   *Understanding events*

Events are also known as publish/subscribe or event emitters. An *event emitter* is a pattern where a component emits events of certain types and passes them arguments, and any interested parties can subscribe to events of interest and react to the event and the provided arguments. Many different ways exist to implement an event emitter, most of which involve prototypal inheritance in one way or another. But you could also attach the necessary methods to an existing object, as you'll see in section 6.4.2.

Events are natively implemented in browsers, too. Native events might be an AJAX request getting a response, a human interacting with the DOM, or a WebSocket carefully listening for any action coming its way. Events are asynchronous by nature, and they're sprinkled all over the browser, so it's your job to manage them appropriately.

6.4.1   *Events and the DOM*

Events are one of the oldest asynchronous patterns of the web, and you can find them in the bindings that connect the browser DOM with your JavaScript code. The following example registers an event listener which will be triggered every time the document body gets clicked:

```
document.body.addEventListener('click', function handler () {
  console.log('Click responsibly. Do not click and drive!');
});
```

DOM events are more often than not triggered by a human being who clicks, pans, touches, or pinches on their browser window. DOM events are hard to test for if they aren't abstracted well enough. Even in the trivial case displayed below, consider the implications of having an anonymous function handling the click event:

```
document.body.addEventListener('click', function handler () {
  console.log(this.innerHTML);
});
```

It's hard to test functionality like this because you have no way to access the event handler independently from the event. For easier testing, and to avoid the hassle of simulating clicks to test the handler (which should still be done in integration testing, as you'll see in chapter 8), it's recommended that you either extract the handler into a named function, or you move the main body of the logic into a testable named function. This also favors reusability in case two events can be handled in the same way. The following piece of code shows how the click handler could be extracted:

```
function elementClick handler () {
  console.log(this.innerHTML);
}
var element = document.body;
var handler = elementClick.bind(element);

document.body.addEventListener('click', handler);
```

Thanks to `Function.prototype.bind` you're keeping the element as part of the context. Arguments exist both in favor of and against using `this` in this way. You should pick the strategy you're most comfortable with and stick to it. Either always bind handlers to the relevant element or always bind handlers using a `null` context. Consistency is one of the most important traits of readable (and maintainable) code.

Next up you'll implement your own event emitter, where you'll attach the relevant methods to an object without using prototypes, making for an easy implementation. Let's investigate what that might look like.

6.4.2   Creating your own event emitters

Event emitters usually support multiple types of events, rather than a single one. Let's implement step by step your own function to create event emitters or improve existing objects as event emitters. In a first step, you'll either return the object unchanged or create a new object if one wasn't provided:

```
function emitter (thing) {
  if (!thing) {
    thing = {};
  }
  return thing;
}
```

Using multiple event types is powerful and only costs you an object to store the mapping of event types to event listeners. Similarly, you'll use an array for each event type, so you can bind multiple event listeners to each event type. You'll also add a simple function that registers event listeners. The following listing (found as ch06/11_event-emitter in the samples) displays how you could turn existing objects into event emitters.

Listing 6.24   Promoting objects to event emitter status

```
function emitter (thing) {
  var events = {};
```
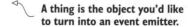 A thing is the object you'd like to turn into an event emitter.

```
    if (!thing) {
      thing = {};                              If you don't provide an object,
    }                                          one will be assigned to you.

    thing.on = function on (type, listener) {     Attach an event listener to an
      if (!events[type]) {                        existing or non-existing event type.
        events[type] = [listener];
      } else {
        events[type].push(listener);
      }
    };

    return thing;
}
```

Now you can add event listeners once an emitter is created. This is how it works. Keep in mind that listeners can be provided with an arbitrary number of arguments when an event is fired; you'll implement the method to fire events next:

```
var thing = emitter();

thing.on('change', function changed () {
  console.log('thing changed!');
});
```

Naturally, that works like a DOM event listener. All you need to do now is implement the method that fires the events. Without it, there wouldn't be an event emitter. You'll implement an `emit` method that allows you to fire the event listeners for a particular event type, passing in an arbitrary number of arguments. The following listing shows how it looks.

Listing 6.25   Firing event listeners

```
thing.emit = function emit (type) {
  var evt = events[type];
  if (!evt) {
    return;
  }
  var args = Array.prototype.slice.call(arguments, 1);
  for (var i = 0; i < evt.length; i++) {
    evt[i].apply(thing, args);
  }
};
```

The `Array.prototype.slice.call(arguments, 1)` statement is an interesting one. Here you'll apply `Array.prototype.slice` on the `arguments` object and tell it to start at index 1. This does two things. It casts the arguments object into a true array, and it gives a nice array with all of the arguments that were passed into `emit`, except for the event type, which you don't need to invoke the event listeners.

EXECUTING LISTENERS ASYNCHRONOUSLY

There's one last tweak to do, which is executing the listeners asynchronously so they don't halt execution of the main loop if one of them blows up. You could also use a try/catch block here, but let's not get involved with exceptions in event listeners; let the consumer handle that. To achieve this, use a `setTimeout` call, as shown in the following listing.

Listing 6.26 Event emission

```
thing.emit = function emit (type) {
  var evt = events[type];
  if (!evt) {
    return;
  }
  var args = Array.prototype.slice.call(arguments, 1);
  for (var i = 0; i < evt.length; i++) {
    debounce(evt[i]);
  }
  function debounce (e) {
    setTimeout(function tick () {
      e.apply(thing, args);
    }, 0);
  }
};
```

You can now create emitter objects, or you can turn existing objects into event emitters. Note that, given that you're wrapping the event listeners in a timeout, if a callback throws an error, the rest will still run to completion. This isn't the case in synchronous implementations of event emitters, as an error will stop execution on the current code path.

As a fun experiment, I've prepared a listing using event emitters and thoroughly exploiting `Function.prototype.bind` in the following listing. Can you tell how it works and why?

Listing 6.27 Using event emitters

```
var beats = emitter();
var handleCalm = beats.emit.bind(beats, 'ripple', 10);

beats.on('ripple', function rippling (i) {
  var cb = beats.emit.bind(beats, 'ripple', --i);
  var timeout =  Math.random() * 150 + 50;
  if (i > 0) {
    setTimeout(cb, timeout);
  } else {
    beats.emit('calm');
  }
});

beats.on('calm', setTimeout.bind(null, handleCalm, 1000));

beats.on('calm', console.log.bind(console, 'Calm...'));
beats.on('ripple', console.log.bind(console, 'Rippley!'));

beats.emit('ripple', 15);
```

Obviously this is a contrived example that doesn't do much, but it's interesting how two of the listeners control the flow, while the others control the output, and a single emit fires an unstoppable chain of events. As usual, you'll find a fully working copy of this snippet in the accompanying samples under ch06/11_event-emitter. While you're at it, make sure to read the samples for all the previous examples!

The power of event emitters stems from their flexibility, and one possible way to use emitters is by inverting their meaning. Imagine you control a component with an event emitter, and you expose the emit functionality, rather than the "listen" functionality. Your component can now be passed by arbitrary messages, and process them, while at the same time it might also emit its own events and let others process them, resulting in effective communication across components.

I have one last topic for you in this chapter: ES6 generators. Generators are a special kind of function in ES6 that can be iterated over lazily, and provide amusing value. Let's inspect them more closely.

6.5 Glimpse of the future: ES6 generators

JavaScript generators, heavily inspired by Python, are an interesting new perk coming our way, which allow you to represent sequences of values, such as the Fibonacci sequence, on which you can iterate. Although you're already capable of iterating over arrays, generators are lazy. Lazy is good because it means it's possible to create an infinite sequence generator and iterate over it without falling victim to an infinite loop or stack overflow exception. Generator functions are denoted with an asterisk, and items in the sequence must be returned using the `yield` keyword.

6.5.1 Creating your first generator

In the following listing you'll see how to create a generator function that represents a never-ending Fibonacci sequence. By definition, the first two numbers in the series are 1 and 1, and each subsequent number is the sum of the previous two.

Listing 6.28 Using a Fibonacci sequence

```
function* fibonacci () {
  var older = 0;
  var old = 1;

  yield 1;

  while (true) {
    yield old + older;
    var next = older + old;
    older = old;
    old = next;
  }
}
```

Once you have a generator, you may want to consume the values it produces, and to do that, you need to call the generator function, which will give you an iterator. The iterator can be used to get values from the generator, one at a time, by calling `iterator.next()`. That function call will result in an object such as `{ value: 1, done: false }` for iterators using the generator in the previous listing. The `done` property will become true when the iterator's done going through the generator function, but in this example it would never finish because of the infinite `while(true)` loop. The following example demonstrates how you could iterate over a few values using the never-ending `fibonacci` generator:

```
var iterator = fibonacci();
var i = 10;
var item;

while (i--) {
  item = iterator.next();
  console.log(item.value);
}
```

The easiest way to run the examples in this section is visiting http://es6fiddle.net, which will run ES6 code for you, including anything that uses generators. Alternatively, you could get Node v0.11.10 or later, which you can easily fetch from https://nodejs.org/dist. Then, doing `node --harmony <file>` when executing a script will enable ES6 features such as generators, including the `function* ()` construct, the `yield` keyword, and the `for..of` construct, which comes next.

ITERATE USING FOR..OF

The `for..of` syntax allows you to shortcut the process of iterating over a generator. Normally you'd call `iterator.next()`, store or use the provided `result.value`, and then check `iterator.done` to see if the iterator is exhausted. The `for..of` syntax handles that for you, trimming down your code. The following is a representation of iterating over a generator with a `for..of` loop. Note that you're using a finite generator, because using a generator such as `fibonacci` would create an infinite loop, unless you use `break` to exit the loop:

```
function* keywords () {
  yield 'buildfirst';
  yield 'javascript';
  yield 'design';
  yield 'architecture';
}

for (keyword of keywords()) {
  console.log(keyword);
}
```

At this point you might wonder how generators can help you deal with asynchronous flows, and we're about to get to that. First, however, we need to go back to generator functions and explain what suspension means.

EXECUTION SUSPENSION IN GENERATORS

Let's look at the first generator example again:

```
function* fibonacci () {
  var older = 1;
```

```
    var old = 0;

  while (true) {
    yield old + older;
    older = old;
    old += older;
  }
}
```

How does that work? Why doesn't it get stuck in an infinite loop? Whenever a `yield` statement is executed, execution in the generator gets suspended and relinquished back to the consumer, passing them the value which was yielded. That's how `itera-tor.next()` gets a value. Let's inspect this behavior more closely using a simple generator, which has side effects:

```
function* sentences () {
  yield 'going places';
  console.log('this can wait');
  yield 'yay! done';
}
```

When you iterate over a generator sequence, execution in the generator will be *suspended* (pausing its execution until the next item in the sequence is requested) immediately after each `yield` call. This allows you to execute side effects such as the `console.log` statement in the previous example, as a consequence of calling `itera-tor.next()` for the second time. The following snippet shows how iterating over the previous generator would flow:

```
var iterator = sentences();

iterator.next();
// <- 'going places'

iterator.next();
// logged: 'this can wait'
// <- 'yay! done'
```

Armed with your newfound knowledge about generators, next you'll try to figure out how to turn the tables and build an iterator that can consume generators in a way that makes asynchronous code easier to write.

6.5.2 *Asynchronicity and generators*

Let's build an iterator that can exploit suspension well enough to combine synchronous and asynchronous flows in a seamless manner. How could you accomplish a `flow` method that would allow you to implement functionality such as that in the following listing (ch06/13_generator-flow)? In this listing, you use `yield` on a method that needs to be executed asynchronously, and then you invoke a `next` function that would be provided by the `flow` implementation once you've fetched all the needed food types. Note how you're still using the callback convention where the first argument is either an error or a false value.

Listing 6.29   Building an iterator to exploit suspension

```
flow(function* iterator (next) {
  console.log('fetching food types...');
  var types = yield get;
  console.log('waiting around...');
  yield setTimeout(next, 2000);
  console.log(types.join(', '));
});

function get (next) {
  setTimeout(function later () {
    next(null, ['bacon', 'lettuce', 'crispy bacon']);
  }, 1000);
}
```

To make the previous listing work, you need to create the `flow` method in such a way that it allows `yield` statements to pause until `next` gets called. The `flow` method would take a generator as an argument, such as the one in the previous listing, and iterate through it. The generator should be passed a `next` callback so you can avoid anonymous functions, and you can, alternatively, yield functions that take a `next` callback and have the iterator pass the `next` callback to them as well. The consumer can let the iterator know that it's time to move on by calling `next()`. Then execution would get unsuspended and pick up where it left off.

You can find how a `flow` function might be implemented in the following listing. It works much like the iterators you've seen so far, except that it also has the capability to let the generator function, which gets passed into `flow`, do the sequencing. The key aspect of this asynchronous generator pattern is the back-and-forth enabled by letting the generator suspend (by using `yield`) and unsuspend (by invoking `next`) the flow of the iteration.

Listing 6.30   Generator flow implementation

```
function flow (generator) {
  var iterator = generator(next);

  next();                          ⟵  Jump start the process by
                                       calling next() by hand.
  function next (err, result) {
    if (err) {
      iterator.throw(err);
    }
    var item = iterator.next(result);
    if (item.done) {
      return;
    }
    if (typeof item.value === 'function') {
      item.value(next);
    }
  }
}
```

Using the `flow` function you can easily mix flows, and have the flow leap into (and out of) asynchronous mode easily. Going forward you'll use a combination of plain old JavaScript callbacks and control flow using the `contra` library, which is a lightweight alternative to `async`.

6.6 *Summary*

That was a lot of ground to cover, so you might want to take a break for a minute and check out the source code samples and play around with them a little more.

- We established what callback hell is, and you learned how to stay away from it by naming your functions or composing your own flow control methods.
- You learned how to use `async` to meet different needs such as asynchronous series, mapping asynchronously, or creating asynchronous queues. You delved into the world of Promises. You understand how to create a Promise, how to compose multiple Promises, and how to mix and match asynchronous and synchronous flows.
- You took an implementation-agnostic look at events and learned how to implement your own event emitters.
- I gave you a glimpse of what's coming in ES6 with Generators, and how you might use them to develop asynchronous flows.

In chapter 7 you'll take a harder look at client-side programming practices. We'll discuss the current state of interacting with the DOM, how to improve on that, and what the future holds in terms of componentized development. We'll detail implications of using jQuery, how it might not be your one-size-fits-all library, and a few alternatives you can gravitate toward. You'll also get your hands dirty with BackboneJS, an MVC framework.

7
Leveraging the
Model-View-Controller

This chapter covers

- Comparing pure jQuery to MVC
- Learning about MVC in JavaScript
- Introducing Backbone
- Building Backbone applications
- Looking at shared-view rendering in the server and browser

Until now, we've discussed topics around application development, such as crafting a build process. We also talked about code-related topics, such as coherent asynchronous flows and modular application design. We haven't yet covered the bulk of an application itself, which is what we'll do in this chapter. I'll explain why jQuery, a popular library that makes interacting with the DOM easier, might be lacking for large-scale application design and what tools you can use to supplement it or how to replace it entirely. You'll look at developing an application using the Model-View-Controller (MVC) design pattern, and you'll create an application to manage a list of to-do items throughout the chapter.

Like modularity, MVC improves software quality by separating concerns. In the case of MVC, this separation is split into three types of modules: Models, Views, and

Controllers. These parts are interconnected to separate internal information representation (Models, what the developer understands) from the presentation layer (Views, what the user sees) from the logic that connects both representations of the same data (Controllers, which also help validate user data and decide what views to show them).

First I'll tell you why jQuery doesn't suffice in large scale application design, and then I'll teach you about MVC in JavaScript through the Backbone.js library. The goal here isn't for you to become a Backbone grandmaster, but rather to get you started in the wonderful world of modern JavaScript application structure design.

7.1 *jQuery isn't enough*

Since its inception, the jQuery library has helped virtually every web developer out there by doing a few things well. It works around known bugs across different browser versions, and it normalizes the web API across browsers, giving the consumer a flexible API that delivers consistent results, making it easy to use.

jQuery helped popularize CSS selectors as the preferred method of querying the DOM in JavaScript. The native `querySelector` DOM API works similarly to querying in jQuery, allowing you to search for DOM elements using a CSS selector string. On its own, however, jQuery isn't enough. Let's discuss why.

CODE ORGANIZATION AND JQUERY

jQuery provides no means for organizing your code base, and that's okay because jQuery wasn't designed to do that. Although jQuery makes it simpler to access the native DOM API, it makes no effort to perform the necessary tasks to take your application closer to a well-structured one. Relying on jQuery alone is fine for traditional web applications where you don't have a need for structure, but doing so isn't suitable for the job of developing single page applications, which tend to have a larger and more complex client-side code base.

Another reason jQuery is so popular even today is because it's a library that plays well with others. This means you're not forced into using jQuery for everything you do. Rather, you can combine it with other libraries, which may or may not be meant to augment jQuery. You may also use jQuery on its own without other libraries. Unless you pair jQuery with an MVC library or framework, it'll be difficult to develop modular components that don't become a maintainability nightmare over time.

The MVC pattern separates your application's concerns into views, models, and controllers; these components interact and collaborate with each other to serve the application. Most of the logic you develop becomes self-contained, meaning that a single complex view won't translate into a complex application, making it a great choice for developing scalable applications. MVC came into existence in the late 1970s, but it only made its way into web applications with Ruby on Rails in 2005. In 2010, Backbone was released, bringing MVC into the client-side JavaScript application development mainstream. Today, dozens of alternatives exist for developing MVC web applications in JavaScript.

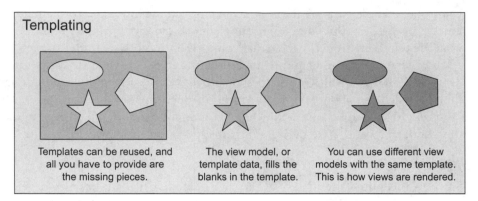

Figure 7.1   Reusing templates with different template data models

VIEW TEMPLATES

First you have the HTML; we'll call that the *view*. This is what defines how your component looks and how it's represented on the user interface. This is also how you define where pieces of data will go. If you use only jQuery, then you'd have to create the DOM elements that make up your component by hand, with their corresponding HTML attribute values and inner text. Typically, though, you'd use a templating engine, which takes a template string (of HTML, in your case) and data, and fills out the template using that data. There might be parts of the template where you loop through an array and create a few HTML elements for each item in the array. That kind of code is tedious to write in plain JavaScript, even if you're using jQuery. You don't have to worry about that if you're using a templating library, because the engine will handle it for you. Figure 7.1 illustrates how templates work as reusable components.

USING CONTROLLERS

Then there's the functionality, giving life to your views; we call this the *controller*. This is how you take your still HTML template and give it life. In the controller you'll do things such as binding DOM events to certain actions or updating the view when something happens. This is an easy thing to do with jQuery; you add events to the DOM, and that's it, right? That's fine for one-time bindings, but what if you want to develop a component using a view like you saw previously and also bind events to the rendered HTML?

For this scenario you'd need a way to consistently create the DOM structure, bind events to it, react to changes, and update it. You also need this to work in isolation, because this is a reusable component, and you want it to work in many places in your application. To be blunt, you'll end up slowly writing your own MVC framework. That's fine, as a learning exercise. In fact, that's exactly how I've come to understand and value MVC in JavaScript. I wrote my own MVC engine for a pet project, my blog, and that's what got me on the path of learning more about other MVC engines in JavaScript. The alternative is to use an existing (and proven) MVC framework.

This primer explains how the MVC pattern works, how it helps develop complex applications, and why it's needed. In section 7.2 you'll learn how it can be applied in

JavaScript. You'll look at different libraries that help write MVC code, and then you'll settle for Backbone. As you would expect, the MVC pattern dictates that your application should be split into

- Models that hold the information necessary to render a view
- Views that are in charge of rendering a model and allowing the human to interact with it
- Controllers that fill the models before rendering their related views and manage human interaction with the component

Figure 7.2 illustrates the interaction between the different elements in a typical MVC application design.

MODELS

Models define the information to be conveyed by the views. This information can be pulled from a service that, in turn, fetches the data from a database source, as we'll cover in chapter 9 when discussing REST API design and the service layer. A model contains raw data, but there isn't any logic in models; they're static collections of

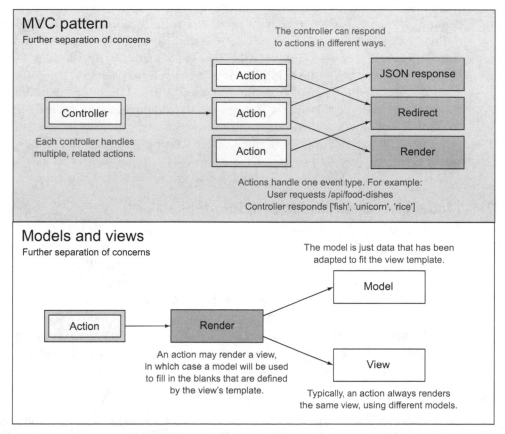

Figure 7.2 **The MVC pattern separates concerns into controllers, views, and models.**

related data. It doesn't know anything about displaying that data, either. That concern is left to views and views alone.

VIEWS

A view is the combination of a template, which gives structure to a data representation of the model, and a model, which contains the data itself. Models can and often are reused across different views. For instance, an "Article" model could be used in both the "Search" view and the "ArticleList" view. Combining a view template with a view model yields a view that can then be used as the response to an HTTP request.

CONTROLLERS

Controllers decide what view to render, and that's one of their primary purposes. The controller will decide on a view to render, prepare a view model containing all the relevant bits and pieces for the view template, and let the view engine render the view using the provided model and template. You can use controllers to add behavior to your views, respond to specific actions, or redirect humans to another view.

ROUTER

The view router is a fundamental piece of MVC in the web, although it's not part of its name. A view router is the first component of MVC applications that gets hit by a request. A router matches URL patterns to controller actions by following previously defined rules. Rules are defined in code, and they capture a request based on a condition: "Whenever a request for `/articles/{slug}` is made, route that request through the `Articles` controller, invoking the `getBySlug` action, passing it the `slug` parameter" (the `slug` is interpolated from the requested URL). The router then delegates to the controller, which will validate the request, decide on a view and render it, redirect to other URLs, and perform similar actions. Rules are evaluated in sequence. If the requested URL doesn't match the rule's pattern, it simply ignores the request, and the next rule is evaluated.

Let's get deeper into JavaScript MVC, which spans the rest of this chapter.

7.2   *Model-View-Controller in JavaScript*

The MVC pattern is nothing new, although it has seen a significant increase in adoption in the last decade, particularly in the client-side web world, which has traditionally been completely devoid of any structure. In this section I'll explain why I chose Backbone as my teaching weapon of choice, and why I discarded the other options I was considering. In section 7.3 I'll show you the basics of MVC through Backbone. Then in section 7.4 you'll dive into a case study where you'll use Backbone to develop a small application so you can learn how to use it to build scalable applications. In chapter 9 you'll take Backbone to the next level, along with everything else you've learned so far, and use it to flesh out a larger application.

7.2.1   *Why Backbone?*

Many different frameworks and libraries exist for performing client-side MVC, let alone server-side MVC, and sadly I can't cover all of them. One of the hardest choices I had to make for this book was picking an MVC framework to use. For a long while, I was torn between React, Backbone, and Angular. Ultimately, I decided Backbone is the best tool for teaching the concepts I want to relay to you. Arriving at that choice wasn't easy, and it came down mostly to maturity, simplicity, and familiarity. Backbone is one of the oldest MVC libraries out there, and therefore one of the most mature. It's also one of the most popular MVC libraries. Angular is an MVC framework developed at Google. It's also mature—in fact it was released before Backbone—but it's also much more complex, having a steep learning curve. React is Facebook's take; it's not as complex as Angular, but it's a much younger project, having been initially released in 2013, and it doesn't provide true MVC capabilities as it's meant to provide only the View in MVC.

Angular introduces concepts that can be hard to grasp at first, and I didn't want to spend the rest of the book explaining these concepts. I felt Angular would've gotten in the way of teaching how to write MVC code, and I would've had to teach how to write Angular code instead. Most importantly, one of the requirements I had going in was to show off how to do shared rendering, reusing the same logic in the server and the browser, to render your views across the stack, and Angular isn't the best solution out there when you want to have both server-side and client-side rendering, as it wasn't developed with that constraint in mind. We'll explore shared rendering in section 7.5.

Understanding progressive enhancement

Progressive enhancement is a technique that helps deliver a usable experience to everyone who uses your site. The technique suggests that you prioritize content, and then progressively add enhancements, such as additional functionality, to the content. Applications that are progressively enhanced must therefore serve the full content of a page without depending on client-side JavaScript to render the view. Once that minimally digestible content is provided to the user, the experience may be enhanced gradually by detecting the features available to the user's browser. After that initial experience is provided, we may then provide a single-page application experience by means of client-side JavaScript.

Developing applications under this philosophy has several benefits. Because you're prioritizing content, everyone visiting your site can get the minimal experience. This doesn't mean that people who have JavaScript disabled can view your site, but that people who are data roaming on mobile networks can see the content faster. Furthermore, if the requests for the JavaScript assets fail to load, at least they'll have access to a readable version of your website.

You can read more about progressive enhancement on my blog at http://ponyfoo.com/articles/tagged/progressive-enhancement.

React introduces more complexity than Backbone does, and it doesn't provide a true MVC solution the way Angular and Backbone does. React helps you write your views, giving you templating capabilities, but it involves more work on your part if you want to use it exclusively as your MVC engine.

Backbone is easier to learn progressively. You don't need to use every feature in it to build a simple application. As you make progress, you can add more components and include extra features in Backbone, such as routing, but you won't need to even know about those features until you need them.

7.2.2 Installing Backbone

In chapter 5, you wrote your client-side code using CommonJS. Later, you'll compile those modules so that browsers can interpret them. The next section is dedicated to laying down an automated compilation process using Grunt and Browserify. For now, let's talk about Backbone. The first thing you'll do is install it through npm, as shown here.

Remember, if you don't have a `package.json` file, you should create one using `npm init`. Check out appendix A on Node.js applications if you get stuck.

```
npm install backbone --save
```

Backbone needs a DOM manipulation library such as jQuery or Zepto to function properly. You'll use jQuery in your examples, because it's more widely known. I recommend you look at Zepto if you're considering this setup for a production-grade application, as it has a significantly smaller footprint. Let's go ahead and install jQuery as well:

```
npm install jquery --save
```

Once you have both Backbone and jQuery, you can start putting together the application. The first few lines of code you'll write are to set up your Backbone library. Backbone expects a jQuery-like library to be assigned to `Backbone.$` before you use it, so you'll need to give it that:

```
var Backbone = require('backbone');
Backbone.$ = require('jquery');
```

Backbone will use jQuery to interact with the DOM, attach and remove event handlers, and perform AJAX requests. That's all there is to getting up and running.

It's time to see Browserify in action! I'll walk you through setting up Grunt to compile the code for the browser. Once that's out of the way, you can make your way through the examples in the next few sections.

7.2.3 Browserifying your Backbone module with Grunt

You already touched on how to Browserify modules in chapter 5, section 5.3.3. The following listing shows how the Gruntfile configuration for Browserify looked back then.

Listing 7.1 Gruntfile configuration for Browserify

```
{
  browserify: {
    debug: {
      files: { 'build/js/app.js': 'js/app.js' },
      options: {
```

```
      debug: true
    }
  }
 }
}
```

This time around, let's do two small tweaks to that configuration. The first tweak is because you want to watch for changes and have Grunt rebuild the bundle. This enables continuous, rapid development, as we addressed in chapter 3. To watch for changes you can use grunt-contrib-watch, as we discussed in chapter 3, using configuration such as the one in the following code:

```
{
    watch: {
      app: {
        files: 'app/**/*.js',
        tasks: ['browserify']
      }
    }
}
```

The tasks property contains any tasks that should run when the matched files change.

The other tweak uses something that's called a transform. *Transforms* allow Browserify to change the source code in your modules, better adjusting it to your needs when it comes to running that code on the browser. In your case, the transform to include is called brfs for "Browser File System." This transform inlines the results of fs.readFileSync calls, making it possible to keep the view templates separate from the JavaScript code. Consider the following module:

```
var fs = require('fs');
var template = fs.readFileSync(__dirname + '/template.html', {
  encoding: 'utf8'
});

console.log(template);
```

That piece of code couldn't be transformed to run in the browser because the browser doesn't have access to files in your server's file system. To work around that issue, you can use brfs by adding it to the list of transforms in your Grunt configuration options for grunt-browserify. The brfs transform will read files referenced by fs.readFile and fs.readFileSync statements and inline them in your bundle, allowing them to work seamlessly in either Node or the browser:

```
options: {
  transform: ['brfs'],
  debug: true
}
```

You'll also need to install the brfs package from npm in your local project, with the following code:

```
npm install brfs --save-dev
```

That's it, as far as Browserifying your CommonJS modules with Grunt goes! Next up, I'll introduce you to the major concepts in Backbone, how they work, and when to use them.

7.3   *Introduction to Backbone*

A few constructs exist in Backbone that you can build your applications around. Here's a list:

- Views render the UI and deal with human interaction.
- Models can be used to track, compute, and validate properties.
- Collections are ordered sets of models, useful for interacting with lists.
- Routers allow you to control the URL, enabling development of single-page applications.

You might've noticed that controllers are nowhere to be found in that list. In reality, Backbone views act as controllers. This subtle fork from traditional MVC is often referred to as Model-View-View-Model (MVVM). Figure 7.3 illustrates the differences between Backbone and traditional MVC, as they were shown in figure 7.2, and explains where routing fits in this structure.

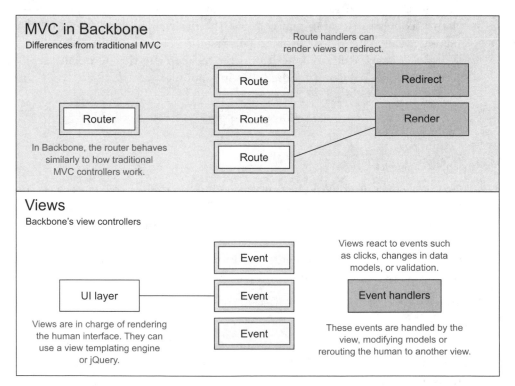

Figure 7.3   Backbone deals with the human-facing aspects of MVC: event handling, validation, and UI rendering.

Naturally, there's more to learn about each one of these constructs. Let's visit each one.

7.3.1 Backbone views

The views are in charge of rendering the UI, and you're in charge of putting together the rendering logic for your views. How to render the UI is entirely up to you. The two preferred options are using jQuery or a templating library.

Views are always associated with an element, which is where the rendering will take place. In the following listing, let's see how a basic view could be rendered. Here you're creating a Backbone view, adding custom render functionality that will set text in the view element. Then you're instantiating the view and rendering the view instance.

Listing 7.2 Rendering a basic view

```
var SampleView = Backbone.View.extend({
  el: '.view',
  render: function () {
    this.el.innerText = 'foo';
  }
});

var sampleView = new SampleView();

sampleView.render();
```

See how you declared the `el` property and assigned `.view` to it? You can assign a CSS selector to that property, and it'll look up that element in the DOM. In the view that element will get assigned to `this.el`. With an HTML page, such as the following one, you could render this minimal Backbone view:

```
<div class='view'></div>
<script src='build/bundle.js'></script>
```

The bundle script file would be the compiled application as I explained in section 7.2.3. Once you run this, the view element would get the `foo` text content. You can check out this example in the accompanying source code; it's listed as ch07/01_backbone-views.

Your view is static as it is, and you probably have a good idea how to render one with jQuery, but that involves more work, because you'd have to create every element, set their attributes, and construct a DOM tree in code. Using templates is easier to maintain and keeps your concerns separate. Let's see how that works.

USING MUSTACHE TEMPLATES

Mustache is a view-templating library that takes a template string and a view model and returns the resulting view. The way you reference model values in your template is by declaring them using the special `{{value}}` notation, which is replaced by the model's `value` property.

Mustache also uses a similar syntax that lets you iterate through arrays, wrapping part of the template in `{{#collection}}` and `{{/collection}}`. When looping a collection, you can access the array item itself using `{{.}}`, and you can also directly access its properties.

To give you a quick example, let's start with an HTML view template:

```
<p>Hello {{name}}, your order #{{orderId}} is now shipping. Your order
    includes:</p>
<ul>
  {{#items}}
  <li>{{.}}</li>
  {{/items}}
</ul>
```

To fill this template, you need to use Mustache, passing it to a model. First, you'll have to install Mustache from npm:

```
npm install mustache --save
```

Rendering this template is a matter of passing it to Mustache as a string, along with a view model:

```
var Mustache = require('mustache');
Mustache.to_html(template, viewModel);
```

To do this in Backbone you'll create a reusable module, shown in the following code snippet, which will know to render any view using Mustache, passing it to the view's template and the view's view model. Here you're creating a base view you can let other views inherit from, sharing basic functionality such as view rendering, so that you don't have to copy and paste this method onto every view you create:

```
var Backbone = require('backbone');
var Mustache = require('mustache');

module.exports = Backbone.View.extend({
  render: function () {
    this.el.innerHTML = Mustache.to_html(this.template, this.viewModel);
  }
});
```

In the previous example, where you had a static view, it was fine to keep all of your application in a single module. But this time around, you're modularizing it a bit. Having a base view is neat, and having a single module for each view is as important. In the snippet below, you're requiring the base view template you saw previously and extending that one. You're using `fs.readFileSync` to load your Mustache template, because `require` only works with JavaScript and JSON files. You won't include the template in the view module itself because it's always nice to keep your concerns separated, particularly if these concerns are in different languages. Also, the view template could arguably be used by many different views.

```
var fs = require('fs');
var base = require('./base.js');
var template = fs.readFileSync(
  __dirname + '/templates/sample.mu', 'utf8'
);
```

```
module.exports = base.extend({
  el: '.view',
  template: template
});
```

Last, you'll adapt your original application module, making it require the view rather than declare it, and declaring a view model before rendering the view. This time around, the view will be rendered with Mustache, as shown in the following listing.

Listing 7.3 Rendering a view with Mustache

```
var SampleView = require('./views/sample.js');
var sampleView = new SampleView();

sampleView.viewModel = {
  name: 'Marian',
  orderId: '1234',
  items: [
    '1 Kite',
    '2 Manning Books',
    '7 Random Candy',
    '3 Mars Bars'
  ]
};
sampleView.render();
```

You can check out this example in the accompanying code samples; it's listed as ch07/ 02_backbone-view-templates. Next up are the models, another crucial part of Backbone applications.

7.3.2 Creating Backbone models

Backbone models (also called data models) hold your application data, which are often copies of the data that can be found in a database. They can be used to observe changes, as well as validate those changes. These aren't to be confused with view models (such as what we've assigned to `sampleView.viewModel` in the previous example, also called template data), which usually contain a combination of Backbone data models, often formatted to fit the prose in the HTML template. For instance, a date might be stored in an ISO format in the data model, but formatted into a human-readable string in the template data. In the same way views get extended off `Backbone.View`, models get extended from `Backbone.Model`, and they can go a great way toward making your data interactive. Models can be validated, testing user input for bad data; they can be observed, helping you react to changes in the data model; and you can also compute properties based on data in the model.

Probably the most impactful thing you can do with your models is observing changes in the model data. This allows your UI to react to changes in the data with little effort. Remember, the same piece of data can be represented in many different ways. For instance, you could represent the same piece of data as an item in a list, as an image, or as a description. Models enable you to update each of those representations as data changes, in real time!

DATA MODELING AND MALLEABILITY

Let's look at an example (found under ch07/03_backbone-models in the samples) where you take a piece of user input and render it as plain text, in binary, and as an anchor link, if it's a URL. To kick things off, you'll create a model to check whether its data looks like a link. The `get` method allows you to access the value of a model property in Backbone.

```
module.exports = Backbone.Model.extend({
  isLink: function () {
    var link = /^https?:\/\/.+/i;
    var raw = this.get('raw');
    return link.test(raw);
  }
});
```

Assuming you had a `binary.fromString` method to convert the model data to a binary string, and you wanted to get the first few characters of the binary stream, you could add a model method for that, because it's also data-related. As a rule of thumb, every method that could be reused that depends solely (or mostly) on model data should probably be a model method. The following is a possible implementation to get the binary string. If the binary code is more than 20 characters, you can trim it using the Unicode ellipsis character, `'\u2026'` or `'…'`:

```
getBinary: function () {
  var raw = this.get('raw');
  var bin = binary.fromString(raw);
  if (bin.length > 20) {
    return bin.substr(0, 20) + '\u2026';
  }
  return bin;
}
```

I mentioned you could listen for changes in your models. Let's learn more about events.

MODELS AND EVENTS

To tie your view to this model, you need to create an instance of the model. One of the most interesting aspects of models is events. For example, you could listen for changes in the model and update your view every time the model changes. You can use the view's `initialize` property to create a model instance, bind your change listener to it, and give the model an initial value, as shown in the following code snippet:

```
initialize: function () {
  this.model = new SampleModel();
  this.model.on('change', this.updateView, this);
  this.model.set('raw', 'http://bevacqua.io/buildfirst');
}
```

Instead of rendering the view from the outside, the view will rerender itself as necessary whenever the model changes. It turns out that's easy to implement. Whenever the model changes, `updateView` is invoked, and you have a chance to update the view model and render the template with the updated values.

```
updateView: function () {
  this.viewModel = {
    raw: this.model.get('raw'),
    binary: this.model.getBinary(),
    isLink: this.model.isLink()
  };
  this.render();
}
```

All that's left for your view to do is allow user input to modify the model. You can conveniently bind to DOM events by adding properties to the `events` property on the view. These properties should have a key in the form of {event-type} {element-selector}; for example, `click .submit-button`. The property value should be the name of an event handler that's available in the view. In the following code snippet, I implement an event handler that updates the model every time the input changes:

```
events: {
  'change .input': 'inputChanged'
},
inputChanged: function (e) {
  this.model.set('raw', e.target.value);
}
```

Whenever a change event is raised, the model data will be updated. That will, in turn, trigger the model's change event listener, which will update the view model and refresh the UI. Keep in mind that if anything else changed the model data, such as incoming server data, that would refresh the UI accordingly as well. That's where the value of using models comes from. As your data gets more complex, you can benefit more from using models to access it, because they're equipped to track and react to changes in the data in such a way that your code isn't tightly coupled.

This is one of the ways in which models help shape your data without repeating logic in your code, and we'll closely inspect the benefits of models, such as data validation, over the next few sections. One last aspect of data organization you'll want to look at is collections. Let's get a quick overview of those before heading to view routing.

7.3.3 *Organizing models with Backbone collections*

Collections in Backbone enable you to group and order a set of models. You can listen for items being added or removed from the collection, and you can even get notified when any model in the collection is modified. In the same way models are helpful in computing data out of their properties, collections are concerned with finding specific models in addition to dealing with CRUD-like (Create Read Update Delete) operations.

A collection takes a model type so that you can add values to it using plain objects, which get converted internally into that model type. The collection created in the following snippet, for example, would create `SampleModel` instances whenever you added an item to it. The collections example can be found at ch07/04_backbone-collections:

```
var SampleModel = require('../models/sample.js');

module.exports = Backbone.Collection.extend({
  model: SampleModel
});
```

Similarly to models or views, collections need to be instantiated for you to take advantage of them. To keep this example short, your view will create an instance of this collection, listen for insertions, and add models to the collection. The toJSON method casts your collection to a plain JavaScript object that can be used to fetch model data when rendering a template, as shown in the following listing.

Listing 7.4 Fetching model data

```
initialize: function () {
  var collection = new SampleCollection();
  collection.on('add', this.report);
  collection.add({ name: 'Michael' });
  collection.add({ name: 'Jason' });
  collection.add({ name: 'Marian' });
  collection.add({ name: 'Candy' });
  this.viewModel = {
    title: 'Names',
    people: collection.toJSON()
  };
  this.render();
},
report: function (model) {
  var name = model.get('name');
  console.log('Someone got added to the collection:', name);
}
```

Collections can also validate models as they're inserted, as you'll see in section 7.4. There's one last item on your checklist before getting there, though. I'm talking about Backbone routers.

7.3.4 *Adding Backbone routers*

Modern web applications are increasingly becoming single-page applications, meaning that the site is loaded once, which results in fewer round-trips to the server, and the client-side code takes over. Routing on the client side can be handled by either changing what comes after the hash in the URL or using paths such as #/users or #/users/13. In modern browsers, it can be modified using the History API, which allows you to change the URL without resorting to the hash hack, resulting in cleaner-looking links, as if the site was getting the pages from the server. In Backbone, you can define and instantiate routers that serve two purposes: changing the URL to give the human a permanent link they can use to navigate to a part of your application, and taking action when the URL changes.

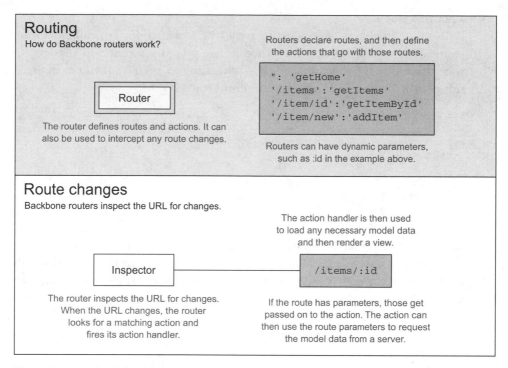

Figure 7.4 Routing in Backbone and the route inspector

Figure 7.4 shows how a router can track your application's state.

As you learned in section 7.1, routers are the first human contact in your application. Traditional routers define rules that route requests to particular controller actions. In the case of Backbone, the controller intermediary doesn't exist, and requests are routed directly to views, which play the role of the controller as well as provide the view templates and rendering logic. The Backbone router inspects the location for changes and invokes action methods, providing them with relevant URL parameters.

ROUTE CHANGES

The following code snippet (available as ch07/05_backbone-routing) instantiates a view router and uses Backbone.history.start to begin monitoring the URL for changes. It'll also check the current URL to see if it matches one of the routes that have been defined, and in that case it'll trigger that route:

```
var ViewRouter = require('./routers/viewRouter.js');
new ViewRouter();

$(function () {
  Backbone.history.start();
});
```

That's all you need to do as far as wiring goes. Let's write your ViewRouter component now.

A ROUTING MODULE

Routers are in charge of connecting each URL to an action. Typically, you'll build your application so that the action method either prepares a view and renders it, or does something that renders a view, such as navigating to a different route. In the following snippet I'm creating a router with different routes:

```
var Backbone = require('backbone');

module.exports = Backbone.Router.extend({
  routes: {
    '': 'root',
    'items': 'items',
    'items/:id': 'getItemById'
  }
});
```

The first route, when humans visit the application root, triggers them to redirect to the default route, as indicated in the following snippet. In this case, that's the items route. This ensures that the user won't be left stranded if they visit the page at the root level rather than at #items, or /items if you're using the history API. The trigger option tells navigate to change the URL and trigger the action method for that route. Next we should add the root method to the object passed to Backbone .Router.extend:

```
root: function () {
  this.navigate('items', { trigger: true });
}
```

As long as all of your views get rendered to the same view container, it could suffice to instantiate the view when a particular action is triggered, such as in the following snippet:

```
items: function () {
  new ItemView();
}
```

You'd have to require the view at the top of your routing module, like this:

```
var ItemView = require('../views/item.js');
```

Last, you might notice that the getItemById route has a named parameter in the form of :id. The router will parse the URL in views, match the items/:id pattern, and call your action method passing in the id as a parameter. Then, it's a matter of using that parameter when rendering the view.

```
getItemById: function (id) {
  new DetailView(id);
}
```

That's all there is to view routing! In section 7.4 you'll expand on all of these concepts to build a small application. Next up, let's investigate how to use your newfound Backbone knowledge to build your first application with MVC in the browser.

7.4 *Case study: the shopping list*

Before you run off and develop your own applications, I want to give you a self-contained example of how to write MVC in the browser using Backbone, putting into practice everything you've learned so far in this chapter.

In this section you'll progressively build a simple shopping list application, which allows you to view shopping list items, remove them from the list, add new ones, and change the quantities. I've divided the exercise into five stages. At each stage, you'll add functionality and refactor what you have so far to keep your code tidy. The five stages are

- Creating a static view with shopping list items
- Adding remove buttons for deleting items
- Building a form to add new items to your shopping list
- Implementing inline editing on the list to change the quantities
- Adding view routing

That sounds like fun! Keep in mind that you have access to the code at any of these five stages in the accompanying code samples.

7.4.1 *Starting with a static shopping list*

Let's go back to basics and put the application together from scratch. The Gruntfile remains the same as it was back in section 7.2.3, and it won't change during the course of this case study, so you don't need to revisit it. Look at the HTML in listing 7.5 (available as ch07/06_shopping-list) to get started. Note that you're including the built Browserify bundle to get the Common.js code working in the browser. The `<div>` will act as your view container in this example. This piece of HTML is called `app.html`, because it's the single page the application will run on.

Listing 7.5   Creating the shopping list

```html
<!doctype html>
<html>
  <head>
    <title>Shopping List</title>
  </head>
  <body>
    <h1>Shopping List</h1>
    <div class='view'></div>
    <script src='build/bundle.js'></script>
  </body>
</html>
```

Next up, this example needs to render a list of shopping items, displaying the quantity and name of each item. Here's a Mustache snippet that can render an array of shopping list items. Mustache templates will go into the `views/templates` directory.

```
<ul>
  {{#shopping_list}}
  <li>{{quantity}}x {{name}}</li>
  {{/shopping_list}}
</ul>
```

Your views will need to render these templates using a view model. This functionality should go in a base view so that it's only implemented once.

RENDERING VIEWS WITH MUSTACHE

To easily render Mustache templates in your views and to avoid repetition, you'll wire up a base view and place it in the `views` directory. The rest of your views will extend this one, allowing you to add functionality that gets shared across every view. If a view needs to be rendered in another way, that's okay; you can override the `render` method again.

```
var Backbone = require('backbone');
var Mustache = require('mustache');

module.exports = Backbone.View.extend({
  render: function () {
    this.el.innerHTML = Mustache.to_html(this.template, this.viewModel);
  }
});
```

Next you'll create items for your List view.

THE SHOPPING LIST VIEW

A static shopping list of items will suffice for now, which is why in the following listing you can set the view model object once and forget about it. Note the `initialize` method, which runs when the view gets instantiated so that the view renders itself when it's created. This view uses the template you saw previously and targets the `.view` element in `app.html`.

Listing 7.6   Creating a list of items

```
var fs = require('fs');
var base = require('./base.js');
var template = fs.readFileSync(
  __dirname + '/templates/list.mu', { encoding: 'utf8' }
);

module.exports = base.extend({
  el: '.view',
  template: template,
  viewModel: {
    shopping_list: [
      { name: 'Banana', quantity: 3 },
      { name: 'Strawberry', quantity: 8 },
      { name: 'Almond', quantity: 34 },
```

```
        { name: 'Chocolate Bar', quantity: 1 }
      ]
    },
    initialize: function () {
      this.render();
    }
});
```

Last, you need to initialize the application. Here's the entry point code where you create an instance of the List view after initializing Backbone. Note that because the view renders itself, you only have to instantiate it.

```
var Backbone = require('backbone');
Backbone.$ = require('jquery');

var ListView = require('./app/views/list.js');
var list = new ListView();
```

You've laid out the ground work for a shopping list application. Let's build on that in the next stage. You'll add delete buttons and refactor to accommodate a dynamic application where the data can change.

7.4.2 *This time with remove buttons*

The first thing you'll do at this stage is update the view template so that it includes buttons to remove items from the shopping list. You'll set a `data-name` attribute on the buttons so you can identify which item should be removed from the list. The updated template can be found in the following snippet:

```
<ul>
  {{#shopping_list}}
  <li>
    <span>{{quantity}}x {{name}}</span>
    <button class='remove' data-name='{{name}}'>x</button>
  </li>
  {{/shopping_list}}
</ul>
```

Before wiring up the Remove button, you need to set up a proper model and a collection.

USING A MODEL AND A COLLECTION

The collection will let you listen for changes to the list, such as when an item gets removed from the list. The model can be used to track changes at the individual level, and it allows you to do validation, as well as computation, as you'll see in the next few stages. For your purposes, you don't need much more than a standard Backbone model, but it's always a good idea to keep your models strictly separated in different modules and well named. The `ShoppingItem` model will be in the `models` directory.

```
var Backbone = require('backbone');

module.exports = Backbone.Model.extend({
});
```

The collection isn't that special, either; it needs a reference to the model. That way, the collection will know what kind of model to create when inserting new objects into the list. To keep things neatly organized, you'll place your collections in a `collections` directory.

```
var Backbone = require('backbone');
var ShoppingItem = require('../models/shoppingItem.js');

module.exports = Backbone.Collection.extend({
  model: ShoppingItem
});
```

Rather than setting the view model once and forgetting about it, and now that you have both the model and the collection in place, you should change your view to use the collection instead. The first change you'll make in your view will be to `require` the collection, as shown in the following code:

```
var ShoppingList = require('../collections/shoppingList.js');
```

Instead of the `viewModel` property, which you'll set dynamically from now on, you'll use a `collection` property to keep track of your models. Note that, as I mentioned previously, I don't have to explicitly create `ShoppingList` instances for my collection, because it already knows that's the model type it has to use.

```
collection: new ShoppingList([
  { name: 'Banana', quantity: 3 },
  { name: 'Strawberry', quantity: 8 },
  { name: 'Almond', quantity: 34 },
  { name: 'Chocolate Bar', quantity: 1 }
])
```

Next, you'll have the view update the UI when it first loads. To do that, you'll set the view model to whatever is in the collection and then render the view. Using the `toJSON` method gives a plain array of model objects.

```
initialize: function () {
  this.viewModel = {
    shopping_list: this.collection.toJSON()
  };
  this.render();
}
```

Last, you'll wire up your shopping list item Remove button.

WIRING UP DOM EVENTS IN BACKBONE

To listen for DOM events, you can assign properties to an `events` object in your views. These properties should be named using an event name and a CSS selector, separated by a space. The following code is what you'll use in your updated view. It'll trigger an action whenever a `click` event occurs in an element matching the `.remove` selector. Keep in mind that these events look for elements inside your view el, in this case the `<div>` you created during the previous stage, and it won't fire events for elements that are outside the view. Last, the event should be set to the name of a method that can be found in your view.

```
events: {
  'click .remove': 'removeItem'
}
```

Let's define `removeItem` now. You'll use a collection filtering method. The button can be accessed through `e.target`, and you'll use its `data-name` attribute to fetch the name. Then you'll use that name to filter the collection to find the shopping list item associated with this particular button.

```
removeItem: function (e) {
  var name = e.target.dataset.name;
  var model = this.collection.findWhere({ name: name });
  this.collection.remove(model);
}
```

Once a model is removed from the collection, the view should be updated again. The naive approach would be to update the view model and render the view after removing an item from the collection. The problem is that items may be removed from a collection in different places throughout an application, particularly if it's a good one. A better approach is to listen to events emitted by the collection. In this case, you can listen for the `remove` event in the collection and refresh the view whenever that event is raised.

The following listing sets up the event listener as you initialize the view, and also includes refactoring so that the code isn't duplicated, staying loyal to the DRY principle.

Listing 7.7 Setting up an event listener

```
initialize: function () {
  this.collection.on('remove', this.updateView, this);
  this.updateView();
},
updateView: function () {
  this.viewModel = {
    shopping_list: this.collection.toJSON()
  };
  this.render();
}
```

That was a big chunk to digest! You may now head over to the accompanying code samples and take a glance at ch07/07_the-one-with-delete-buttons, which is the working example you got as you completed this stage. In the next portion of this walk-through, you'll create a form that humans can use to add items to their shopping list.

7.4.3 Adding items to your cart

In the previous stage you gave life to your shopping list, allowing items to be removed from the list. This time, you'll add the option to add new items as well, so that humans can make their own purchases, instead of removing the items they don't want.

To keep things interesting, let's throw in another requirement. When creating a new item, you need to make sure its name isn't already listed. If the item is already on the grocery list, then the quantity needs to be added to the existing item. That avoids creating duplicate items.

CREATING AN "ADD TO CART" COMPONENT

You'll add the bit of HTML in the following listing to add groceries to the list. This sample can be found as ch07/08_creating-items. You'll use a couple of inputs, and a button that will add the item to the shopping list collection. There's also a field that will only be displayed if an error message is set. You'll use that field for input validation purposes. To keep things simple, this piece of HTML will go into your list template for now. You'll refactor and move it into its own view in the next couple of stages.

Listing 7.8 Setting up an add to cart component

```
<fieldset>
  <legend>Add Groceries</legend>
  <label>Name</label>
  <input class='name' value='{{name}}' />
  <label>Quantity</label>
  <input class='quantity' type='number' value='{{quantity}}' />
  <button class='add'>Add</button>
  {{#error}}
  <p>{{error}}</p>
  {{/error}}
</fieldset>
```

Until now your models never changed. You could remove items but not update them. Now that the models can be changed via human interaction, it's time to add in validation.

INPUT VALIDATION

Human input should never be trusted, because users can easily enter a quantity that isn't numeric, or they can forget to enter a name. Maybe they entered a negative number, and that should be taken into consideration as well. Backbone allows you to validate information by supplying a `validate` method on your models. That method takes an `attrs` object, which is an internal model variable that holds all of the model properties so that you can access them directly. The following listing shows how to implement the validation function. You're checking that the model has a name, a numeric quantity that's not `NaN` (Not a Number). Confusingly, `NaN` is of type `'number'` and `NaN` is not equal to itself either, so you need to test for `NaN` using the native JavaScript `isNaN` method. Last, you'll make sure that the quantity is at least 1.

Listing 7.9 Implementing the validation function

```
validate: function (attrs) {
  if (!attrs.name) {
    return 'Please enter the name of the item.';
  }
```

```
  if (typeof attrs.quantity !== 'number' || isNaN(attrs.quantity)) {
    return 'The quantity must be numeric!';
  }
  if (attrs.quantity < 1) {
    return 'You should keep your groceries to yourself.';
  }
}
```

To make editing simpler, you'll also add a helper method to the model that takes a quantity and updates the model, adding that amount to the current quantity. This change should be validated to make sure that a negative amount doesn't make the resulting quantity go below 1. Models aren't validated by default when changing their values, but you can force that by turning on the `validate` option. The following code shows what that method looks like:

```
addToOrder: function (quantity) {
  this.set('quantity', this.get('quantity') + quantity, { validate: true });
}
```

When adding any amount to the model, validation will be triggered, and if it fails, the model won't be changed, but instead a `validationError` property will be set on the model. Suppose you have a model with a quantity of 6; the following code will fail and set the `validationError` property to the appropriate error message:

```
model.addToOrder(-6);
model.validationError;
// <- 'You should keep your groceries to yourself.'
```

Now that your model protects itself against bad data, you can update the view and give life to your new form.

REFACTORING THE VIEW LOGIC

The first change we'll make to the view is adding a render method that can display an error message while keeping the name and quantity that the human entered, so that they're not cleared when an error occurs. Let's name that method `updateViewWithValidation` for clarity:

```
updateViewWithValidation: function (validation) {
  this.viewModel = {
    shopping_list: this.collection.toJSON(),
    error: validation.error,
    name: validation.name,
    quantity: validation.quantity
  };
  this.render();
}
```

You also need to bind an event listener to click events on your Add button. To do that, add another property to the `events` object in your view. Then all that's left is creating the `addItem` event handler:

```
'click .add': 'addItem'
```

The first couple of things your `addItem` handler should do is get the human input and parse the quantity as a base 10 integer:

```
var name = this.$('.name').val();
var quantity = parseInt(this.$('.quantity').val(), 10);
```

Once you have the user input, the first thing you'll do is figure out if any items in the collection have the same name, and, in that case, you'll use the `addToOrder` method to update the model after validating the input. If the item isn't already in the list, then you create a new `ShoppingItem` model instance and validate it. If the validation passes, then you add the newly created item onto the collection. In code, that looks like the following listing.

Listing 7.10 Validating a shopping item

```
var model = this.collection.findWhere({ name: name });
if (model) {
  model.addToOrder(quantity);
} else {
  model = new ShoppingItem({ name: name, quantity: quantity }, { validate:
      true });
  if (!model.validationError) {
    this.collection.add(model);
  }
}
```

Because you're using the `ShoppingItem` class, you'll have to add the following statement to the top of your module:

```
var ShoppingItem = require('../models/shoppingItem.js');
```

If the validation step fails, you need to render the view again, adding the validation error message so that the user knows what went wrong:

```
if (!model.validationError) {
  return;
}

this.updateViewWithValidation({
  name: name,
  quantity: quantity,
  error: model.validationError
});
```

If validation goes well, the collection will either get a new item or an existing item will change. These cases should be handled by listening to the `add` and `change` events on the collection. You need to add the following couple of lines to the `initialize` method on the view:

```
this.collection.on('add', this.updateView, this);
this.collection.on('change', this.updateView, this);
```

That's all there is to this stage. You now have the ability to add new items to the list, modify the quantity on existing ones, and remove items. In the next stage, you'll make editing more intuitive by adding an inline edit button on each list item.

7.4.4   *Using inline editing*

In this section we'll introduce inline item editing. Each item will get an Edit button. Clicking on it will allow humans to change the quantity and then save the record. That feature in itself is simple, but you're going to take this opportunity and clean house a bit. You're going to split your growing list view into three: an Add Item view that will be in charge of the input form, a List Item view that will be in charge of individual list items, and the original List view that will handle removals and additions to the collection.

COMPONENTIZING YOUR VIEWS

The first order of business will be breaking your list view template in two. You'll use two different view containers: one for the list and another one for the form. The `<div>` you used to have can be replaced by the following code:

```
<ul class='list-view'></ul>
<fieldset class='add-view'></fieldset>
```

This division of labor also means you need to split your Mustache template. Rather than have the `list` template do everything, you'll replace it with two other templates. As you'll soon learn, the list itself won't need any templating; only the form and the individual list items will. The following code is what `views/templates/addItem.mu` looks like. The form remains almost unchanged, except the `fieldset` tag has been promoted to view container status, so it's no longer in the template.

```
<legend>Add Groceries</legend>
<label>Name</label>
<input class='name' value='{{name}}' />
<label>Quantity</label>
<input class='quantity' type='number' value='{{quantity}}' />
<button class='add'>Add</button>
{{#error}}
<p>{{error}}</p>
{{/error}}
```

The List view no longer needs a template itself, because the only element that's needed is the `<ul>` element, bound to your List view through the `el` property, as you'll see in a minute. Each list item will be kept in its own view, and you'll use a view template for them. The List Item view model will hold a property to track whether the item is being edited or not. This property is checked in the view template to decide if you need to render a label and the action buttons or the inline editing form. The list item template looks like the following listing and goes into `views/templates/listItem.mu`.

Listing 7.11   Viewing a list item template

```
{{^editing}}
<span>{{quantity}}x {{name}}</span>
<button class='edit'>Edit</button>
<button class='remove'>x</button>
{{/editing}}
{{#editing}}
<span>{{name}}</span>
```

```
<input class='edit-quantity' value='{{quantity}}' type='number' />
<button class='cancel'>Cancel</button>
<button class='save'>Save</button>
{{/editing}}
{{#error}}
<span>{{error}}</span>
{{/error}}
```

You'll still create the collection in the List view, but you need to pass that collection to the addItem view. This couples both views tightly, because the addItem view needs a List view that can create a collection, and that isn't modular. This is what your entry point, app.js, looks like now. You'll sort out the coupling issues in the next stage; this code snippet is about turning your components smaller:

```
var Backbone = require('backbone');
Backbone.$ = require('jquery');

var ListView = require('./views/list.js');
var listView = new ListView();

var AddItemView = require('./views/addItem.js');
var addItemView = new AddItemView({ collection: listView.collection });
```

Let's continue by creating the Add Item view.

A MODULAR "ADD TO CART" VIEW

The Add Item view is similar to what you had in the List view before starting to componentize it. First, the following listing shows how the view is initialized, and how it uses the .add-view selector to find the <fieldset>, which will be used as the view container.

Listing 7.12   Initializing the view

```
var fs = require('fs');
var base = require('./base.js');
var template = fs.readFileSync(
  __dirname + '/templates/addItem.mu', { encoding: 'utf8' }
);
var ShoppingItem = require('../models/shoppingItem.js');

module.exports = base.extend({
  el: '.add-view',
  template: template,
  initialize: function () {
    this.updateView();
  },
  updateView: function (vm) {
    this.viewModel = vm || {};
    this.render();
  }
});
```

This view is only concerned with adding models to the collection, and it shows. It'll have a click event handler on the Add button that will look almost exactly identical to your old `addItem` method. The only difference is that in this version you update the view every time the `addItem` event handler is fired, as shown in the following listing.

Listing 7.13   Updating the view

```
events: {
  'click .add': 'addItem'
},
addItem: function () {
  var name = this.$('.name').val();
  var quantity = parseInt(this.$('.quantity').val(), 10);
  var model = this.collection.findWhere({ name: name });
  if (model) {
    model.addToOrder(quantity);
  } else {
    model = new ShoppingItem(
      { name: name, quantity: quantity },
      { validate: true }
    );

    if (!model.validationError) {
      this.collection.add(model);
    }
  }

  if (!model.validationError) {
    this.updateView();
    return;
  }
  this.updateView({
    name: name,
    quantity: quantity,
    error: model.validationError
  });
}
```

The only thing the Add Item view has to do is add items, so that's all there is to it! Let's put together the List item view next.

CREATING A LIST ITEM COMPONENT

The list item component will be in charge of rendering any changes made to its model and provide the opportunity to edit or remove items from the list. Let's go over this view from scratch. First off, there are the usual suspects. You need to read the template file and extend the base view. The `tagName` property means that this view will get rendered to an `<li>` element. Start with the following code snippet:

```
var fs = require('fs');
var base = require('./base.js');
var template = fs.readFileSync(
  __dirname + '/templates/listItem.mu', { encoding: 'utf8' }
);

module.exports = base.extend({
  tagName: 'li',
  template: template
});
```

This view will take the model and collection properties as they're created, as you'll see when refactoring the List view, which you'll do next. Whenever the model changes, you'll render the view again. The view also needs to be rendered when it's initialized. In case a validation error occurs while using the inline editing feature, you'll track that with the view model as well. Here's how that looks in code:

```
initialize: function () {
  this.model.on('change', this.updateView, this);
  this.updateView();
},
updateView: function () {
  this.viewModel = this.model.toJSON();
  this.viewModel.error = this.model.validationError;
  this.render();
}
```

The remove event handler is much simpler now, because all you have to do is remove the model from the collection, and you still have both of those in the properties of your view. This is how it looks in code:

```
events: {
  'click .remove': 'removeItem'
},
removeItem: function (e) {
  this.collection.remove(this.model);
}
```

Next you'll wire up the edit and cancel methods, which are similar. The first one puts the item in edit mode, while the second leaves edit mode. All these methods need to do is change the `editing` property. The rest will be handled by the model change event listener, which will make sure to render the view again. When switching the edit mode on or off, you'll clear the `validationError` property as well. The following listing introduces these event handlers.

Listing 7.14 Adding edit and cancel methods

```
events: {
  'click .edit': 'editItem',
  'click .cancel': 'cancelEdit',
  'click .remove': 'removeItem'
},
removeItem: function (e) {
  this.collection.remove(this.model);
}
editItem: function (e) {
  this.model.validationError = null;
  this.model.set('editing', true);
},
cancelEdit: function (e) {
  this.model.validationError = null;
  this.model.set('editing', false);
}
```

The last task of the List Item view will be saving edits made to a record. You'll bind to clicks on the Save button, parse the input, and update the quantity. You'll get out of edit mode only if the validation succeeded. Keep in mind I'm not repeating all of the previous event handlers, for brevity:

```
events: {
  'click .save': 'saveItem'
},
saveItem: function (e) {
    var quantity = parseInt(this.$('.edit-quantity').val(), 10);
    this.model.set('quantity', quantity, { validate: true });
    this.model.set('editing', this.model.validationError);
  }
});
```

List items don't have any other responsibilities, but the list should add and remove this partial view to the UI. When saying partial view, I mean that it only represents a portion of an object, in this case a portion of the list rather than the whole. The List view needs to hold as many list item views as it has to.

REBUILDING THE LIST VIEW

Previously, your List view would rerender every time an item was added or deleted. Now your list will only render individual items and append them to the DOM or remove existing items from the DOM. This is not only faster than rerendering the whole list, but it's also more modular. The list is only managing the big picture actions, when items are added or removed. The individual items will each be in charge of maintaining their own state and updating their own UI representation.

For this to work, the List view will no longer rely on the view.render method, but manipulate the DOM directly instead. The aspects of the old List view that you kept, such as the hard-coded collection data, extending from the base view, and the el property declaration are shown in the following listing. Note that the view container has changed to match your <ul> element.

Listing 7.15 Aspects of the old list view

```
var base = require('./base.js');
var ShoppingList = require('../collections/shoppingList.js');

module.exports = base.extend({
  el: '.list-view',
  collection: new ShoppingList([
    { name: 'Banana', quantity: 3 },
    { name: 'Strawberry', quantity: 8 },
    { name: 'Almond', quantity: 34 },
    { name: 'Chocolate Bar', quantity: 1 }
  ])
});
```

Because you no longer desire to repaint the entire view every time an item changes, you'll rely on two new methods, addItem and removeItem, to do the DOM manipulation. You'll run these methods whenever the collection is updated, keeping the UI up to date at all times. You can also use the `addItem` method to render the initial representation of the collection, by running it on each model in the collection when initializing the view. The `initialize` method will look like the following code snippet. I'll explain the `partials` variable next.

```
initialize: function () {
  this.partials = {};
  this.collection.on('add', this.addItem, this);
  this.collection.on('remove', this.removeItem, this);
  this.collection.models.forEach(this.addItem, this);
}
```

Before you can see the `addItem` method, I'll mention that it needs to `require` the List Item view. You'll use that to create partial views, one for each model in the collection. Let's add that to the top of the List view module:

```
var ListItemView = require('./listItem.js');
```

You're now ready to implement the `addItem` method. That method will take a model and create an instance of the `ListItemView`. Then the view element, which is an `<li>`, will be appended to `this.$el`, which is your `<ul>` element. To cleanly find and remove items from the list, you'll track them in the `partials` variable. Backbone models have a unique ID property that can be accessed through `model.cid`, so you can use that as the keys in your `partials` object. The code is as follows:

```
addItem: function (model) {
  var item = new ListItemView({
    model: model,
    collection: this.collection
  });
  this.$el.append(item.el);
  this.partials[model.cid] = item;
}
```

Removing elements is now merely a matter of looking at the `partials` object, accessing the partial by means of the `model.cid` key, and removing the element. You should then make sure that it gets removed from the `partials` object as well.

```
removeItem: function (model) {
  var item = this.partials[model.cid];
  item.$el.remove();
  delete this.partials[model.cid];
}
```

Phew! That was an intense refactoring session, but it paid off. Now you have a few different views working on the same collection, and they're much more self-contained now. The Add Item view only adds items to the collection, the List view only cares about creating new List Item views or removing them from the DOM, and the List Item view is only concerned about changes to an individual model.

Give yourself a congratulatory pat on the back, and check out the accompanying code samples to make sure you understand all the changes you've made at this stage and the current state of the shopping list application. You'll find the example listed as ch07/09_item-editing.

You accomplished a nice separation of concerns at this stage, but you can do better. Let's examine that in the last stage of this process.

7.4.5   *A service layer and view routing*

This last stage introduces two changes to your organization. You'll add a thin service layer and introduce view routing into your application design. By creating a service that provides a unique shopping list collection, you give your views the ability to actively ask the service for the shopping list data. This dramatically decouples your views, which previously generated the data and shared it with each other.

Note that in this case you're still hard coding an array of items, but you could as easily pull them from an Ajax request and provide access to them through a Promise, as you saw in chapter 6. For the time being, the following listing will do. This should be placed in the `services` directory.

Listing 7.16   Hard coding an array of items

```
var ShoppingList = require('../collections/shoppingList.js');

var items = [
  { name: 'Banana', quantity: 3 },
  { name: 'Strawberry', quantity: 8 },
  { name: 'Almond', quantity: 34 },
  { name: 'Chocolate Bar', quantity: 1 }
];
module.exports = {
  collection: new ShoppingList(items)
};
```

Once that's in place, both the Add Item and the List views should `require` the service, and assign `shoppingService.collection` to their `collection` properties. In doing that, you no longer need to pass around a reference to the collection that was previously initialized by the List view.

Let's turn to the routing changes, rounding up your shopping list adventure.

ROUTING FOR THE SHOPPING LIST

You're also going to implement routing at this stage. To keep things interesting, you'll move the Add Item view to a different route. The code in the following listing should go into its own module. Place it at `routers/viewRouter.js`. The `'root'` action helps redirect humans when they open up the application, and there's no other hash location set.

Listing 7.17   Moving the Add Item view to a different route

```
var Backbone = require('backbone');
var ListView = require('../views/list.js');
var AddItemView = require('../views/addItem.js');
module.exports = Backbone.Router.extend({
```

```
  routes: {
    '': 'root',
    'items': 'listItems',
    'items/add': 'addItem'
  },
  root: function () {
    this.navigate('items', { trigger: true });
  },
  listItems: function () {
    new ListView();
  },
  addItem: function () {
    new AddItemView();
  }
});
```

As I mentioned back in section 7.3.4 when I first introduced Backbone routers, you'll have to go back to `app.js` and replace what you had in there with the code in the following listing. This will wire up your view router and activate it. Rather than statically defining the first view served to the human, it'll depend on from which URL they visit your application.

Listing 7.18 Activating the view router

```
var Backbone = require('backbone');
var $ = require('jquery');

Backbone.$ = $;

var ViewRouter = require('./routers/viewRouter.js');
new ViewRouter();

$(function () {
  Backbone.history.start();
});
```

The last change you need to make to have routing has to do with views and templating. First, you'll revert back to the single view container you used to have before the last stage:

```
<div class='view'></div>
```

Second, you need to set the `el` property to `'.view'` in both the Add Item view and the List view. You also have to change the view templates around a bit. For example, the Add Item view template should have a Cancel button that goes back to the List view. It should look like the following code:

```
<a href='#items' class='cancel'>Cancel</a>
```

Last, you'll give your List view a well-deserved view template, which will be small. It needs the `<ul>` that will keep the list and an anchor link that matches the route for the Add Item view. The following code snippet shows how the template, placed in views/templates/list.mu, should look:

```
<ul class='items'></ul>
<a href='#items/add'>Add Item</a>
```

The List view should render this template when initialized and look up the list element:

```
this.render();
this.$list = this.$('.items');
```

When adding an item to the list, rather than appending them to $el, which is now the shared view container, you should append them to $list:

```
this.$list.append(item.el);
```

That's all there is to it! Make sure to check out the code in the accompanying repository. The last stage can be found under ch07/10_the-road-show, and it contains everything you've worked on so far. Next up, you'll learn about Rendr, a technology you can use to render client-side Backbone views on the server side, which is useful for improving human-perceived performance when developing Node.js applications.

7.5   *Backbone and Rendr: server/client shared rendering*

Rendr boosts the perceived performance of Backbone applications by rendering them on the server side. This allows you to display the rendered page before Java-Script code is executed in the browser and Backbone kicks in. The first time the page gets loaded, the human will see the content sooner. After that first load, Backbone will take over and handle routing on the client side. The first load is extremely important and rendering the application on the server before the human gets any content is better than having them wait for Backbone to pull your data, fill your views, and render your templates. That's why server-side rendering is still vital to the web application development process. Let's start with a quick dive into the world of Rendr.

7.5.1   *Diving into Rendr*

Rendr uses a conventional approach to application building. It expects you to name your modules in a certain way and place them in certain directories. Rendr also has opinions about the kinds of templates you should use and how your application should access its data. By default, this means Rendr expects you to have a REST API to access the application data; you'll investigate REST API design in chapter 9.

Rendr runs on Node.js, acting as middleware in your HTTP stack. It works by intercepting requests and rendering views server-side before handing the prerendered results to the client. In its conventional approach, it helps separate concerns by defining controllers, where you can fetch data, render views, or perform redirects. Rather than having to reference your templates in your views, Rendr uses well-defined naming policies that abstract away dependencies, which are mostly managed by the Rendr engine. This will become clearer once you look at the code in section 7.5.2.

PROBLEMS IN PARADISE

Not all is peaches and cream. At the time of this writing, Rendr (v0.5) includes "peculiar" design choices that ultimately made me decide not to use it throughout this chapter, as it would've complicated the examples. For instance, Rendr uses Browserify to bring the modules you write into the browser, but it has three distinct hacks in the way it compiles your CommonJS modules using Browserify:

1 jQuery needs to be shimmed through `browserify-shim`. This is problematic because the server-side version of Rendr uses its own version of jQuery, and there could be versioning discrepancies. If you try to use the CommonJS version obtained through `npm`, it won't work.

2 It needs aliases for part of its `require` calls to work as expected, which is an issue because it translates into the next deficiency, as well.

3 You can't use the `brfs` transform with Rendr.

The decision to not go deeper into Rendr mostly had more to do with it being less broadly applicable. If you chose a server-side language other than Node.js, you couldn't carry as many of the concepts I'll teach into your designs. Beside these problems, there definitely is value in learning about the conventional MVC capabilities Rendr provides to your Backbone applications. Many conventional MVC frameworks exist in server-side languages, providing similar features as those resulting from combining Backbone and Rendr, but you rarely learn about those when talking about client-side JavaScript. The ability to perform shared rendering definitely boosts its appeal. As with most things when deciding on a technology stack, it's a tradeoff. Note that Facebook's React is a good example of a library that's capable of doing both server-side and client-side rendering without any additional tooling needed.

DIVING IN

To showcase Rendr, I've settled for a slightly modified version of an example AirBnB (the company behind Rendr) uses to teach how Rendr works. You can find the code as ch07/11_entourage in the accompanying code samples.

First, let's talk about the templates. Rendr encourages you to use a superset of Mustache called Handlebars. Handlebars provides extra features, mostly in the form of helper methods you can use, such as an `if` convenience method. Rendr expects you to compile the Handlebars templates and place the bundled result in `app/templates/compiledTemplates.js`. To do that, start by installing the Grunt plugin for Handlebars:

```
npm install --save-dev grunt-contrib-handlebars
```

To configure the Handlebars Grunt plugin, you have to add the code in the following listing to the `Gruntfile`. The `options` passed to the `handlebars:compile` task target are needed by Rendr, which expects the templates to be named in a certain way.

Listing 7.19   Configuring the Handlebars plugin

```
handlebars: {
  compile: {
```

```
    options: {
      namespace: false,
      commonjs: true,
      processName: function (filename) {
        return filename.replace('app/templates/', '').replace('.hbs', '');
      }
    },
    src: 'app/templates/**/*.hbs',
    dest: 'app/templates/compiledTemplates.js'
  }
}
```

The Browserify configuration is, at the moment, also tied to Rendr's expectations. You'll need to shim jQuery, rather than install it from npm. You're expected to provide an alias so Rendr can access rendr-handlebars, the Handlebars adapter used by Rendr. Last, Rendr needs you to provide a few mappings so it can access your application's modules. The code to configure Browserify to play nice with Rendr can be found in the following listing.

Listing 7.20   Configuring Browserify to work with Rendr

```
browserify: {
  options: {
    debug: true,
    alias: ['node_modules/rendr-handlebars/index.js:rendr-handlebars'],
    aliasMappings: [{
      cwd: 'app/',
      src: ['**/*.js'],
      dest: 'app/'
    }],
    shim: {
      jquery: {
        path: 'assets/vendor/jquery-1.9.1.min.js',
        exports: '$'
      }
    }
  },
  app: {
    src: ['app/**/*.js'],
    dest: 'public/bundle.js'
  }
}
```

That's it, as far as build configuration goes. It might not be ideal, but once it's in there you can forget about it. Let's go into the sample application code and see how it works.

7.5.2   *Understanding boilerplate in Rendr*

The first step you'll take in putting together your Rendr application is creating the entry point for the Node program. You'll name this file app.js and place it in your application root. As I mentioned previously, Rendr works as a middleware in your HTTP stack, sitting inside Express.

EXPRESS MIDDLEWARE FOR RENDR

Express is a popular Node.js framework that wraps the native http module, providing more functionality and allowing you to perform routing and a few other things. Past this section, most of what we'll discuss is inherent to Rendr and not part of Express. Rendr enhances Express to make its conventions work, though.

```
npm install express --save
```

Have a look at the following piece of code. You're using the express package to set up an HTTP server in Node. Calling express() will create a new Express application instance, and you can add middleware to that instance with app.use. Invoking app.listen(port) will keep the application running and react on incoming HTTP requests on the chosen port. Best practice dictates that the listening port for your application should be configurable as an environment variable and have a sensible default value.

```
var express = require('express');
var app = express();
var port = process.env.PORT || 3000;

app.use(express.static(__dirname + '/public'));
app.use(express.bodyParser());
app.listen(port, function () {
  console.log('listening on port %s', port);
});
```

The static middleware tells Express to serve all of the content in the specified directory as static assets. If a human requests http://localhost:3000/js/foo.js, and the public/js/foo.js file exists, that's what Express will respond with. The bodyParser middleware is a utility that will parse request bodies that are detected to be in JSON or form data format.

The following listing configures Rendr for your example. The middleware will take care of everything else, as you'll see next. The data adapter configuration tells Rendr what API it should query. The beauty of Rendr lies in that, both on the client side as well as on the server side, it'll query the API whenever it needs to fetch data.

Listing 7.21 Configuring Rendr

```
var rendr = require('rendr');
var rendrServer = rendr.createServer({
  dataAdapterConfig: {
    default: {
      host: 'api.github.com',
      protocol: 'https'
    }
  }
});

app.use(rendrServer);
```

SETTING UP RENDR

Rendr provides a series of base objects you're expected to extend when building your application. The `BaseApp` object, which extends from `BaseView`, should be extended and placed in `app/app.js` to create a Rendr app. In this file you could add app initialization code that runs in both the client and the server and is used to maintain the application's global state. The following snippet of code will suffice:

```
var BaseApp = require('rendr/shared/app');

module.exports = BaseApp.extend({
});
```

You also need to create a router module, which you could use to track page views whenever there's a route change, although for now you'll merely create an instance of the base router. The router module should be placed at `app/router.js`, and it should look like the following code:

```
var BaseClientRouter = require('rendr/client/router');

var Router = module.exports = function Router (options) {
  BaseClientRouter.call(this, options);
};

Router.prototype = Object.create(BaseClientRouter.prototype);
Router.prototype.constructor = BaseClientRouter;
```

Let's turn our attention to how the meat of your Rendr application should look.

7.5.3　*A simple Rendr application*

You've configured Grunt and Express to comply with Rendr's needs. Now it's time to develop the application itself. To make this example easier to understand, I'll show you the code in the logical order Rendr uses to serve its responses. To keep your example self-contained, yet interesting, you'll create three different views:

1　Home is the welcome screen for your app.
2　Users keeps a list of GitHub users.
3　User contains the details of a specific user.

These views will have a one-to-one relationship with routes. The home view will sit at the application root, `/`; the user list will be at `/users`; and the user details view will be at `/users/:login`, where `:login` is the user login on GitHub (bevacqua in my case). Views are rendered by controllers.

Figure 7.5 shows what the user list will look like when you're done.

Figure 7.5　A list of users in your GitHub browser built using Rendr

Let's start with routing and then learn how controllers operate.

ROUTES AND CONTROLLERS

The following code matches routes to controller actions. The controller actions should be defined as the controller name, followed by a hash, and then the action name. This module goes into `app/routes.js`.

```
module.exports = function (match) {
  match('',                    'home#index');
  match('users'          ,    'users#index');
  match('users/:login',       'users#show');
};
```

Controllers fetch any data that's required to render a view. You have to define each action that's expected by the routes. Let's put the two controllers together. By convention, controllers should be placed in `app/controllers/{{name}}_controller.js`. The following code snippet, your Home controller, should be placed at `app/controllers/home_controller.js`. It should expose an `index` function, matching the `index` route. This function takes a parameters object and a callback that, once called, will render the view:

```
module.exports = {
  index: function (params, callback) {
    callback();
  }
};
```

The `user_controller.js` module is different. It has an `index` action as well, but it also has a `show` action. In both cases, you need to call `this.app.fetch` with parameters to get the model data and then invoke the callback once you're done, as shown in the following listing.

Listing 7.22   Retrieving model data

```
module.exports = {
  index: function (params, callback) {
    var spec = {
      collection: {
        collection: 'Users',
        params: params
      }
    };
    this.app.fetch(spec, function (err, result) {
      callback(err, result);
    });
  },
  show: function (params, callback) {
    var spec = {
      model: {
        model: 'User',
        params: params
      },
      repos: {
```

```
      collection: 'Repos',
      params: { user: params.login }
    }
  };
  this.app.fetch(spec, function (err, result) {
    callback(err, result);
  });
  }
};
```

Fetching this data wouldn't be possible if you didn't have matching models and collections. Let's flesh those out next.

MODELS AND COLLECTIONS

Models and collections need to extend the base objects provided by Rendr, so let's create those. The following code is for your base model, placed at `app/models/base.js`:

```
var RendrBase = require('rendr/shared/base/model');

module.exports = RendrBase.extend({});
```

The base collection is similarly thin. Having your own base objects, though, is necessary to easily share functionality across your models:

```
var RendrBase = require('rendr/shared/base/collection');

module.exports = RendrBase.extend({});
```

We'll have to define your models using the endpoint you want to use to fetch the models, in this case from the GitHub API. Your models should also export a unique identifier that's the same as what you used when calling `app.fetch` in your User controller. The following code shows what the User model looks like. This should be placed at app/models/user.js:

```
var Base = require('./base');

module.exports = Base.extend({
  url: '/users/:login',
  idAttribute: 'login'
});
module.exports.id = 'User';
```

As long as your models don't have any validation or computed data functions, they'll look similar: a `url` endpoint, the unique identifier, and the name of the parameter that's used to look up a single model instance. When you look at REST API design in chapter 9, constructing a URL in this way will feel more natural to you. Here's what the Repo model looks like:

```
var Base = require('./base');

module.exports = Base.extend({
  url: '/repos/:owner/:name',
  idAttribute: 'name'
});
module.exports.id = 'Repo';
```

As in your case study in section 7.4, collections need to reference a model to learn what kind of data they're dealing with. Collections are similar to models and use a unique identifier to teach Rendr what kind of collection they are and a URL from which you can fetch data. The following code shows the Users collection in code. It should be placed in `app/collections/users.js`:

```
var User = require('../models/user');
var Base = require('./base');

module.exports = Base.extend({
  model: User,
  url: '/users'
});
module.exports.id = 'Users';
```

The Repos collection is almost identical, except it uses the Repo model, and it has a different URL for fetching the data from the REST API. The code is as follows, and it should go in `app/collections/repos.js`:

```
var Repo = require('../models/repo');
var Base = require('./base');

module.exports = Base.extend({
  model: Repo,
  url: '/users/:user/repos'
});
module.exports.id = 'Repos';
```

At this point, the user requested a URL, and the router decided which controller action that should direct them to. The action method probably fetched data from the API and then it invoked its callback. At last, let's learn how views behave to render the HTML.

VIEWS AND TEMPLATES

As with most things Rendr, the first step in defining your views is creating your own base view, which is an extension of Rendr's base view. The base view should go in `app/views/base.js` and look like the following code:

```
var RendrBase = require('rendr/shared/base/view');

module.exports = RendrBase.extend({});
```

Your first view is the Home view. It should be placed at `app/views/home/index.js` and look like the following. As you can see, views also need to export an identifier:

```
var BaseView = require('../base');

module.exports = BaseView.extend({
});
module.exports.id = 'home/index';
```

Given that your views consist mostly of links to each other, but not much functionality, they're mostly empty. The Users view is almost identical to the Home view. It goes in `app/views/users/index.js`, and its code follows:

```
var BaseView = require('../base');

module.exports = BaseView.extend({
});
module.exports.id = 'users/index';
```

The User Details view goes in `app/views/users/show.js`. This view has to tamper with the template data, which is what I've referred to as the view model, to make the `repos` object available to the template, as shown in the following listing.

Listing 7.23 Making the `repos` object available to the template

```
var BaseView = require('../base');

module.exports = BaseView.extend({
  getTemplateData: function () {
    var data = BaseView.prototype.getTemplateData.call(this);
    data.repos = this.options.repos;
    return data;
  }
});
module.exports.id = 'users/show';
```

The last view you'll put together is a partial to render a list of repositories. It should be placed in `app/views/user_repos_view.js`, and as you can see, partials barely differ from other views, and they need a view controller like any other view:

```
var BaseView = require('./base');

module.exports = BaseView.extend({
});
module.exports.id = 'user_repos_view';
```

Last, there are the view templates. The first view template you'll look at is the `layout` `.hbs` file. This is the HTML that will serve as a container for all your templates. You can find the code in the following listing. Note that you're bootstrapping the application data and initializing it using JavaScript. This is required by Rendr. The `{{{body}}}` expression will be replaced by the views dynamically as the route changes.

Listing 7.24 Bootstrapping the application data

```
<!doctype html>
<html>

  <head>
    <title>Entourage</title>
  </head>

  <body>
    <div>
      <a href='/'>GitHub Browser</a>
    </div>
    <ul>
```

```
      <li><a href='/'>Home</a></li>
      <li><a href='/users'>Users</a></li>
    </ul>

    <section id='content' class='container'>
      {{{body}}}
    </section>

    <script src='/bundle.js'></script>
    <script>
    (function() {
      var App = window.App = new (require('app/app'))({{{json appData}}});
      App.bootstrapData({{{json bootstrappedData}}});
      App.start();
    })();
    </script>
  </body>
</html>
```

Next you have the Home view template. Here are a few links with no view model data access going on. This template goes in `app/templates/home/index.hbs`. Note that Backbone will capture navigation to any links in your application that match one of its routes and behave as a single-page application. Rather than reloading the entire page whenever a link is clicked, Backbone will load the corresponding view.

```
<h1>Entourage</h1>
<p>
  Demo on how to use Rendr by consuming GitHub's public API.
</p>
<p>
  Check out <a href='/repos'>Repos</a> or <a href='/users'>Users</a>.
</p>
```

Now things get more interesting. Here you're looping through the list of models that were fetched in the controller action, and rendering a list of users and links to their account details. This template goes in `app/templates/users/index.hbs`:

```
<h1>Users</h1>

<ul>
{{#each models}}
  <li>
    <a href='/users/{{login}}'>{{login}}</a>
  </li>
{{/each}}
</ul>
```

Next up you have the User Details template, which goes in `app/templates/users/show.hbs`. You can find the template code in the following listing. Take into account how you're telling Handlebars to load the `user_repos_view` partial and how that name matches exactly the identifier that was defined in its view.

Listing 7.25 Setting up the User Details template

```
<img src='{{avatar_url}}' width='80' height='80' /> {{login}}
    ({{public_repos}} public repos)

<br />

<div>
  <div>
    {{view 'user_repos_view' collection=repos}}
  </div>

  <div>
    <h3>Info</h3>
    <br />
    <table>
      <tr>
        <th>Location</th>
        <td>{{location}}</td>
      </tr>
      <tr>
        <th>Blog</th>
        <td>{{blog}}</td>
      </tr>
    </table>
  </div>
</div>
```

The User Repos view is your last view template, a partial in this case. It has to be located at `app/templates/user_repos_view.hbs`, and it's used to iterate through a collection of repositories, displaying interesting metrics about each repository, as shown in the following listing.

Listing 7.26 Setting up the User Repos template

```
<h3>Repos</h3>
<table>
  <thead>
    <tr>
      <th>Name</th>
      <th>Watchers</th>
      <th>Forks</th>
    </tr>
  </thead>
  <tbody>
  {{#each models}}
    <tr>
      <td>{{name}}</td>
      <td>{{watchers_count}}</td>
      <td>{{forks_count}}</td>
    </tr>
  {{/each}}
  </tbody>
</table>
```

That's it! Phew. As you can see, once you get past the vast amount of boilerplate code around your application, creating a Rendr app isn't that hard. I'm sure over time they'll reduce the amount of boilerplate around the meat of your Rendr applications. The nice aspect of creating an application using Rendr, Backbone, and CommonJS is how modular your code can become. Modularity is one of the characteristic properties of testable code.

7.6   *Summary*

Wow, we certainly accomplished big results in this chapter:

- You learned why jQuery isn't enough, and how a more structured approach would help you with the application development process.
- You got an overview of how Model-View-Controller patterns are supposed to work.
- You went on a Backbone adventure after learning about the basic concepts in Backbone.
- You exploited CommonJS and Browserify to get modular Backbone components interoperating in the browser.
- You took advantage of Rendr to bring a Backbone application to the server side, improving perceived performance.

Let's use this momentum to learn more about testability and how to write good tests. All kinds of testing await; turn the page already!

Testing JavaScript
components

By writing tests, you'll improve the reliability of the modules and applications you build and insure they work the way you intend. In typical Build First fashion, you'll get the necessary insight to automate those tests and run them on the cloud. This chapter includes a few guidelines that will help you write tests, and you will also get hands-on experience in testing components. In some cases I'll walk you through the tests that you may write for a given piece of code, helping you visualize the thought process behind writing thoughtful unit tests.

While I'm not an advocate for the Test-Driven Development (TDD) paradigm, which encourages you to write tests before you develop any functionality, I think tests are important, and you should write them. In this chapter we'll go back and forth between process design and application design. You'll look at how to write tests, and then I'll give you the tools to automate testing.

What do you mean you're not an advocate for TDD?

That's right. I wouldn't recommend you use TDD, so let me elaborate on that. I don't have anything against TDD itself, but writing tests is already a large commitment. If you're getting started and throw TDD into your learning process, it probably won't work out well for you. It definitely didn't work for me when I was first getting into testing! TDD can be overwhelming, and maybe you don't write any tests because you don't know where to start. Or maybe you write pointless ones, testing against the implementation itself rather than testing the underlying interfaces and their expected behavior. Before attempting to learn TDD, I suggest that you try writing a few tests for existing code. That way when (and if) you decide to go down the TDD route you'll know how your tests should be structured, what parts are important to test, and what parts are not. More importantly, you'll know whether writing a particular test case is necessary or even helpful. That being said, if you already have experience writing unit tests, and Test-Driven Development suits you, then I have nothing against that!

You learned about modularity, mostly in chapter 5; improving your asynchronous flows, as discussed in chapter 6; and structuring your code in a more organized manner, thanks to the MVC pattern in chapter 7. All that modularity helps drive down the complexity in your application designs by creating smaller components that are easier to work on and understand. A benefit of the work you've accomplished so far in part 2 is that testing becomes much simpler.

8.1 JavaScript testing crash course

The essence of testing lies in learning how to isolate functionality so that it can be easily tested. This is the reason modularity is so important for attaining more testable code, which in turn improves quality, the cornerstone of Build First. Modular, loosely coupled code is easier to test because you have fewer things to account for, and your tests can be contained in small units that are only concerned with one small piece of code getting something right. In contrast, monolithic, tightly coupled code is harder to test because more things can go wrong, many of which might be completely unrelated to the piece of functionality you were attempting to test.

8.1.1 Logical units in isolation

Consider the following contrived example for reference. You have a method that queries an API endpoint (you'll learn about API design in chapter 9, so hang tight), and then crunches numbers before returning a value. Suppose you want to make sure the data, whatever it was, was correctly multiplied by 555:

```
function getWorkDone () {
  return get('/api/data').then(function (res) {
```

```
    return res.data * 555;
  });
}
```

In this case, you don't care about the bits of this method that don't have to do with the computational part, and they get in the way of your testing. Testing becomes harder, as you now need to deal with the Promise stuff to verify that the data gets computed correctly. You might want to consider refactoring this into two smaller methods, one that does computation only, and one that deals with querying the API:

```
function getWorkDone () {
  return get('/api/data').then(function (res) {
    return compute(res.data);
  });
}
function compute (data) {
  return data * 555;
}
```

This kind of separation of concerns enables reusability, because you could run the computation in other places in your code that might need it. More importantly, it's much easier to test the computation in isolation now. The following piece of code is good enough at making sure the `compute` method works as intended:

```
if (compute(3) !== 1665) {
  throw new Error('assertion failed!');
}
```

Things become much easier when you use a library equipped to help with testing requirements, and I'll teach you how to use the Tape library, which adheres to a unit testing protocol called Test Anything Protocol[1] (TAP). Other popular JavaScript testing libraries include Jasmine and Mocha, but we'll stay away from those. They involve more complicated setups, often requiring a test harness and filling the global namespace with global variables. We'll be using Tape, which doesn't rely on globals or a test harness, and makes it easy to test code regardless of whether it's written for Node.js or the browser.

8.1.2 *Using the Test Anything Protocol (TAP)*

TAP is a test protocol implemented in a variety of languages, including Node.js. There are a few ways in which you can execute `tap` tests:

- Using `node` to run the tests directly in your terminal
- In a browser, compiling the tests to client-side JavaScript using Browserify
- Remotely, using automation services such as Travis-CI, the way you did in chapter 4

---

[1] Visit http://testanything.org to learn more about the Test Anything Protocol.

To get things started, you'll look at how to use Tape in your local environment by plainly firing up a browser. In section 8.4 you'll learn how to automate this process using Grunt to avoid firing up the browser on your own, and I'll explain how to include it in your CI workflows.

Getting started with JavaScript unit tests that need a browser can be confusing at first. You'll set up a pointless unit test in Node first, and then you'll run that in the browser before getting to unit testing principles and advice, which you'll find in section 8.2.

8.1.3   Putting together our first unit test

To create your first unit test and run it in the browser, start with the `compute` function from the previous examples in this chapter, placed in a CommonJS module. This example is available as ch08/01_your-first-tape-test in the samples. You can save this file in `src/compute.js`:

```
module.exports = function (data) {
  return data * 555;
};
```

In the following code you'll find the unit test written using `tape`, which provides an interface to perform basic assertions. Once you create a test, you can give it a name and a function will provide an interface to write your test. You'll learn more about assertions in section 8.2. Each test case in Tape can be defined using a description and a test method. You'll place this file in `test/compute.js`:

```
var test = require('tape');
var compute = require('../src/compute.js');

test('compute() should multiply by 555', function (t) {
  t.equal(1665, compute(3));
  t.end();
});
```

Note that you have to `require` the `compute` function to test it. Tape won't load your source code for you. Similarly, the `tape` module should also be `required`. The API is fairly simple and requires you to call `t.end()` to denote when a test has finished. Tape is mostly concerned with assertions about your assumptions and tracking test results. To run any tests written using `tape`, you merely need to run the code using Node:

```
node test/compute.js
```

Let's see what it takes to run these tests in the browser as well.

8.1.4   Tape in the browser

Running Tape tests in the browser is mostly a matter of Browserifying your tests. You could do this once by using the global Browserify package, or you could automate it using Grunt. Let's automate it. You'll need to use `grunt-browserify` to do that:

```
npm install --save-dev grunt grunt-browserify
```

Once you've installed `grunt-browserify`, you need to set up a Gruntfile the way you did throughout part 1, and configure the browserify task to compile your CommonJS code down to something browsers can interpret seamlessly. In the case of the unit test you've seen, your configuration could look like the following listing (you can find this example under ch08/02_tape-in-the-browser).

Listing 8.1 Compiling code for a browser to interpret

```
module.exports = function (grunt) {
  grunt.initConfig({
    browserify: {
      tests: {
        files: {
          'test/build/test-bundle.js': ['test/**/*.js']
        }
      }
    }
  });
  grunt.loadNpmTasks('grunt-browserify');
};
```

Using the `browserify:tests` target, you can compile the code so it can be referenced in an HTML file. As a last step you need to put together the HTML file. Luckily, you won't need to touch it once it's put together, because the JavaScript will be taken care of by the Browserify bundler, and you won't need to change the script tags by hand or anything else in your HTML, as shown in the following listing.

Listing 8.2 Compiling code to be referenced by the HTML file

```
<!doctype html>
<html>
<head>
  <meta charset='utf-8'>
  <title>Unit Testing JavaScript with Tape</title>
</head>
<body>
  <script src='build/test-bundle.js'></script>
</body>
</html>
```

Running the tests will only be a matter of opening this HTML file with a browser. You'll come back to Grunt later in the chapter to look at automating your testing process. Let's talk about testing principles and how to apply them in JavaScript tests.

8.1.5 *Arrange, Act, Assert*

Writing unit tests is often made out to be a difficult and tedious process, but it doesn't have to be. If your code is written with modularity and testability in mind, it'll be much easier to test. Monolithic, tightly coupled code does turn testing into a complicated process. That's because tests are most effective when they can verify small components in isolation, so you shouldn't have to worry about dependencies. This type of

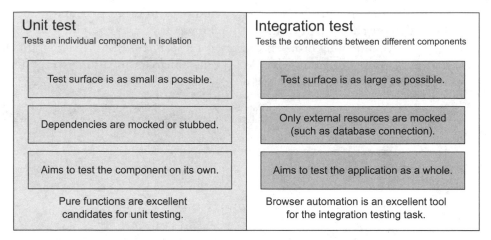

Figure 8.1   **Differences between unit and integration testing strategies. Note that a combination of the two should be used. Unit tests and integration tests are not exclusive. Pure functions are discussed in section 8.1.15.**

testing is referred to as *unit testing*. The second most common type of testing is *integration testing*, which involves testing that the interaction between components works as expected, focusing on how the network of components operates. Figure 8.1 compares both types of testing.

8.1.6   *Unit testing*

In contrast with integration tests, which focus on interaction, good unit tests actively disregard interaction, only focusing on how a single component works in isolation. Furthermore, good unit tests don't care about a component's implementation details; they only focus on the component's public API. That means good unit tests can be read as examples of how a component is expected to work. Even though not ideal, sometimes unit tests are the next best thing when a package's documentation is lacking.

Good unit tests often follow the "Arrange Act Assert" (AAA) pattern, creating fake versions of dependencies in unit tests and spying on methods to make sure they are invoked. The following subsections explore those concepts. Before you get to section 8.3, you'll go through real unit testing case scenarios.

The AAA pattern can help you to develop concise and organized unit tests. It consists of building your unit tests in three stages:

- Arrange: You create instances of everything needed by your test.
- Act: You execute your tests and track their results.
- Assert: You verify whether the results match the expected output.

Following these simple steps, it's easy to find your place when skimming through a unit test. Assertions are used to verify, for instance, the result of `typeof {}` matches `object`. Note that when these steps can be simplified into a single, readable line, you probably should do so.

8.1.7 *Convenience over convention*

Some purists will tell you to do only a single assertion per unit test. I suggest you stay pragmatic and allow yourself to write a few assertions in the same test, as long as they test the same specific piece of functionality. It won't hurt if you do, because the test harness (Tape, in your case) will tell you exactly which assertion failed in which test. Using a single assertion per test often leads to massive code duplication and frustrating testing sessions.

8.1.8 *Case study: unit testing an event emitter*

Let's write tests against the emitter method, which augments objects allowing them to emit and listen to events that we saw back in chapter 6. That should give you a good idea what a real unit test might look like. The following listing (available as ch08/03_arrange-act-assert in the samples) shows the full method in all its glory. This is the same event emitter method you implemented in section 6.4.2.

Listing 8.3   Your event `emitter` implementation

```
function emitter (thing) {
  var events = {};

  if (!thing) {
    thing = {};
  }

  thing.on = function (type, listener) {
    if (!events[type]) {
      events[type] = [listener];
    } else {
      events[type].push(listener);
    }
  };

  thing.emit = function (type) {
    var evt = events[type];
    if (!evt) {
      return;
    }
    var args = Array.prototype.slice.call(arguments, 1);
    for (var i = 0; i < evt.length; i++) {
      evt[i].apply(thing, args);
    }
  };

  return thing;
}
```

How do you test all of that? It's pretty big! Repeat after me: test against the interface. The rest doesn't matter that much. You want to make sure that, given the correct parameters, each of the public API methods does what you expect it to do. In the case of the emitter function, the API consists of the emitter function itself, the on method, and the emit method. The API is anything that can be accessed by the consumer, which is what you want to verify.

You can think of writing good unit tests as asserting the right things. The assertions your tests will verify should be deterministic, and they should also disregard implementation details, such as how the event listeners are stored. Private methods are typically implementation details, and you shouldn't worry about testing them; only the public interface matters. If you want to test private methods, you'll have to expose them so that they can be unit tested like any other public interface method.

8.1.9   *Testing the event emitter*

To get things going, let's start with a test asserting whether calling emitter with different arguments results in an emitter object. This is a basic test in which you'll verify that an object is returned with the expected properties (on and emit) on it.

Listing 8.4   Your first test using TAPE

```
var test = require('tape');
var emitter = require('../src/emitter.js');

test('emitter(thing) should always return an emitter', function (t) {    ←  Always define test cases
  // Act                                                                      using meaningful names.
  isEmitter(emitter());
  isEmitter(emitter({}));
  isEmitter(emitter([]));

  function isEmitter (thing) {          The second argument describes
    // Assert                           the assertion that's being made.
    t.ok(thing, 'should be truthy');    ←
    t.ok(thing.on, 'should have on property');    ←  Does it have a .on property?
    t.ok(thing.emit, 'should have emit property');
  }

  t.end();      ←  Let Tape know the test has ended.
});
```

It's always good to have unit tests that assert the basics of how something is expected to operate. Keep in mind that you only need to write these tests once, and they'll help you assert these validations anytime. Let's write a few more basic assertions in the following listing, making sure the returned object is indeed the same object you provided.

Listing 8.5   Writing basic assertions

```
test('emitter(thing) should reference the same object', function (t) {
  var data = { a: 1 };          // Arrange
  var thing = emitter(data);    // Act
  t.equal(data, thing);         // Assert
  t.end();
});
```

```
test('emitter(thing) should reference the same array', function (t) {
  var data = [1, 2];            // Arrange
  var thing = emitter(data);    // Act
  t.equal(data, thing);         // Assert
  t.end();
});
```

In the "basic JavaScript unit test" department, you'll sometimes find tests asserting whether something that's supposed to be a function is indeed a function. Although it's true that any other test would fail if `emitter` wasn't a function, redundancy is a good thing to have when it comes to unit testing. In addition, your tests should fail at assertions rather than while arranging or acting. If your tests fail somewhere else, it might indicate it's time to add more tests to assert that doesn't happen, or maybe the problem lies with your code.

Testing for object types might seem trivial, but it can pay off. Even more important is testing return value types. The first test you wrote made sure the properties were there, but it didn't check if they were functions. Let's rework it, adding type checks. These will seem like trivial changes, but you want to be explicit about the purposes of an assertion, for clarity.

Listing 8.6 Type checking in your tests

```
test('emitter(thing) should be a function', function (t) {
  t.ok(emitter, 'should be truthy');
  t.ok(typeof emitter === 'function', 'should be a method');
  t.end();
});
```
Test for function type rather than truthy values.

```
test('emitter(thing) should always return an object', function (t) {
  // Act
  isEmitter(emitter());
  isEmitter(emitter({}));
  isEmitter(emitter([]));

  function isEmitter (thing) {
    // Assert
    t.ok(thing, 'should be truthy');
    t.ok(typeof thing.on === 'function', 'should have on method');
    t.ok(typeof thing.emit === 'function', 'should have emit method');
  }

  t.end();
});
```

8.1.10 *Testing for the .on method*

Next we'll write tests for the `.on` method. This time around, we'll be content if calling `.on` does not throw. In a bit, we'll make sure that the listeners work when we test the `emit` method. Note how I wrote two different tests which are almost identical, even though they have different purposes. In testing, it's fairly common to find duplicate code, and it's fine to copy and paste, although it's not encouraged to abuse it.

Listing 8.7   Testing the `.on` function

```
test('on(type, listener) should attach an event listener', function (t) {
  // Arrange
  var thing = emitter();

  function listener () {}

  // Assert
  t.doesNotThrow(function () {                    In this case, make sure
    // Act                                        thing.on doesn't throw.
    thing.on('foo', listener);
  });
  t.end();
});

test('on(type, listener) should attach many event listeners to the same
    event', function (t) {
  // Arrange
  var thing = emitter();

  function listener () {}

  // Assert
  t.doesNotThrow(function () {                    Multiple calls to .on
    // Act                                        shouldn't throw either.
    thing.on('foo', listener);
    thing.on('foo', listener);
    thing.on('foo', listener);
  });
  t.end();
});
```

Last, you need to test the `emit` function. To do that, you'll attach a few listeners, as before, and then you'll emit the event. Then you'll assert that the listeners fired correctly, once for each call to `.on`. Notice how if you changed `emit` to be asynchronous by wrapping the event handlers in a `setTimeout` call, this test would fail. In those cases, you can either adapt the test to the new functionality or avoid changing the functionality in the first place.

Listing 8.8   Testing the `.emit` function

```
test('emit(type) should emit to the event listeners', function (t) {
  // Arrange
  var thing = emitter();              Note that steps are cleanly
  var listens = 0;                    separated into Arrange, Act, Assert.
                                      Do that in your testing.
  function listener () {
    listens++;
  }

  // Act
  thing.on('foo', listener);
```

```
thing.on('foo', listener);
thing.emit('foo');

// Assert                                Sometimes counting how many times
t.equal(listens, 2);        ◁           a function was invoked is sufficient.
t.end();
});
```

Finally, let's add one more method to make sure that emit passes any arguments to the event listener the way we expect.

Listing 8.9   Further testing on .emit

```
test('emit(type) should pass params to event listeners', function (t) {
  // Arrange
  var thing = emitter();
  var listens = 0;

  function listener (context, value) {
    t.equal(arguments.length, 2);      ◁     Making sure you get exactly what
    t.equal(context, thing);                 you expect, but nothing more
    t.equal(value, 3);
    listens++;
  }

  // Act
  thing.on('foo', listener);
  thing.on('foo', listener);
  thing.emit('foo', thing, 3);

  // Assert
  t.equal(listens, 2);
  t.end();
});
```

That's it! Your event emitter implementation is fully tested. You only wrote assertions that verify how the public API works, and you didn't meddle with implementation details. At this point, you could add tests that deal with unconventional usage of the API, such as calling emit() without any arguments. Then you could decide whether you'd want emit to throw an exception in that particular case. Think of your tests as a formal and stricter API documentation.

In the following section you'll learn about creating mocks, spying on function calls, and proxying require statements.

8.1.11 *Mocks, spies, and proxies*

Sometimes you want greater isolation, even though two parts of an application can't be decoupled any further. The application might need to query a real database, fetch data using a service, or connect together different modules, or there may be some other reason why you can't decouple the implementation. You can use a variety of different tools, such as mocks, spies, and proxies, to circumvent the testing issues

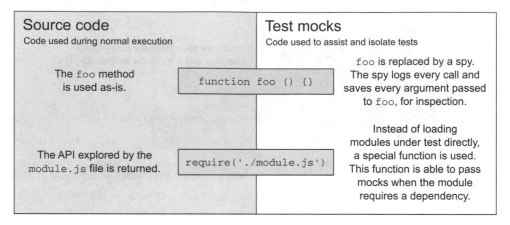

Figure 8.2 Using source code as-is versus using mocks when testing

introduced by tight coupling. Figure 8.2 depicts the issue and the solution provided by these stubs.

Next up you'll learn about mocking dependencies, which can come in handy if you're working with a component that has external dependencies.

8.1.12 *Mocking*

Mocking creates fake instances of the dependencies (such as services or other objects) in your System Under Test (SUT). In statically typed languages, mocking often involves access to the compiler, often referred to as Reflection. One of the advantages of Java-Script being a dynamically-typed language is that you can create an object with a couple of properties and that's it. Suppose you have to test the following snippet of code:

```
function (http, done) {
  http.get('/api/data', done);
}
```

In a real application, maybe that snippet accessed the network and queried an end-point, getting back data from the application's API. You should never need to connect to external services to run a unit test, making this an ideal scenario for mocking. In this case in particular, you're making a GET request and calling back a done function with an optional error and data in return.

Mocking the http object using plain JavaScript, as it turns out, is easy. Note how you're using setTimeout to keep the method asynchronous, the way the original code expected, and how you can conjure up any response you like to fit your test:

```
{
  get: function (endpoint, done) {
    setTimeout(function () {
      done(null, { data: 'dummy' });
    }, 0);
  }
}
```

The server-side aspect of this test, querying the real HTTP endpoint, should be handled in server tests, which isn't a client-side concern anymore. Another option might be testing these things in integration tests, which is a topic you'll navigate later in the chapter. I'll introduce Sinon.js next. Sinon is a library for creating mocks, spies, and stubs. It also allows you to fake XHR requests, server responses, and timers. Let's look at it.

8.1.13 Introducing Sinon.js

Sometimes it's not enough to mock values by hand, and in those more advanced case scenarios, using a library such as Sinon.js might come in handy. Sinon helps you easily test `setTimeout` delays, dates, XHR requests, and even set up fake HTTP servers to use in your tests. Using Sinon, it's trivial to create functions called spies. *Spies* are functions that are prepared to tell you whether they've been called, how many times, and what arguments they were invoked with. As it turns out, you've already used a custom flavor of spies in listing 8.9, where we had a `listener` function that kept track of how many times it was called. Let's see how using spies helps assert function calls.

8.1.14 Spying on function calls

Spies can be used whenever a function you're testing requires function parameters, and you can use them to easily assert whether they've been used and how.

Let's go through a simple example (found as ch08/04_spying-on-function-calls). Here's a pair of functions that take a callback function parameter:

```
var maxwell = {
  immediate: function (cb) {
    cb('foo', 'bar');
  },
  debounce: function (cb) {
    setTimeout(cb, 0);
  }
};
```

Sinon makes it easy to test these. Without the need to construct a custom callback, you can ensure that `immediate` invoked your callback exactly once:

```
test('maxwell.immediate invokes a callback immediately', function (t) {
  var cb = sinon.spy();

  maxwell.immediate(cb);

  t.plan(2);
  t.ok(cb.calledOnce, 'called once');
  t.ok(cb.calledWith('foo', 'bar'), 'arguments match expectation');
});
```

Note how I switched from `t.end` to `t.plan`. Using `t.plan(n)` allows you to define how many assertions you expect to be made during the execution of your test case. The test will fail if it doesn't exactly match the number of asserts. This is most useful for asynchronous tests, where your code may or may not end up invoking a callback where you had a few more asserts. Using `t.plan` verifies that the correct amount of asserts were indeed executed.

Testing delayed execution is a bit trickier, but Sinon provides an easy-to-use interface for that, as shown in the following listing. By calling `sinon.useFakeTimers()`, any subsequent calls to `setTimeout` or `setInterval` are going to be faked. You also get a simple `tick` API to manually change the clock.

Listing 8.10   Testing delayed execution

```
test('maxwell.debounce invokes a callback after a timeout', function (t) {
  var clock = sinon.useFakeTimers();
  var cb = sinon.spy();

  maxwell.debounce(cb);

  t.plan(2);
  t.ok(cb.notCalled, 'not called before tick');
  clock.tick(0);
  t.ok(cb.called, 'called after tick');
});
```

Sinon.js has more tricks you can perform, such as creating fake XHR requests. The last topic I want to discuss regarding mocking is the case where you need to create a mock for the results provided by invoking `require` on any given module. Let's check out how that works!

8.1.15 *Proxying require calls*

The issue here is that sometimes modules require other modules, which in turn require additional modules, and you don't want all that in unit tests. Unit tests are about controlling the environment, detecting the absolutely necessary pieces that are needed to execute a test, and mocking everything else. There's a nice npm package called `proxyquire` that can help with that situation. Consider that you'd like to test the code in the following listing (available as ch08/05_proxying-your-dependencies in the samples), in which you'd like to fetch a user from the database and then return a subset of the model for security reasons.

Listing 8.11   Using the `require` method

```
var User = require('../models/User.js');

module.exports = function (id, done) {
  User.findOne({ id: id }, function (err, user) {
    if (err || !user) {
      done(err); return;
    }
    done(null, {
      name: user.name,
      email: user.email
    })
  });
};
```

Let's consider a small refactor for a moment. It's always best to isolate "pure" functionality. A *pure function* is a concept that comes from functional programming, and it describes a function whose outputs are defined solely by its inputs and nothing else. Pure functions return the same value every time they receive the same inputs. In the example above, your pure and reusable piece of functionality is mapping the user model to its "safe" subset, so let's extract that into its own function, and make your code a little prettier and easier to follow through.

Listing 8.12   Creating a pure function

```
var User = require('./models/User.js');

function subset (user) {
  return {
    name: user.name,
    email: user.email
  };
}

module.exports = function (id, done) {
  User.findOne({ id: id }, function (err, user) {
    done(err, user ? subset(user) : null);
  });
};
```

As you can see, though, unless you expose the `subset` function on its own, you're stuck with querying the database to get a user. You could argue that the module should get a `user` object, instead of merely an `id`, and you're right. Sometimes, however, you have to query the database. Maybe you have a `user` parameter and do something with it, but you also want to ask the database about his permissions or the groups he belongs to. In those cases, as well as in the previous case, assuming you don't refactor it any further, a good way to get around the situation is to return a fake result from `require` calls.

The good news is that using `proxyquire` means you don't have to change the application code at all. The following listing demonstrates how to use `proxyquire` to mock up a required module without resorting to a database at all. Note how the mock object you're passing to `proxyquire` is a map of `require` paths and the results you want to get (rather than what you'd normally get).

Listing 8.13   Mocking up a required module

```
var proxyquire = require('proxyquire');

var user = {
  id: 123,
  name: 'Marian',
  email: 'marian@company.com'
};
```

```
var mapperMock = {
  './models/User.js': {
    findOne: function (query, done) {
      setTimeout(done.bind(null, null, user));
    }
  }
};

var mapper = proxyquire('../src/mapper.js', mapperMock);
```

Once you isolate the mapping functionality without resorting to a database connection, the test becomes trivial. You're using the `mapper` function, complete with fake database access, and asserting whether it gives back an object with the `name` and `email` properties on it. Note that you're using Sinon's `cb.args` to figure out the arguments when the `cb` spy was first called.

Listing 8.14   Creating spies with Sinon

```
var test = require('tape');
var sinon = require('sinon');

test('user mapper returns a subset of user', function (t) {
  // Arrange
  var clock = sinon.useFakeTimers();
  var cb = sinon.spy();

  // Act
  mapper(123, cb);                    This call will fire any setTimeout functions
  clock.tick(0);                      that had a delay of 0 milliseconds.
  var result = cb.args[0][1];
  var actual = Object.keys(result).sort();
  var expected = ['name', 'email'].sort();

  // Assert
  t.plan(2);
  t.ok(cb.calledOnce);
  t.deepEqual(actual, expected);
});
```

In the following section I'll go a bit deeper into client-side testing, talking about fake XHR (XMLHttpRequest). You'll also get a feel for DOM interaction testing before you look at other forms of automation and a mention of non-unit testing flavors.

8.2   *Testing in the browser*

Testing client-side code is typically a hassle because of both AJAX requests and DOM interaction. That, often paired with a complete lack of modularity and code organization, spells chaos for the client-side JavaScript test developer. That being said, in chapter 5 you resolved your browser modularity concerns by settling for Browserify. Browserify allows you to use self-contained CommonJS modules even in client-side code but at the cost of an extra build step.

You also resolved code organization issues by resorting to an MVC framework on the client side, to keep your concerns properly separated. In chapter 9, you'll learn about REST API design, which you'll apply to future web applications you write, getting rid of the endpoint chaos that usually characterizes front-end application development.

In the next section, you'll learn how to write tests for your client-side code by mocking XHR requests and isolating DOM interaction so that you can write tests against it. Let's start with the easy part: mocking up XHR requests and server responses.

8.2.1 *Faking XHR and server communication*

Similarly to the way you created fake `require` results with `proxyquire`, you can use Sinon to mock any XHR requests you'd like, without modifying your source code. Use Sinon to simulate server responses and snoop request data. Those are the only reasons you'll need to deal with XHR. Figure 8.3 shows how these mocks can help you to isolate and test code that would normally depend on an external resource.

To see how that might look in code, here's a snippet of client-side JavaScript that makes an HTTP request and gives you the response text (see sample ch08/06_fake-xhr-requests). I'm using the `superagent` module to make the HTTP requests, because it works seamlessly in the server or the browser. Perfect for Browserifying action!

```
module.exports = function (done) {
  require('superagent')
    .get('https://api.github.com/zen')
    .end(cb);

  function cb (err, res) {
    done(null, res.text);
  }
};
```

In this case you don't want to write tests for `superagent` itself. You don't want to test the API call, either. You probably want to make sure that an AJAX call is made, though.

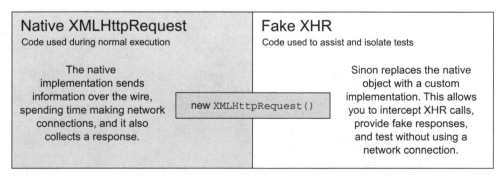

Figure 8.3   Native XMLHttpRequest compared with fake XHR mocks during tests

The method is supposed to call you back with the response text, so you should test for that as well, as shown in the following listing.

> **Listing 8.15   Creating a method that sends response text**

```
var test = require('tape');
var sinon = require('sinon');

test('qotd service should make an XHR call', function (t) {
  var quote = require('../src/qotdService.js');
  var cb = sinon.spy();

  quote(cb);

  t.plan(2);

  setTimeout(function () {
    t.ok(cb.called);
    t.ok(cb.calledWith(null, sinon.match.string));
  }, 2000);
});
```

That's fine for testing the outcome, but you can't afford to have tests depend on network conditions or to spend that long waiting to make assertions. The right way to test your method is to simulate the responses. Sinon allows you to do this by creating a fake server, which provides two-fold value. It captures real requests made by your code and transforms them into testable objects it controls. It also allows you to create responses for those requests within your tests, simulating an operational server. To get that functionality, create the fake server using `sinon.fakeServer.create()` before invoking the method under test. Then, once the method that's supposed to create an AJAX request is invoked, you can respond to the request, setting your response's status code, headers, and body. Let's update your test method to reflect those changes.

> **Listing 8.16   Testing the "Quote of the Day" service**

```
test('qotd service should make an XHR call', function (t) {
  var quote = require('../src/qotdService.js');
  var cb = sinon.spy();

  var server = sinon.fakeServer.create();
  var headers = { 'Content-Type': 'text/html' };

  quote(cb);

  t.plan(4);
  t.equals(server.requests.length, 1);
  t.ok(cb.notCalled);

  server.requests[0].respond(200, headers, 'The cake is a lie.');

  t.ok(cb.called);
  t.ok(cb.calledWith(null, 'The cake is a lie.'));
});
```

As you can see, you verified that a single request was made and that you got called back with exactly the same value as the response text.

The last piece of browser testing to dabble in before heading over to the automation department is DOM interaction testing. Much like testing AJAX calls, DOM testing is complicated because you're interacting with something that's across a gap. Mind the gap.

8.2.2 Case study: testing DOM interaction

Client-side development and testing are funny in that way. You have three layers: HTML, JavaScript, and CSS, all working together to serve a sophisticated concoction of bits. Yet, as any good developer will, you must keep the concerns separated across the three technologies, trying not to couple them too tightly together. CSS is easy to leave untied. You create classes in CSS and assign them to DOM elements by giving them their matching `class` attributes. Your CSS starts falling apart when it makes assumptions about the structure of your HTML. The best pieces of CSS are those that don't depend on the HTML being structured exactly in a particular way, those that aren't tightly coupled to the HTML.

JavaScript and HTML are similar to CSS and HTML in that your HTML shouldn't make any assumptions about your JavaScript. HTML should work fairly well even with JavaScript turned off; this is called progressive enhancement and it helps deliver primary content to your users faster, resulting in a better experience overall. The problem is that your JavaScript code must make assumptions about your HTML. Finding the inner text for a DOM node, attaching event listeners, reading data attributes, setting attributes, or any other form of DOM manipulation, leads with the assumption that a DOM node is there.

Let's get to your imaginary application where events come to party and decimal numbers get rounded.

SETTING UP THE HTML

In this application, you have an input where you're meant to enter decimal numbers and then click on a button to get the rounded version of that same number back. Each result is written into a list that's displayed on the page. There's also another button to clear the result list. Figure 8.4 depicts how the application should look.

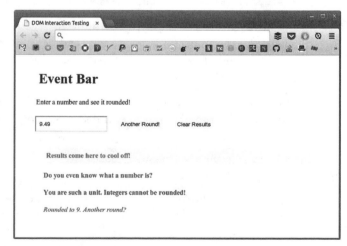

Figure 8.4   The application you'll be building in this case study

We'll start by going through the application, and explain the choices made along the way. Then, I'll show you what you should be testing in this small application, and how you can get test coverage on those factors without worrying about implementation details.

Consider the following piece of HTML. Note that you're not writing any JavaScript in the DOM directly. Keeping your concerns separated is extremely important to testability:

```
<h1>Event Bar</h1>
<p>Enter a number and see it rounded!</p>
<input class='square' placeholder='Decimals only please.' />
<button class='barman'>Another Round!</button>
<button class='clear'>Clear Results</button>
<div class='result'>
  <h4>Results come here to cool off!</h4>
</div>
```

Next you'll learn how to implement JavaScript functionality.

IMPLEMENTING THE JAVASCRIPT FUNCTIONALITY

Next we'll discuss a small JavaScript application that interacts with the HTML shown in the previous example, using the JavaScript DOM API. To begin, you'll use `query-Selector`, a (relatively) little-known but powerful native browser API that allows you to find DOM nodes in a similar fashion to how jQuery works, using CSS selectors. `query-Selector` is supported in all major browsers, going as far back as Internet Explorer 8. The API is present on the document root as well as on any DOM nodes, allowing you to limit the search to their children. If you want to look for many elements, instead of the first one, you can use `querySelectorAll` instead.

```
var barman = document.querySelector('.barman');
var square = document.querySelector('.square');
var result = document.querySelector('.result');
var clear = document.querySelector('.clear');
```

> **NOTE** I never use the `id` attribute in HTML. It causes all sorts of problems, such as CSS selector precedence, leading to developers using `!important` style rules and the inability to reuse the value, because HTML `id` attributes are meant to be unique.

Let's implement the code in charge of figuring out how your input did. If it's not a number, then that's a mistake. If it's an integer, that's a problem too. Otherwise, you'll return the rounded value:

```
function rounding (number, done) {
  if (isNaN(number)) {
    done(new Error('Do you even know what a number is?'));
  } else if (number === Math.round(number)) {
    done(new Error('You are such a unit. Integers cannot be rounded!'));
  } else {
    done(null, Math.round(number));
  }
}
```

The done callback should create a new paragraph in your result list and fill it with the error message, if any, or the rounded value, if present. You'll also set a different CSS class if you see an error than when you're successful, to help a designer style the page accordingly without you making additional changes to your JavaScript, as shown in the following listing.

Listing 8.17   Using the done callback

```
function report (err, value) {
  var p = document.createElement('p');

  if (err) {
    p.className = 'error';
    p.innerText = err.message;
  } else {
    p.className = 'rounded';
    p.innerText = 'Rounded to ' + value + '. Another round?';
  }
  result.appendChild(p);
}
```

The last piece to the puzzle is binding the click event and parsing the input before handing it off to the two methods you put together in listing 8.17. The following code snippet will do:

```
barman.addEventListener(click, round);

function round () {
  var number = parseFloat(square.value);
  rounding(number, report);
}
```

Wiring up the Reset button is even easier. Your listener should remove every paragraph created by the barman; that's as straightforward as it gets! The following listing shows how you might do it.

Listing 8.18   Wiring a Reset button

```
clear.addEventListener(click, reset);

function reset () {
  var all = result.querySelectorAll('.result p');
  var i = all.length;

  while (i--) {
    result.removeChild(all[i]);
  }
}
```

That's it; your application is fully operational. How can you make sure future refactorings don't break existing code? You need to identify tests that ensure your code works as intended and then write those tests.

IDENTIFYING THE TEST CASES

First off, let me go on a tangent to mention that you need to completely disregard the HTML at the beginning of this case study. You shouldn't write any HTML in your tests. If you need a DOM, you should build it using JavaScript inside your tests. As you'll see when you implement the tests, this can be even easier than writing HTML. Separating concerns is one of the most important aspects of unit testing.

Next, you should try and identify your application concerns and differentiate them from implementation details. For the sake of this experiment, consider everything you wrote previously to be implementation details, because your application doesn't provide an API or even build a public-facing object of any sort. When everything in the implementation is an implementation detail, you can still unit test, but you need to test against what the application is supposed to do, as opposed to what each method is supposed to do.

The test cases are supposed to assert that the statements you can find in the application definition presented previously, quoted here, hold true when checked against its implementation.

> **APPLICATION DEFINITION** In this application you have an input where you enter decimal numbers and then click on a button to get the rounded version of that same number back. Each result is written into a list that's displayed on the page. There's also another button to clear the result list.

Several test cases are noted in the following list. These were derived from the quoted definition and other logic constraints imposed in the implementation (which you'd like to turn into part of the definition). Keep in mind you could prepare any test cases you want, as long as they satisfy the definition. These are the ones I designed:

- Clicking barman without input should result in an error message.
- Clicking barman with an integer should result in an error message.
- Clicking barman with a number should result in a rounded number.
- Clicking barman twice, with two values should produce two results.
- Clicking clear when the list is empty does not throw.
- Clicking clear removes any results in the list.

Let's get to the testing. I mentioned earlier that you'd create the DOM in code in every test. You'll do that by creating a Setup task, called before every test, and a Teardown task, called after every test. Setup will create the elements. Teardown will remove them. This gives every test a clean slate even after another test has run.

SETUP AND TEARDOWN

Most JavaScript testing frameworks, for baffling reasons, include globals in your test program. For instance, if you want to run a task before each test when using the Mocha test framework (Buster.js and Jasmine also do this), you'd pass a callback function to the `beforeEach` global method. In fact, test cases should be described with other globals, such as `describe` and `it`, as shown in the following listing.

Listing 8.19   Using `describe` to describe test cases

```
function setup () {
  // prepare something
}

describe('foo()', function () {
  beforeEach(setup);

  it('should not throw', function () {
    assert.doesNotThrow(function () {
      foo();
    });
  });
});
```

This is terrible! Indiscriminate use of globals, even in tests, shouldn't be the norm. Luckily tape doesn't submit to this nonsense, and it's still easy to run something before each test. The following listing shows the same piece of code, using tape instead.

Listing 8.20   Using `tape` to describe test cases

```
var test = require('tape');

function testCase (name, cb) {
  var t = test(name, cb);
  t.once('prerun', setup);
}

function setup () {
  // prepare something
}

testCase('foo() should not throw', function (t) {
  assert.doesNotThrow(function () {
    foo();
  });
});
```

Granted, it looks more verbose, but it doesn't pollute the global namespace, breaking one of the oldest conventions. In tape, tests emit events, such as prerun, at different points in the test run. To set up and tear down our tests, you'll need to create and use a testCase method. The name is irrelevant, but I find testCase applies well in this situation:

```
function testCase (name, cb) {
  var t = test(name, cb);
  t.once('prerun', setup);
  t.once('end', teardown);
}
```

Now that you know how to run these methods for every test, it's time to code them!

PREPARING THE TEST HARNESS

In the setup method, you need to create each DOM element you'll need in the tests and set any default values made available through the HTML. Note that testing the HTML itself isn't part of these tests, which is why you completely disregard it. Your concern is that, assuming the HTML is what you expect, the application will run successfully. Testing the HTML is a concern of integration testing.

The setup method is found in the following listing. The bar module is your application's code, wrapped in a function so you can execute it whenever you want. In this case, you need to run the application before every test. That will attach event listeners to your freshly baked DOM elements.

> **Listing 8.21   Using the setup method**

```
var bar = require('../src/event-bar.js');

function setup () {
  function add (type, className) {
    var element = document.createElement(type);
    element.className = className;
    document.body.appendChild(element);
  }
  add('input', 'square');
  add('div', 'barman');
  add('div', 'result');
  add('div', 'clear');
  bar();
}
```

The teardown method is even easier, because you give it a few selectors and iterate through them, removing the elements created during setup:

```
function teardown () {
  var selectors = ['.barman', '.square', '.result', '.clear'];
  selectors.forEach(function (selector) {
    var element = document.querySelector(selector);
    element.parentNode.removeChild(element);
  });
}
```

Woo-hoo! Onto the tests.

CODING YOUR TEST CASES

As long as you keep your concerns cleanly separated between Arrange, Act, and Assert, you shouldn't have any issues writing or reading your tests. In the first one you get the barman element, click it, and get any results. You verify there's one result. Then you assert that the CSS class and text in that result are correct, as shown in the following listing.

> **Listing 8.22   Asserting the CSS class and text are correct**

```
testCase('barman without input should show an error', function (t) {
  // Arrange
  var barman = document.querySelector('.barman');
```

```
    var result;

    // Act
    barman.click();
    result = document.querySelectorAll('.result p');

    // Assert
    t.plan(4);
    t.ok(barman);
    t.equal(result.length, 1);
    t.equal(result[0].className, 'error');
    t.equal(result[0].innerText, 'Do you even know what a number is?');
});
```

The next test also does error checking. Making sure your error checking works as expected is as important as making sure the happy path does indeed work. In the following listing, you're also setting a value in the input, before the click.

Listing 8.23 Error checking your code

```
testCase('barman with an int should show an error', function (t) {
    // Arrange
    var barman = document.querySelector('.barman');
    var square = document.querySelector('.square');
    var result;

    // Act
    square.value = '2';
    barman.click();
    result = document.querySelectorAll('.result p');

    // Assert
    t.plan(4);
    t.ok(barman);
    t.equal(result.length, 1);
    t.equal(result[0].className, 'error');
    t.equal(result[0].innerText, 'Integers cannot be rounded!');  ⟵
});
```

The complete text for the assertion is "You are such a unit. Integers cannot be rounded!"

By now you should start to see the pattern. See how easy it is to identify what each test does when they follow the AAA convention? This next one, shown in the following listing, verifies that the happy path works as intended. It sets the input to a decimal value and clicks on the button, and then it checks that the result was a rounded number.

Listing 8.24 Verifying the path works

```
testCase('numbers should be rounded', function (t) {
    // Arrange
    var barman = document.querySelector('.barman');
    var square = document.querySelector('.square');
    var value = 2.4;
    var result;

    // Act
    square.value = value.toString();
```

```
barman.click();
result = document.querySelectorAll('.result p');

// Assert
t.plan(4);
t.ok(barman);
t.equal(result.length, 1);
t.equal(result[0].className, 'rounded');
t.equal(result[0].innerText, 'Rounded to ' + Math.round(value));    ←
});
```

The complete text for the assertion is "Rounded to %s. Another round?"

It's certainly good to write tests that interact with your code the way you expect humans to interact with it. Sometimes humans do the unexpected, and that should be tested for as well.

TESTING POSSIBLE OUTCOMES

We're wired in a certain way, where we believe in three possible outcomes: something either never works, works once, or it always works. I often joke that only three numbers exist: 0, 1, and infinite. As shown in the following listing, asserting that making two clicks works as intended should be enough. You can always go back and add more tests.

Listing 8.25 Making sure two clicks works

```
testCase('two inputs should produce two results', function (t)
  // Arrange
  var barman = document.querySelector('.barman');
  var square = document.querySelector('.square');
  var value = 2.4;
  var result;

  // Act
  square.value = value.toString();
  barman.click();
  square.value = '3';
  barman.click();
  result = document.querySelectorAll('.result p');

  // Assert
  t.plan(6);
  t.ok(barman);
  t.equal(result.length, 2);
  t.equal(result[0].className, 'rounded');
  t.equal(result[0].innerText, 'Rounded to ' + Math.round(value));
  t.equal(result[1].className, 'error');
  t.equal(result[1].innerText, 'Integers cannot be rounded!');    ←
});
```

The complete text for the assertion is "You are such a unit. Integers cannot be rounded!"

When developing code, you might find that your code is throwing errors, wearing down your productivity. Simple tests such as the one in the following listing that asserts a method call does not throw are helpful in these types of cases. The next section talks about automated testing, which definitely helps as well.

Listing 8.26 Asserting a method call does not throw errors

```
testCase('clearing empty list does not throw', function (t) {
  // Arrange
  var clear = document.querySelector('.clear');

  // Assert
  t.plan(2);
  t.ok(clear);
  t.doesNotThrow(function () {
    clear.click();
  });
});
```

The last test in your embarrassingly small suite is close to an integration test. It clicks repeatedly, and then it asserts that clicking the Clear button does indeed remove the accumulated results.

Listing 8.27 Verifying the Clear button works

```
testCase('clicking clear removes any results in the list', function (t) {
  // Arrange
  var barman = document.querySelector('.barman');
  var square = document.querySelector('.square');
  var clear = document.querySelector('.clear');
  var result;
  var resultCleared;

  // Act
  square.value = '3.4';
  barman.click();
  square.value = '3';
  barman.click();
  square.value = '';
  barman.click();
  result = document.querySelectorAll('.result p');
  clear.click();
  resultCleared = document.querySelectorAll('.result p');

  // Assert
  t.plan(2);
  t.equal(result.length, 3);
  t.equal(resultCleared.length, 0);
});
```

The most value in your tests always comes when it's time to refactor. Suppose you changed the implementation of your Event Bar program. You run the tests again. If they succeed, all is good, unless you find a bug testing by hand, in which case you add more tests and fix the issue. If they fail, two possibilities exist. The tests now may be outdated. For example, the Clear button may have been changed to "remove only the oldest result" when clicked. In that case you should update the tests to reflect those changes. The other reason why the tests may fail is because of an oversight in your changes, which would break functionality. The fact that these tests are forever repeatable, at no extra cost, is what makes them so valuable.

You can check out the fully working example, with all the code I've shown you, in the accompanying code samples, as ch08/07_dom-interaction-testing. Next up we'll go back to the case study we developed during chapter 7 and add unit tests to it.

8.3   *Case study: unit testing the MVC shopping list*

In chapter 7 we reached quite a few milestones in developing an MVC shopping list application, and in this section we'll unit test one of the iterations of that application. Concretely, you'll pair with me in unit testing the application at the end of section 7.4, right before we added Rendr to the solution in section 7.5. You can check out the source code for that application at ch07/10_the-road-show in the samples. Its unit-tested counterpart can be found under ch08/07b_testability-boulevard.

The Road Show was a small-sized application, yet large enough to show how you could slowly add tests to an application and end up having a well-tested application. Taking this gradual approach to testing would have been much harder if we hadn't put effort into modularizing our application, but we learned to do that in chapter 5 and applied those concepts when putting together the application in chapter 7. This section guides us through writing tests for the view router, and model validation. You are then free to explore adding test coverage for the view controllers.

8.3.1   *Testing the view router*

The first step you always need to take before any testing can begin is configuring the environment so tests can run. In this case that means you'll copy the application (from ch07/10_the-road-show) to be used as a starting point, and then add the test harness built in this chapter for running Tape in the browser (the ch08/02_tape-in-the-browser sample) on top of that.

Once the initial setup is put together (ch08/07b_testability-boulevard in the samples), you can start fleshing out your tests using Tape. We'll start with the router (which was shown in listing 7.18 in chapter 7) because that's the simplest module we want to test. For reference, the following listing is how the module looks at the moment.

Listing 8.28   Testing the module

```
var Backbone = require('backbone');
var ListView = require('../views/list.js');
var AddItemView = require('../views/addItem.js');

module.exports = Backbone.Router.extend({
  routes: {
    '': 'root',
    'items': 'listItems',
    'items/add': 'addItem'
  },
```

```
  root: function () {
    this.navigate('items', { trigger: true });
  },
  listItems: function () {
    new ListView();
  },
  addItem: function () {
    new AddItemView();
  }
});
```

We want to assert a few things in testing this module. You want to know that

- There are three routes.
- Their associated route handlers do in fact exist.
- The `root` route handler properly redirects to the `listItems` action.
- View routes would render the correct view in each case.

You may already be drooling over the possibilities, considering creating mocks for the views, or maybe using `proxyquire` to stub those modules altogether. To get started, we'll assert that three routes are in fact registered, and that their route handlers exist on the router.

To achieve this, the following listing uses `proxyquireify` (a flavor of `proxyquire` that works on the client side) combined with `sinon` and `tape` to put together the `routes.js` test module.

Listing 8.29 The first View Router tests

```
var proxyquire = require('proxyquireify')(require);    Setup is involved in making
var sinon = require('sinon');                          proxyquire work in the browser.
var ListView;
var AddItemView;
                                      This method uses a combination of sinon and proxyquire to
                                      stub out the view modules, because we're only interested
function getStubbedRouter () {        in testing the view router, and not the views themselves.
  ListView = sinon.spy();
  AddItemView = sinon.spy();
  var ViewRouter = proxyquire('../app/routers/viewRouter.js', {
    '../views/list.js': ListView,
    '../views/addItem.js': AddItemView
  });                                               We use the relative
  return ViewRouter;                                path from the
}                                                   router to each view.

test('there are three routes and route handlers', function (t) {
  // Arrange
  var ViewRouter = getStubbedRouter();       Get a stubbed instance
                                             of the view router.
  // Act
  var router = new ViewRouter();

  // Assert
  var routes = Object.keys(router.routes);        Assert there are exactly
  t.equal(routes.length, 3);                      three route handlers.
```

```
    routes.forEach(exists);              ⟵  Ensure each route
    t.end();                                 handler exists.

    function exists (route) {
      var handlerName = router.routes[route];
      var handler = router[handlerName];
      t.ok(handler, util.format('route handler for "%s" exists', route));
    }
});
```

Route handler property name for the current route. For example, listItems.

Once the test file is ready, you can verify that the tests pass by going through the same process as in section 8.4: opening up a browser with the compiled test bundle and checking the developer console for any error messages.

TEST RUNNER HTML FILE

First off, you'll need a test runner HTML file like the following one. There's nothing special about it, except that it loads the built test bundle:

```html
<!doctype html>
<html>
<head>
  <meta charset='utf-8'>
  <title>Unit Testing JavaScript with Tape</title>
</head>
<body>
  <script src='build/test-bundle.js'></script>
</body>
</html>
```

Once you've created both the `routes.js` test module and the `runner.html` test runner, you should create a Grunt task to build the bundle.

CREATE A GRUNT TASK TO BUILD THE BUNDLE

Because you've learned how to write your own tasks, and as a way of reinforcing that knowledge, you'll create your own task to compile the Browserify bundle! To make that work, you should include all of the following listing in a `Gruntfile`. It uses the `browserify` package directly, without the `grunt-browserify` plugin intermediary. Sometimes using a package directly instead of through a plugin can offer greater flexibility in what your tasks can do.

Listing 8.30   Creating a custom Browserify task

```
var fs = require('fs');
var glob = require('glob');
var mkdirp = require('mkdirp');
var browserify = require('browserify');
var proxyquire = require('proxyquireify');

function browserifyTests () {
  var done = this.async();
  var dir = __dirname + '/test/build';

  mkdirp.sync(dir);
  var bundle = browserify()
```

This is an asynchronous task; call done when it ends.

This is the public interface to the Browserify API.

Create a directory structure so the task works even if the directories don't exist yet.

Globbing gives you all the test entry files. Currently you have routes.js.

Map the relative globbed paths to absolute paths.

Pipe that bundle into a file.

```
      .transform('brfs')
      .plugin(proxyquire.plugin);

      glob
    .sync('./test/*.js')
    .map(resolve)
    .reduce(include, bundle)
    .bundle()
    .pipe(fs.createWriteStream(dir + '/test-bundle.js'))
    .on('done', done);

  function include (bundle, file) {
    bundle.require(file, { entry: true });
    return bundle;
  }
}

function resolve (file) {
  return require.resolve(file);
}
```

The brfs transform is used when compiling Mustache view templates into their JavaScript counterparts.

The proxyquireify plugin allows us to intercept require calls and stub implementations.

Call bundle.require for each test module, while returning the bundle to enable chaining.

Create the browser-enabled JavaScript bundle.

When the data transfer is completed, tell Grunt the task has finished.

Using bundle.require allows external access to the module. The entry flag adds the module as an entry point.

```
grunt.registerTask('browserify_tests', browserifyTests);
```

SEE TEST EXECUTION

When everything is set up, you can run the following command and see the tests being executed in your browser:

```
grunt browserify_tests
open test/runner.html
```

A browser window should pop up. If we open the developer console, we'd see the output shown in figure 8.5.

There are a few more routing tests to be had. Next up, you'll make sure that each route handler does what it's meant to, whether it's meant to redirect users to a different route or render a particular view.

Figure 8.5 Developer Tools showing the results for the tests we've provided

A FEW MORE TESTS

The following listing contains the code for the remaining tests. You can add it to the end of the routes.js test suite.

> **Listing 8.31   Testing route handlers individually**

```
test('route # redirects to the #items route', function (t) {
    // Arrange
    var ViewRouter = getStubbedRouter();

    // Act
    var router = new ViewRouter();
    var handler = getRouteHandler(router, '');
    router.navigate = sinon.spy(); #C
    handler();

    // Assert
    t.ok(router.navigate.calledOnce, 'called router.navigate');
    t.ok(router.navigate.calledWith('items', { trigger: true }), 'called
        router.navigate with proper arguments');
    t.end();
});

test('route #items renders ListView', function (t) {
    // Arrange
    var ViewRouter = getStubbedRouter();

    // Act
    var router = new ViewRouter();
    var handler = getRouteHandler(router, 'items');
    handler();

    // Assert
    t.ok(ListView.calledOnce, 'called ListView once');
    t.ok(ListView.calledWithNew(), 'called new ListView()');
    t.end();
});

test('route #items/add renders AddItemView', function (t) {
    // Arrange
    var ViewRouter = getStubbedRouter();

    // Act
    var router = new ViewRouter();
    var handler = getRouteHandler(router, 'items/add');
    handler();

    // Assert
    t.ok(AddItemView.calledOnce, 'called AddItemView once');
    t.ok(AddItemView.calledWithNew(), 'called new AddItemView()');
    t.end();
});
```

Use a spy so the real .navigate method isn't used.

Every test begins by getting a mocked version of the view router.

The getRouteHandler method returns the route handler for a view route.

Ensure that the route handler calls .navigate and redirects the user to the correct route.

Ensure that the route handler invokes the constructor for ListView.

Ensure that the route handler invokes the constructor for AddItemView.

```
function getRouteHandler (router, route) {
  var routeHandler, key, i;
  var routes = Object.keys(router.routes);
  for (i = 0; i < routes.length; i++) {
    key = routes[i];
    if (route === key) {
      routeHandler = router.routes[key];
      return router[routeHandler].bind(router);
    }
  }
}
```

Loop through all the routes until the provided route is found.

Get the route patterns registered with this router.

Return the route handler for the provided route, bound to the router so "this" is properly assigned.

Once all of the tests are in your routes.js file, you can run the Grunt task again and reload the browser. Figure 8.6 contains the results of executing the new test suite.

While our tests for the router are minimal, in that they don't assert much, we're at least ensuring that the routes exist and that their route handlers do what they're expected to. Routing in an application is typically a convergence point where configuration is plumbed together, and tests help ensure that the correct modules are used.

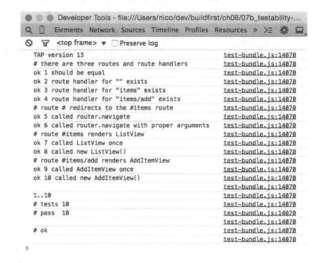

Figure 8.6 Reveals the results of our modest test suite and its ten assertions

8.3.2 *Testing validation on a view model*

The application also needs to test model validation with a few different inputs, making sure that a model is invalid under certain circumstances, and valid when every validation condition is met. For reference, code for the Shopping Item module is included in the following listing.

Listing 8.32 Testing validation

```
var Backbone = require('backbone');

module.exports = Backbone.Model.extend({
  addToOrder: function (quantity) {
    this.set('quantity', this.get('quantity') + quantity, {
      validate: true
    });
  },
  validate: function (attrs) {
    if (!attrs.name) {
```

```
        return 'Please enter the name of the item.';
      }
      if (typeof attrs.quantity !== 'number' || isNaN(attrs.quantity)) {
        return 'The quantity must be numeric!';
      }
      if (attrs.quantity < 1) {
        return 'You should keep your groceries to yourself.';
      }
    }
  });
```

Validation brings us to an interesting use case for JavaScript when it comes to testing. Given that we want to set up a test for each possible validation scenario, we could set up a list of test cases in an array, and then create a single test for each test case.

The following listing shows one possible way to stay DRY in our tests by using a test case factory and a battery of test cases. I've thrown in a test that's not part of the test cases array for contrast.

Listing 8.33 Model validation test case battery

The model doesn't depend on any modules other than Backbone. We don't need proxyquire here.

```
var test = require('tape');
var ShoppingItem = require('../app/models/shoppingItem.js');
var cases = [
  ['must be constructed with a name', {}],
  ['must be constructed with a quantity', { name: 'Chocolate' }],
  ['cannot have NaN quantity', { name: 'Chocolate', quantity: NaN }],
  ['cannot have negative quantity', { name: 'Chocolate', quantity: -1 }],
  ['cannot have zero quantity', { name: 'Chocolate', quantity: 0 }],
  ['is valid when both a name and a positive quantity are provided', {
    name: 'Chocolate', quantity: 1
  }, true]
];

cases.forEach(testCase);

function testCase (c) {
  test('ShoppingItem ' + c[0], function (t) {
    // Arrange
    var expectation = !c[2]; // t.true or t.false
    var expectationText = ' is ' + (expectation ? 'invalid' : 'valid');

    // Act
    var item = new ShoppingItem(c[1], { validate: true });

    // Assert
    t[expectation](item.validationError, JSON.stringify(c[1]) +
    expectationText);
    t.end();
  });
}

test('consumer can increase quantity of a shoppingItem', function (t) {
```

Each test case consists of a description, a model, and the expected validation result.

The testCase factory is executed for every test case.

Tape's test method is called every time, creating individual tests.

Create a ShoppingItem with the model for this test case.

Test whether validation passed and matches our expectations.

Nothing stopping you from writing traditional tests as well!

```
      // Arrange
      var item = new ShoppingItem({
        name: 'Chocolate', quantity: 1
      }, { validate: true });
      // Act
      item.addToOrder(4);
      // Assert
      t.equal(item.validationError, null);
      t.equal(item.get('quantity'), 5, 'four items got added to the order');
      t.end();
    });
```

> Add a few items to the order and later verify that the quantity gets updated.

Imagine if you had to write each test case as an individual test: much copy-pasting would ensue, breaking the DRY principle.

Following the practices we've discussed in this chapter, you could write tests for the views as well. Good test cases could be

- Making sure the template assigned to the view is the one intended for that view
- Checking that event handlers are declared in the events property
- Ensuring those event handlers do what they're expected to

You could use sinon to mock the different properties in the view before invoking each method under test. I'll leave those test cases as an exercise for you.

When you finish writing your tests for the view controllers, it'll be time to shift your attention toward more automation. This time, you'll automate Tape tests using Grunt, and you'll also learn how to run these tests continuously on a remote integration server.

8.4 Automating Tape tests

You automated the Browserify process using Grunt in section 8.1.4. How can you add the tape tests to your Grunt builds? Running the tests on Node is significantly easier than executing them on the browser. As you learned earlier, you could run them on Node by providing the node CLI with the test file path:

```
node test/something.js
```

Automating the process shown in the previous code by using the grunt-tape plugin couldn't be easier. The following code snippet (found as ch08/08_grunt-tape-node in the samples) is all you need in your Gruntfile to run the tape tests in Grunt. Note that you don't have to run Browserify because, in this case, the tests will run in Node:

```
module.exports = function (grunt) {
  grunt.initConfig({
    tape: {
      files: ['test/something.js']
    }
  });
  grunt.loadNpmTasks('grunt-tape');
  grunt.registerTask('test', ['tape']);
};
```

That was fast. How about in the browser?

8.4.1   *Automating Tape tests for the browser*

Running `tape` tests on browsers from your command line is also fairly easy. You can use `testling` to do it. Testling (also known as substack) is a tool written by James Halliday, a tremendously prolific Node contributor, who's also the author of Tape, and a modularity fanatic. There wasn't a readily available `grunt-testling` package in existence, but I decided not to disappoint. I created `grunt-testling` so that you could run Testling from Grunt. The `grunt-testling` package doesn't require any Grunt configuration. But you need to configure `testling` itself. Testling is configured by placing a `'testling'` property in your `package.json` and telling it where the test files are. The following listing (found as ch08/09_grunt-tape-browser) is a sample `package.json` to do that.

Listing 8.34   Automating Tape tests

```
{
  "name": "buildfirst",
  "version": "0.1.0",
  "author": "Nicolas Bevacqua <buildfirst@bevacqua.io>",
  "homepage": "https://github.com/bevacqua/buildfirst",
  "repository": "git://github.com/bevacqua/buildfirst.git",
  "devDependencies": {
    "grunt": "^0.4.4",
    "grunt-contrib-clean": "^0.5.0",
    "grunt-testling": "^1.0.0",
    "tape": "~2.10.2",
    "testling": "^1.6.1"
  },
  "testling": {
    "files": "test/*.js"
  }
}
```

Once you've configured `testling`, installed `grunt-testling`, and added it to your Gruntfile, you should be all set!

```
module.exports = function (grunt) {
  grunt.initConfig({});
  grunt.loadNpmTasks('grunt-testling');
  grunt.registerTask('test', ['testling']);

};
```

You can now run the tests in a browser entering the following command into your terminal:

`grunt test`

Figure 8.7 shows the results of using Testling with Grunt.

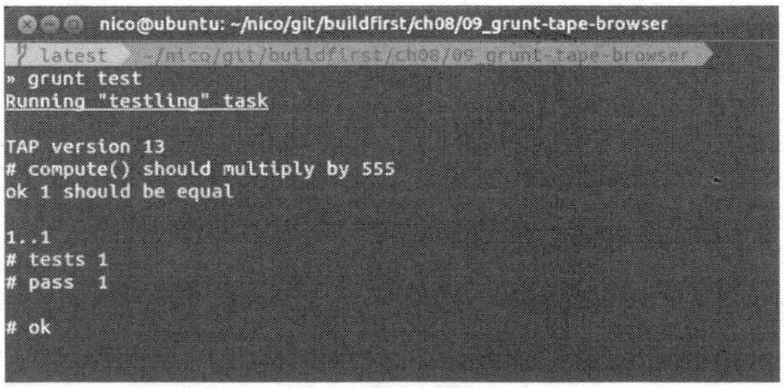

Figure 8.7   Driving tests through the Testling CLI using Grunt

Next up let me briefly reiterate a concept you first saw in chapter 3: continuous development adapted to testing.

8.4.2 Continuous testing

An important aspect of running tests is to do so on every change, making sure you don't spend a long time with broken code in your local development environment. You might recall a particular `watch` configuration snippet in chapter 3 that allowed you to run specific tasks when file changes were detected somewhere in your code base. The following listing is an adapted version of that snippet to run tests and lint when files change.

Listing 8.35 Running tests and lint when files change

```
watch: {
  lint: {
    tasks: ['lint'],
    files: ['src/**/*.less']
  },
  unit: {
    tasks: ['test'],
    files: ['src/**/*.js', 'test/**/*.js']
  }
}
```

Automating tests in both Node and the browser is important. Watching for changes and running those tests locally again is also important. At this point you might want to check out chapter 4, section 4.4 again, where I discussed continuous integration, which is fundamental to setting up your project so tests are executed on every push to your version control system.

Testing components in isolation isn't the only way to test an application. In fact, countless types of testing exist, and we'll briefly discuss a few interesting ones in the next section.

8.5 Integration, visual, and performance testing

As I mentioned a few times before, testing comes in various sizes and shapes. Integration testing, for instance, allows you to test different paths in your application workflow, making sure that component interaction works as expected. Components were already tested in isolation, and integration testing provides both a redundancy layer and the ability to capture bugs that aren't evident without executing an application and seeing for yourself.

8.5.1 Integration testing

Integration tests are no different from unit tests in the sense of tooling. You can still use Tape, Sinon, and Proxyquire to run these tests. The difference lies in what should be tested. In integration, you no longer strive to test a completely isolated version of a component, but rather test as many interconnections as you can get away with, and mock the rest. For instance, you might run your application's web server, hit it with real HTTP requests, and check if the response matches your assertions.

You may also use Selenium, a browser automation tool, to help drive these comprehensive tests on the client side. Selenium uses a web server to communicate with a browser through its API, which is supported in a variety of languages. You can send commands to the browser through a Selenium server. You could write down a series of steps for your test to follow, and then Selenium fires up a browser and does those actions for you. A running web server and browser automation, working together, allow you to automate tests that you might do by hand. Remember, you only have to put together the test once! Then you can run it as many times as needed. You can always go back and change the tests, too. I'm not going to lie to you, though. Setting up Selenium is cumbersome and generally frustrating, and it's poorly documented. But once you've put together a few tests, you'll reap the benefits.

Integration tests aren't limited to browser automation with a tool like Selenium, though. You could run integration tests that work solely on your back-end stack or merely in the front end.

8.5.2   *Visual testing*

Visual testing mostly consists of taking screenshots of an application, at different viewport dimensions, and validating that the layout isn't broken. You can perform these validations by either comparing a screenshot to what you expect or by superimposing the latest screenshot with the previous one, generating what's called a "diff." These diffs let you quickly identify what changed from one version to another by highlighting the differences and shading the parts of the screenshot that haven't changed. Many Grunt plugins can take screenshots of an application for you. Several even go the extra mile and compare the latest screenshot with the previous one, showing you where the differences may lie. One such Grunt plugin is `grunt-photobox`. Configuring it is mostly a matter of deciding which URL you want to load and what resolution you want the viewport to be when taking the screenshots. This is particularly useful if your site follows the Responsive Web Design paradigm, which uses CSS media queries to change the appearance of a page based on the dimensions of the viewport and other variables. The following code snippet shows how you might configure `grunt-photobox` to take pictures of a page in three different sizes. Let me go over the options:

- The `urls` field is an array of pages you want to take pictures from.
- In `screenSizes` you can define the width of each screenshot you want to take; the height will be the full height of the page. Make sure you use strings. Note that Photobox will take a picture of each site in each of the resolutions you've decided on:

```
photobox: {
  buildfirst: {
    options: {
      urls: ['http://bevacqua.io/bf'],
      screenSizes: ['320', '960', '1440'] // these must be strings
```

```
        }
      }
    }
```

Once you've configured Photobox in Grunt, you can run the following command and Photobox will generate a site you can browse to compare the screenshots:

```
grunt photobox:buildfirst
```

You can find the fully working example in the accompanying code samples as ch08/ 10_visual-testing. Finally, let's shift our attention to performance testing.

8.5.3 Performance testing

Keeping tabs on the performance of your application can help quickly identify the root cause of performance issues. You can monitor performance in web applications using tools such as Google PageSpeed or Yahoo YSlow. Both tools give you similar insights, and they can both be automated using Grunt plugins. They do have a few differences between their services. The PageSpeed Grunt tool gives you more insight into what improvements you should make to your site. For example, it might let you know that you aren't caching your static assets as aggressively as you should. The YSlow plugin gives you a more compact version, telling you how many requests were made, how long the page took to load, how much content was downloaded, and a performance score.

The PageSpeed plugin, `grunt-pagespeed`, requires you to get an API key from Google.[2] You can then configure the plugin as shown in listing 8.36 (sample ch08/ 11_pagespeed-insights). In the code, you're telling PageSpeed which URL you want it to hit, what locale you want the results to be generated in, what strategy to use (`'desktop'` or `'mobile'`), and the minimum score (out of 100) to consider the test successful. Note that you're purposely avoiding including the API key in the Grunt-file. Instead, you'll get it from an environment variable to keep the secret safe.

Listing 8.36   Configuring the PageSpeed plugin

```
pagespeed: {
  desktop: {
    url: 'http://bevacqua.io/bf',
    locale: 'en_US',
    strategy: 'desktop',
    threshold: 80
  },
  options: {
    key: process.env.PAGESPEED_KEY
  }
}
```

To run the example, you'll have to take the key you got from Google and enter the following command into your terminal:

```
PAGESPEED_KEY=$YOUR_API_KEY grunt pagespeed:desktop
```

---

[2]   Get the API key from https://code.google.com/apis/console.

For more information about the reasons for storing secrets in environment variables, go back to chapter 3, section 3.2.

In the case of `grunt-yslow`, the Grunt plugin for YSlow, you won't need to get any API keys, which makes matters considerably simpler. Configuring the plugin is a matter of specifying the website URL you want to hit and setting the threshold levels for page weight, page load speed, performance score (out of 100), and request count, as shown in the following listing (sample ch08/12_yahoo-yslow).

Listing 8.37 Configuring the YSlow plugin

```
yslow: {
  options: {
    thresholds: {
      weight: 1000,
      speed: 5000,
      score: 80,
      requests: 30
    }
  },
  buildfirst: {
    files: [
      { src: 'http://bevacqua.io/bf' }
    ]
  }
}
```

To run these YSlow tests, enter the following command into your terminal:

```
grunt yslow:buildfirst
```

All of these examples can be found in the accompanying source code samples, under ch08. Make sure to check them out!

8.6 Summary

That was exciting! We covered many concepts in a short time:

- You got a crash course on unit testing and learned how to tune your components, making them more suitable to test.
- I explained Tape and how you can use it to seamlessly run tests on both the client side and the server side, without duplicating your code.
- You learned about mocks, spies, and proxies; why you need them; and how you can use them in JavaScript code.
- I showed you several case studies to help you figure out what things you should be testing for and how you should test them.
- You looked at automation using Grunt to run Tape tests on both the server and the browser without leaving the command line.
- I introduced you to integration and visual testing, and you learned how to automate those tasks using Grunt.

If you're interested in learning more about testing, I suggest you check out *Test-Driven JavaScript Development,* by Christian Johansen (Developer's Library, 2010).

REST API design and layered service architectures

This chapter covers

- Designing API architectures
- Understanding the REST constraint model
- Learning about API paging, caching, and throttling schemes
- API documentation techniques
- Developing layered service architectures
- Consuming a REST API on the client side

I've described how to approach build processes, and you've learned about deployments and configuring the different environments your application will live on. You also learned about modularity, dependency management, asynchronous code flows in JavaScript, and the MVC approach to developing scalable application architectures. To round things out, this chapter focuses on designing a REST API architecture and consuming it on the client side, allowing you to tie the front end to a back-end persistence layer using a transparent and clean API.

251

9.1   *Avoiding API design pitfalls*

If you've ever worked on the front end of a web project for a large enterprise, then I'm sure you can relate to the complete lack of cohesion in the design of the back-end API. Do you need to access a list of product categories? You should do an AJAX request `GET /categories`. Do you have products belonging to a category? Sure thing; use `GET /getProductListFromCategory?category_id=id`. Do you have products in two categories? Use `GET /productInCategories?values=id_1,id_2,...id_n`. Need to save changes to the product description? Tough luck, you'll have to send the entire product again through the wire. `POST /product`, appending a large JSON blob in the body. Need to send a customized email to a particular human? `POST /email-customer` with their email and the email message data.

If you can't find anything wrong with that API design, chances are you've spent too much time working with similar APIs. The following list details issues with how it was designed:

- Each new method has its own set of naming conventions: the `GET` verb is repeated in the endpoint, camelCase, hyphen-delimited, or underscore_separated. You namc it!

- Beside naming conventions, endpoints aren't marked in any way that differentiates them from those that render views.

- Argument intake preference also varies wildly with no clear distinction through the query string or the request body. Maybe cookies could do the trick!

- It's not clear when to use each HTTP verb (`HEAD`, `GET`, `POST`, `PUT`, `PATCH`, `DELETE`). As a result, only `GET` and `POST` are used.

- Inconsistency throughout the API. Well-designed APIs are not only well documented, but also present consistency across the board that allows consumers to hack through the API, as well as implementers to easily build on the existing API by copying what it does.

This isn't merely the work of a madman who decided to mix naming and argument-passing conventions, along with glossing over any kind of standardization and cohesion across API endpoints. The most likely scenario for how the API got to the state it is in today is employee rotation on the project maintaining the API. Yes, it could also be a single person who doesn't know any better, but in that case you'll observe at least some degree of consistency across the API methods. A well-designed API enables consumers to infer documentation for a method once they've used a few related methods. That's because methods would be named in a consistent manner, they would take similar parameters, and those parameters would be named and ordered consistently as well. When an API is poorly designed, or doesn't follow a set of consistency guidelines, it's harder to achieve this state where the how can be inferred from simply using the API. Inference can only be attained when the API is consistently designed to be straightforward.

In this chapter I'll teach you how to design cohesive, consistent, and coherent APIs for direct consumption in your web projects and elsewhere. The API consumed by the front end is one area where we could do better. Together with JavaScript testing, I'd say that these are two of the most commonly undervalued aspects of frontend development.

REST stands for Representational State Transfer, and it's a comprehensive set of guidelines that you can use to design API architectures. Once you understand REST, I'll give you a tour of how to design a typical layered service architecture to go with that API. Before signing off, you'll gain insight into developing client-side code to interact with the REST API, allowing you to react to responses from the API. Let's get going!

9.2   *Learning REST API design*

REST is a set of architectural constraints that aid you when developing an API over HTTP. Imagine you start developing a web API in "anything goes" mode—a clean slate. Then add REST constraints into the mix, one by one. The end result will be a standardized API that most developers will feel comfortable developing and consuming. Note that there are different interpretations of how a REST API should be designed, and that several of my interpretations are sprinkled throughout this chapter. These are the interpretations that work well for me, but in the end that's simply my opinion.

Roy Fielding wrote a dissertation that introduced REST to the world,[1] and it has only seen an increase in adoption since its publication in 2000. I'll only cover the constraints relevant to our purposes: putting together a dedicated REST API for the front end of your application to consume. Among other constraints, you'll touch on how to construct the endpoints that make up your API, how to handle requests, and what kinds of status codes you should use. Later we'll go into more advanced HTTP communication topics, such as paging results, caching responses, and throttling requests.

The first such constraint that you'll visit is that REST is stateless, meaning requests should contain all the information necessary for the back end to understand what you want, and the server shouldn't take advantage of any additional context stored in the server. In practical terms, you get "pure" endpoints where the output (response) is defined solely by the inputs (request).

The other constraint that interests us is that REST expects a uniform interface. Each endpoint in the API is expected to take parameters, affect the persistence layer, and respond in a certain, predictable way. To expand on these, you'll need to understand that REST deals in resources.

REST resources

In REST, a *resource* is an abstraction of information, any information. For your purposes you could act as if resources and database models were equivalents. Users are a resource, and so are Products and Categories. Resources can be queried through the uniform interface I described.

---

[1]   Fielding, Roy Thomas. Architectural Styles and the Design of Network-Based Software Architectures. Doctoral dissertation, UC Irvine, 2000. http://bevacqua.io/bf/rest.

Let's bring the discussion closer to the ground and describe in practical terms what this means for the way you structure the front-end API.

9.2.1   *Endpoints, HTTP verbs, and versioning*

Have you ever used an API and felt it was great? Felt that you "get it," and in fact you could guess the names of their methods, their methods worked in the way you expected them to, and there were no surprises? A couple of examples of well-executed APIs come to my mind; the first one is the language API in the Ruby standard library, with methods that clearly define what their purpose is, are consistent in the parameters they take, and have mirror methods that do exactly their opposite.

The `String` class in Ruby has a `.capitalize` method; it creates an uppercase copy of a string. Then there's `.capitalize!`, which capitalizes the original string rather than creating a copy. You also have `.strip`, which returns a copy where leading and trailing whitespace is gone. You probably guessed the next one: `.strip!`, which is the same as `.strip` but on the original string.

Facebook has other good examples. Their Graph REST API is easy to use, and it's cohesive in that endpoints work mostly the same way. You can also chop parts of the URL and hack your way through their website; for example, http://facebook.com/me takes you to your own profile, as their API recognizes `me` as the currently authenticated user.

This kind of consistent behavior is critical to a great API. In contrast, bad API design leads to confusion and is characterized by the lack of a naming convention, ambiguous or poor documentation, or even worse: undocumented side effects. PHP is a notorious guide to writing a poor API. The issue arises because of the lack of a specification and different authors taking over different parts of the PHP language API. As a result, PHP functions have wildly varying signatures, names, and even casing conventions. You have no way to guess the name of a given function. Sometimes these issues can be solved by wrapping the existing API in a consistent one, which is a big part of how jQuery became popular—by abstracting the DOM API in a more convenient and consistent API.

The single most important aspect in API design is consistency, and that starts with endpoint naming conventions.

NAMING YOUR ENDPOINTS

To begin with, you need to define a prefix for all API endpoints. If you have a subdomain to use, such as `api.example.com`, that'll work too. For front-end API efforts, using `example.com/api` as a prefix should work. A prefix helps discern API methods from view routes and sets an expectation for the kind of responses they produce (typically JSON in modern web applications).

The prefix on its own isn't enough, though. Putting together a coherent API mostly relies on following strict guidelines when naming your endpoints. Here's a set of guidelines to get you started:

- Use all lowercase, hyphenated endpoints such as `/api/verification-tokens`. This increases URL "hackability," which is the ability to manually go in and modify the URL by hand. You can pick any naming scheme you like, as long as you're consistent about it.

- Use a noun or two to describe the resource, such as `verification-tokens`, `users`, or `products`.
- Always describe resources in plural: `/api/users` rather than `/api/user`. This makes the API more semantic, as you'll see in a minute.

These guidelines get us to an interesting point. Let's make an example out of `/api/products` to see how you can design the API in a way that's RESTful and consistent.

HTTP VERBS AND CRUD CONSISTENCY

First, getting a list of products is probably the most basic task you could perform against the products API. The `/api/products` endpoint is prime for the task, so you implement a route on the server that returns a list of products as JSON, and you start feeling pretty good about yourself. Next, you want to return individual products; this will be used when humans visit the product details page. In this case, you might be tempted to define the endpoint as `/api/product/:id`, but one of your guidelines was to always use plurals, so that'll end up looking like `/api/products/:id`.

Both of those methods are clearly defined as GET requests, because they interact with the server in a read-only fashion. What about removing a product? Typically, non-REST interfaces use methods such as POST `/removeProduct?id=:id`. Sometimes the GET verb is used, which results in web crawlers such as Google wiping out important database information by following GET links on a site.[2] REST suggests you use the DELETE HTTP verb instead, on the same endpoint that you used to GET a single product, `/api/products/:id`. Taking advantage of one of the building blocks of HTTP—their verbs—you can compose more semantic and consistent APIs.

Inserting items of a given resource type involves a similar thought process. In non-REST scenarios you might've had POST `/createProduct` and a body of relevant data, whereas in REST you should use the more semantic PUT verb, along with the consistent `/api/products` endpoint. Last, edits should use the PATCH verb and an endpoint such as `/api/products/:id`. We'll reserve the POST verb for operations that don't merely involve creating or updating database objects, such as `/notifySubscribers` via email. Relationships are one last type of endpoint that can be considered part of basic storage operations (Create, Read, Update, Delete, or CRUD for short). Given all of what I've described so far, it probably won't be hard for you to imagine how GET `/api/products/:id/parts` is a great starting point for a request that responds with the individual parts that make up a particular product.

That's it, as far as CRUD goes. What happens if you want to use something other than CRUD? Use your best judgment. Usually, you could use the POST verb, ideally constraining yourself to a particular resource type, which doesn't necessarily need to be a

---

2 Read this article for a similar story on how Google wiped clean the content on a website just by following links: http://bevacqua.io/bf/spider.

database model reference. For instance, `POST /api/authentication/login` can handle login attempts on the front end.

As a summary, Table 9.1 shows the verbs and endpoints discussed so far per a typical REST API design. I omitted the `/api` prefixes for brevity. Note that I use `products` as an example resource type to make the example easier to relate to, but this applies to any resource type.

Table 9.1   Product endpoints in a typical REST API

Verb	Endpoint	Description
GET	/products	Gets a list of products
GET	/products/:id	Gets a single product by ID
GET	/products/:id/parts	Gets a list of parts in a single product
PUT	/products/:id/parts	Inserts a new part for a particular product
DELETE	/products/:id	Deletes a single product by ID
PUT	/products	Inserts a new product
HEAD	/products/:id	Returns whether the product exists through a status code of 200 or 404
PATCH	/products/:id	Edits an existing product by ID
POST	/authentication/login	Most other API methods should use POST requests

Please note that the HTTP verbs chosen for each type of action aren't set in stone. It is, in fact, a topic of heated arguments, where people argue POST should be used for inserts, or any other operation that's not idempotent, and endpoints using the other verbs (GET, PUT, PATCH, DELETE) must result in idempotent operations—repeated requests on those endpoints shouldn't alter the outcome.

Versioning is also an important aspect of REST API design, but is it necessary for front-end operations?

API VERSIONING

In traditional API scenarios, versioning is useful because it allows you to commit breaking changes to your service without demolishing the interaction with existing consumers. Two main schools of thought exist in the REST API versioning department.

One school of thought is convinced that the API version should be set in HTTP headers, and that if a version isn't specified in the request, you should get a response from the latest version of the API. This formal approach is closer to what the original dissertation for REST proposed, but an argument is that if the API is poorly executed it can lead to breaking changes inadvertently.

Instead, they propose that the version is embedded into the API endpoint prefix: `/api/v1/....` This also identifies right away which version of the API your application wants by looking at the requested endpoint.

Truth is, it doesn't change that much from having the v1 be in the endpoint or in a request header, so it's mostly a matter of preference for the API implementer. When it comes to web applications and their accompanying API, you don't necessarily need to implement any versioning, and that's why I'm inclined to go with the request header approach. That way, if somewhere down the line you decide you do need versioning, you can easily define a "latest version" as the default, and if consumers still want the previous version they can add a header explicitly asking for the old one. That being said, requesting a specific version of the API is always more desirable than blindly accepting whatever the latest API may be, so as not to break functionality unexpectedly.

I mentioned you don't need to necessarily implement versioning in the REST API consumed by the front end, and that depends on two factors:

- Is the API public facing as well? In this case, versioning is necessary, baking a bit more predictability into your service's behavior.
- Is the API used by several applications? Are the API and the front end developed by separate teams? Is there a drawn-out process to change an API endpoint? If any of these cases apply, you're probably better off versioning your API.

Unless your team and your application are small enough that both live in the same repository and developers touch on both indistinctly, go for the safe bet and use versions in your API.

Time to move on and study what requests and responses may look like.

9.2.2 Requests, responses, and status codes

As I've mentioned before, consistency by following REST conventions is key in developing a highly usable API. This applies to requests and responses as well. An API is expected to take arguments consistently; the way this usually works is that you take the ID via the endpoint. In the case of the product by ID route, `/api/products/:id`, when requesting the `/api/products/bad0-bab8` URL, assume `bad0-bab8` is the requested resource identifier.

REQUESTS

Modern-day web routers have no trouble dissecting the URL and providing the specified request parameters. For instance, the following code shows how Express, a Node.js web framework, lets you define a dynamic route that captures requests for products via an identifier. Then it parses the request URL and hands you the appropriately parsed parameters:

```
app.get('/api/products/:id', function (req, res, next) {
  // req.params.id contains the extracted id
});
```

Having the identifier as part of the request endpoint is great because it allows DELETE and GET requests to use the same endpoint, making for a more intuitive API, like I mentioned previously about Ruby. You should decide on a consistent data-transfer strategy to upload the data to the server when making PUT, PATCH, or POST requests that modify a resource in the server. Nowadays, JSON is used almost ubiquitously as the data transport of choice due to its simplicity, the fact that it's native to browsers, and the high availability of JSON parsing libraries across server-side languages.

RESPONSES

Like requests, responses should conform to a consistent data-transfer format, so you have no surprises when parsing the response. Even when an error occurs on the server side, the response is still expected to be valid according to the chosen transport; for example, if our API is built using JSON, then all the responses produced by our API should be valid JSON (granted the user is accepting a JSON response in the HTTP headers).

You should figure out the envelope in which you'll wrap your responses. An envelope, or message wrapper, is crucial for providing a consistent experience across all your API endpoints, allowing consumers to make certain assumptions about the responses the API provides. A useful starting point may be an object with a single field, named data, that contains the body of your response:

```
{
  "data": {} // the actual response
}
```

Errors may be another useful field, only present when an error occurs, containing an object that may expose properties such as an error message, reason, and accompanying metadata. Suppose you query the API on the GET /api/products/baeb-b00f endpoint, but a baeb-b00f product doesn't exist in the database:

```
{
  "error": {
    "code": "bf-404",
    "message": "Product not found.",
    "context": {
      "id": "baeb-b00f"
    }
  }
}
```

Using an envelope and the appropriate error fields in your responses aren't enough on their own. As a REST API developer you should also be conscious about the status codes that you choose for your API's responses.

HTTP STATUS CODES

In the case of a product not being found, you should respond with the 404 Not Found status code, in addition to the properly formatted response that describes the error. Status codes are particularly important in allowing API consumers to make assumptions about the responses. When you respond with status codes in the 2xx Success class, the response body should contain all of the relevant data that was requested. Here's an example showing the response to a request on a product that could be found, alongside with the HTTP version and status code:

```
HTTP/1.1 200 OK
{
  "data": {
    "id": "baeb-b001",
    "name": "Angry Pirate Plush Toy",
    "description": "Batteries not included.",
    "price": "$39.99",
    "categories": ["plushies", "kids"]
  }
}
```

Then there's the 4xx Client Error class codes, which mean the request most likely failed due to an error made by the client side (the user wasn't properly authenticated, for instance). In these cases, you should use the `error` field to describe why the request was faulty. For instance, if input validation fails on a form while attempting to create a product, you could return a response using a `400 Bad Request` status code, as shown in the following listing.

Listing 9.1   Describing an error

```
HTTP/1.1 400 Bad Request
{
  "error": {
    "code": "bf-400",
    "message": "Some required fields were invalid.",
    "context": {
      "validation": [
        "The product name must be 6-20 alphanumeric characters",
        "The price can't be negative",
        "At least one product category should be selected"
      ]
    }
  }
}
```

Another kind of error in the 5xx status code range is an unexpected error such as `500 Internal Server Error`. These should be presented to the consumer in the same way as 4xx errors. Suppose the previous request results in an error; you should then respond with a 500 status code and a snippet of data in the response body, similar to the following:

```
HTTP/1.1 500 Internal Server Error
{
  "error": {
    "code": "bf-500",
    "message": "An unexpected error occurred while accessing the database."
    "context": {
      "id": "baeb-b001"
    }
  }
}
```

It's usually relatively easy to capture these kinds of errors when everything else fails and respond with a 500 message, passing in a bit of context as to what went wrong.

Up to this point I've covered endpoints, request bodies, status codes, and response bodies. Setting proper response headers is another REST API design aspect that's worth mentioning for a variety of reasons.

9.2.3 *Paging, caching, and throttling*

Although not as important in small applications, paging, caching, and throttling all play a part in defining a consistent and highly usable API. Paging in particular is often a necessity, because a complete lack of paging would easily cripple your application by allowing the API to query and transfer massive amounts of data from the database to the clients.

RESPONSE PAGING

Going back to the first REST endpoint example I used, suppose I make a query to your API for `/api/products`. How many products should that endpoint return? All of them? What if there are a hundred? A thousand? Ten? A million? You have to draw the line somewhere. You could set a default pagination limit across the API and have the ability to override that default for each individual endpoint. Within a reasonable range, the consumer should have the ability to pass in a query string parameter and choose a different limit.

Suppose you settle for 10 products per request. You then have to implement a paging mechanism to access the rest of the products available on your application. To implement paging, you use the `Link` header.

If you query the first products page, the response's `Link` header should be similar to the following code:

```
Link: <http://example.com/api/products/?p=2>; rel="next",
      <http://example.com/api/products/?p=54>; rel="last"
```

Note that the endpoints must be absolute so the consumer can parse the `Link` header and query them directly. The `rel` attribute describes the relationship between the requested page and the linked page.

If you now request the second page, `/api/products/?p=2`, you should get a similar `Link` header, this time letting you know that "previous" and "first" related pages are also available:

```
Link: <http://example.com/api/products/?p=1>; rel="first",
      <http://example.com/api/products/?p=1>; rel="prev",
      <http://example.com/api/products/?p=3>; rel="next",
      <http://example.com/api/products/?p=54>; rel="last"
```

Cases exist where data flows too rapidly for traditional paging methods to behave as expected. For instance, if a few records make their way into the database between requests for the first page and the second one, the second page results in duplicates of items that were on page one but were pushed to the second page as a result of the inserts. This issue has two solutions. The first solution is to use identifiers instead of page numbers. This allows the API to figure out where you left off, and even if new records get inserted, you'll still get the next page in the context of the last range of identifiers that the API gave you. The second approach is to give tokens to the consumer that allow the API to track the position they arrived at after the last request and what the next page should look like.

If you deal with the kind of large datasets that require paging to work efficiently, then you'll probably get big returns from implementing caching and throttling. Caching will probably yield better results than throttling, so let's discuss that first.

RESPONSE CACHING

Typically it's up to the end client to cache API results as deemed necessary. The API, however, can make suggestions with varying degrees of confidence on how its responses should be cached. What follows is a crash course on HTTP caching behaviors and the related HTTP headers.

Setting the `Cache-Control` header to `private` bypasses intermediaries (such as proxies like `nginx`, other caching layers like Varnish, and all kinds of hardware in between) and only allows the end client to cache the response. Similarly, setting it to `public` allows intermediaries to store a copy of the response in their cache.

The `Expires` header tells the browser that a resource should be cached and not requested again until the expiration date has elapsed:

```
Cache-Control: private
Expires: Thu, 3 Jul 2014 18:31:12 GMT
```

It's hard to define future `Expires` headers in API responses because if the data in the server changes, it could mean that the client's cache becomes stale, but it doesn't have any way of knowing that until the expiration date. A conservative alternative to `Expires` headers in responses is using a pattern known as "conditional requests."

Conditional requests can be time-based, specifying a `Last-Modified` header in your responses. It's best to specify a `max-age` in the `Cache-Control` header, to let the browser invalidate the cache after a certain period of time even if the modification date doesn't change:

```
Cache-Control: private, max-age=86400
Last-Modified: Thu, 3 Jul 2014 18:31:12 GMT
```

The next time the browser requests this resource, it will only ask for the contents of the resource if they're unchanged since this date, using the `If-Modified-Since` request header:

```
If-Modified-Since: Thu, 3 Jul 2014 18:31:12 GMT
```

If the resource hasn't changed since `Thu, 3 Jul 2014 18:31:12 GMT`, the server will return with an empty body with the `304 Not Modified` status code.

An alternative to the `Last-Modified` negotiation is to use the `ETag` (also known as Entity Tag) header, which is usually a hash that represents the resource in its current state. This allows the server to identify if the cached contents of the resource are different than the most recent version:

```
Cache-Control: private, max-age=86400
ETag: "d5aae96d71f99e4ed31f15f0ffffdd64"
```

On subsequent requests, the If-None-Match request header is sent with the ETag value of the last requested version for the same resource:

```
If-None-Match: "d5aae96d71f99e4ed31f15f0ffffdd64"
```

If the current version has the same ETag value, your current version is what the client has cached and a 304 Not Modified response will be returned. Once you have caching in place, request throttling could also mitigate server load.

REQUEST THROTTLING

Throttling, also known as rate limiting, is a technique you can use to limit the number of requests a client can make to your API in a certain window of time. You have numerous criteria to rely on to rate limit consumers, but one of the most common ways to do so is to define a fixed rate limit and reset the quota after a certain period of time. You also have to decide how you're going to enforce such limiting. Maybe the limit is enforced per IP address, and you could also have a more permissive limit for authenticated users.

Suppose you define a rate limit of 2,000 requests per hour for unauthenticated users; the API should include the following headers in its responses, with every request shaving off a point from the remainder. The X-RateLimit-Reset header should contain a UNIX timestamp describing the moment when the limit will be reset:

```
X-RateLimit-Limit: 2000
X-RateLimit-Remaining: 1999
X-RateLimit-Reset: 1404429213925
```

Once the request quota is drained, the API should return a 429 Too Many Requests response, with a helpful error message wrapped in the usual error envelope:

```
HTTP/1.1 429 Too Many Requests
X-RateLimit-Limit: 2000
X-RateLimit-Remaining: 0
X-RateLimit-Reset: 1404429213925
{
  "error": {
    "code": "bf-429",
    "message": "Request quota exceeded. Wait 3 minutes and try again.",
    "context": {
      "renewal": 1404429213925
    }
  }
}
```

This kind of safeguarding is usually unnecessary when dealing with an internal API, or an API meant only for your front end, but it's a crucial measure to take when exposing the API publicly. Together with paging and caching, these measures help relieve the strain on your back-end services.

When something unexpected happens as the consumer is using your API, thorough documentation will be the last bastion of the highly usable services you design. The next section explains the essentials of properly documenting an API.

9.2.4 Documenting an API

Any API worth using is well-documented, regardless of whether it's public facing or not. When everything else fails, consumers refer to the API documentation. You can get away with auto-generating the API based on metadata sprinkled throughout your code base, often in the form of code comments, but you have to make sure the documentation stays up to date and relevant.

Good API documentation should

- Explain how the response envelope looks.
- Demonstrate how error reporting works.
- Show how authentication, paging, throttling, and caching work on a high level.
- Detail every single endpoint, explain the HTTP verbs used to query those endpoints, and describe each piece of data that should be in the request and the fields that may appear in the response.

Test cases can sometimes help as documentation by providing up-to-date working examples that also indicate best practices in accessing an API. Documentation enables API client developers to rapidly sift through any issues they may have because they didn't fully understand the kind of data the API expected from them. Another desirable component in API documentation is a changelog that briefly details the changes that occur from one version to the next. Refer to section 4.2.2 for more information about changelogs.

Documentation may be useful even when the API and the web application live together, because it helps reduce time spent researching what the API is supposed to expect or how it works. Instead of sifting through code, developers can read the documentation. When asked something about the API, you can direct them to the docs. In this regard, documentation doesn't present benefits only when maintaining a REST API, but it makes sense for any kind of service, library, or framework. In the case of a library—take jQuery, for example—the documentation should cover each of the library's public API methods, clearly detailing the possible arguments and response combinations. The docs may also explain the underlying implementation in those cases where it helps the consumer understand why the API is shaped the way it is. Well-executed API documentation examples include Twitter, Facebook, GitHub, and Stack-Exchange.[3]

---

[3] You can find these examples at http://bevacqua.io/bf/api-twitter, http://bevacqua.io/bf/api-fb, http://bevacqua.io/bf/api-github, and http://bevacqua.io/bf/api-stack, respectively.

Armed with the knowledge needed to design a REST API, in the next section you'll explore the possibility of creating a series of layers for the API. These layers will define the API and help you keep your service modularly structured and testable.

9.3   *Implementing layered service architectures*

If your API is small enough and dedicated to the front end, chances are that it'll live in the same project. If that's the case, then it makes sense that the API lives in the same layer as the web application's controllers.

A common approach is to have a so-called service layer that handles the core of the data processing task, while having a data layer that's in charge of interacting with the database. Meanwhile, the API should be designed as a thin layer on top of the others. This architecture is pictured in figure 9.1.

Looking at the figure from the top down, you can see the basic parts of each API layer.

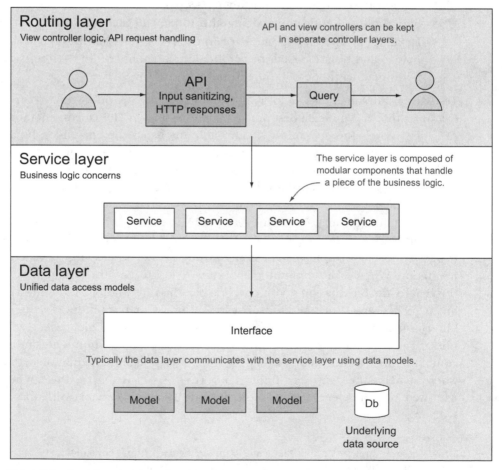

Figure 9.1   Overview of a three-tiered service architecture

9.3.1 *Routing layer*

The API layer is in charge of dealing with throttling, paging, caching headers, parsing request bodies, and preparing responses. All of that, however, should be accomplished by using the service layer as the only way to access or modify the data, for the following reasons:

- Controllers must validate request data before producing a response.
- The API asks the service for the different pieces of data it needs to properly fulfill the response.
- When the service jobs are complete, the API controller responds with a proper status code and relevant response data.

9.3.2 *Service layer*

The service layer can be architected to defer all data access to a third layer: the data layer. This layer is in charge of dealing with computation for any missing data that can't be directly extracted from the data stores:

- The service layer is composed of many small services. Each of them handles a subset of the business.
- The service layer queries the data layer, computes business logic rules, and validates request data on a model level.
- CRUD operations typically end up being a pass-through to the data layer.
- Tasks such as sending out emails, where no persistence access is involved, may be handled entirely by a component of the service layer without resorting to a data store.

9.3.3 *Data layer*

The data layer is in charge of communicating with the persistence medium such as a database, flat file, memory, and so on. Its purpose is to provide access to any of those mediums through a consistent interface. The goal of having such an interface in place is that you can easily swap persistence layers (database engines, or in-memory key-value stores, for example), also making it easier to test:

- The data access layer provides an interface to the data in the underlying data store. This makes it easier to interact with different data sources and change vendors.
- Models stay the same independently of the underlying data store; they're part of the interface.
- The underlying data models are kept away from the interface. This makes swapping out data stores easier, because data layer consumers won't be affected.

That was a frantic overview! Let's slow down and pace ourselves through this three-tiered architecture in greater detail. Note that this type of architecture isn't limited to API design but could also fit typical web applications and possibly other types of applications too, if they deserve the extra infrastructure.

9.3.4   *Routing layer*

Controllers are the public-facing layer in this type of architecture. At this layer you'll define the routes your application can be accessed from. The routing layer is also in charge of parsing any parameters found in the requested URL and in the request body.

Before even trying to fulfill the request, you may have to validate that the client didn't exceed their allowed quota, and if that were the case, you can kill the request right then, passing the appropriate response and status code of `429 Too Many Requests`.

As we all know, user input can't be trusted, and this is where you're meant to validate and sanitize user input most aggressively. Once the request is parsed, make sure that the request provided exactly what's needed to fulfill the request, nothing less and also nothing more. Once you've made sure all of the required fields are provided, you should sanitize them and make sure that the inputs are valid. For example, if the provided email address isn't a valid email, your API should know to respond with a `400 Bad Request` and an appropriately formatted response body.

Once the request is parsed and its inputs validated, you're ready to hand it to the service layer, which will trade the inputs provided by the request into the outputs it requires. (Bear with me for a minute; we'll go deeper into the service layer.) Once the service layer gets back to you, you can finally figure out if the request can be fulfilled or not and respond with the corresponding status code and response data. What exactly is the service layer supposed to do, then? Glad you asked!

9.3.5   *Service layer*

At the service level, also known as the business logic layer, the request is processed, data is pulled from the data layer, and a representation of that data is returned. At this point it makes sense to validate business rules, whereas it wasn't a responsibility of the routing layer.

For instance, if a user tries to create a new product with a price of `very expensive` or `-1`, it's up to the routing layer to figure out that's not a valid money input. If the selected product category expects products in the `$20 - $150` range and the product is priced `$200`, then it's up to the service layer to figure out that the request can't be fulfilled.

The service layer is also responsible for doing any necessary data aggregation. Although it's likely that the routing layer will only have to make a single call into the service layer to get what it needs, the same isn't true for the interaction between the service and data layers. As an example, the service layer may need to get a list of articles on a news site and hand that over to a service that performs a processing task on the contents of those articles, finding commonalities and eventually returning a list of articles related to each other.

In this regard, the service layer is the event organizer in the architecture, in that it will query and command other layers to provide it with the means to produce a meaningful response. Let's quickly comb through the specifics of how the data layer should be shaped.

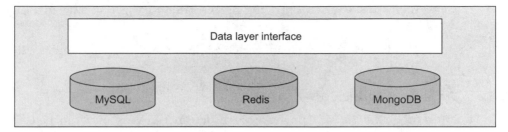

Figure 9.2   The data layer interface and a few underlying data stores

9.3.6   *Data layer*

The data layer is the only layer that's meant to access a persistence component, which would be your database. The goal of the data layer is to ensure a consistent API is provided, regardless of the underlying data store being used. If you're persisting data in MongoDB, MySQL, or Redis, the API offered by the data layer will hide that detail from the service layer by providing a consistent API that isn't tied to any particular persistence model.

Figure 9.2 shows the potential data stores that could be behind the data layer's interface. Note that this interface doesn't necessarily hide a single type of backing data store: you could be using both Redis and MySQL, for instance.

The data layer is typically thin, bridging the gap between the service and persistence layers. Results produced by the data layer are also expected to be consistent, because changing the underlying persistence model truly won't make a difference.

Although not recommended, in small projects it's plausible to merge the service layer and the data layer if there won't be any significant changes in the persistence model of the application. Keep in mind that splitting the two is easy at first, but doing so once you have dozens of services that consume dozens of different data models becomes increasingly complex and nontrivial. That's why, if possible, it's recommended to split these two layers from the get-go.

The last topic we'll go over in this chapter is how services like these should be consumed on the client side.

9.4   *Consuming a REST API on the client side*

When intensively interacting with a REST API layer on the client side of a web application, it's often prudent to come up with a thin layer to act as an intermediary between the API and the core of your application. This layer relies on creating a shared infrastructure to emit requests against the API in exchange for the following list of benefits enumerated:

- A high-level overview of the requests taking place in your application
- Allows you to perform caching and avoid extra requests
- Manage errors in a single place in your application, providing a consistent UI experience

- Ability to shoot down pending requests when navigating away in a single-page application

I'll start by describing what creating such a layer would entail, and then we'll move on to the specifics.

9.4.1   *The request handling layer*

Putting together such a layer can be tackled in two ways. You can patch the XHR implementation in browsers, guaranteeing that any AJAX requests made by your application will have to go through the proxy you patched into XHR, or you can create a wrapper around XHR and use it every time an AJAX request takes place. The latter approach is typically regarded as being "cleaner," because it doesn't affect the native behavior provided by the browser the way the monkey-patching approach does, which sometimes leads to unexpected behavior. This is often reason enough to prefer creating a simple wrapper around XHR calls and using that instead of the native APIs.

I've created a library called `measly` exactly with this purpose in mind. It takes the less invasive wrapper approach, because that way it won't affect code that's unaware of how Measly behaves, and it allows you to easily associate requests with different parts of the DOM. It also allows for caching and event handling, both of which can be limited to the context of a particular DOM element or global. I'll walk you through several key features in `measly`. To get started, you'll have to install it from npm. It's also available on Bower under the same name.

```
npm install --save measly
```

After you install `measly`, you'll be ready to get into the next section, where we'll explore how to use it to make sure requests don't end up causing unintended side effects.

9.4.2   *Shooting down old requests*

Single-page web applications are all the rage these days. In traditional web applications, the user agent aborts all pending requests when navigating away to another page, but what about single-page applications (SPA)? If you're developing an SPA, chances are that you hope stray requests won't corrupt the state of your application when a human navigates to another page.

The following code is a generic example assuming a client-side MVC framework that broadcasts events when entering and leaving views. In this example you're creating a `measly` layer on the view container element and aborting all requests on that layer when leaving the view:

```
view.on('enter', function (container) {
  measly.layer({ context: container });
});
view.on('leave', function (container) {
  measly.find(container).abort();
});
```

Whenever you need to make an AJAX call, you'll have to look up the layer first. You can keep a reference around for convenience, as well. Using the `measly` layer to create requests is fairly straightforward. In this case you're making a request for `DELETE` `/api/products/:id`, deleting a product by ID using a REST API:

```
var layer = measly.find(container);

deleteButton.addEventListener('click', function () {
  layer.delete('/api/products/' + selectedItem.id);
});
```

Whenever you make a request, `measly` emits a series of events, letting you react to them. For example, if you want to know when a request succeeds you can use the `data` event, and if you want to listen for errors you can subscribe to the `error` event. You have two different places where you can listen for errors:

- At the request level directly, where you're notified only if a particular request results in an error.
- At a layer level, where you can learn about any requests that result in an error.

Each of these methods has obvious use cases. You definitely want to know when a request succeeds so you can do something specific armed with the response data.

You may also need to learn about any errors that originate in your application on a global scale, so you can display the corresponding UI elements to notify the human about those errors or to send reports to a logging service.

9.4.3 Consistent AJAX error management

The following listing explains how you can show a UI dialog whenever an AJAX error occurs, but only if the status code in the response equals 500, meaning there was an internal server error. You'll fill the dialog with the error message provided by the response, and after a short timeout, you'll hide it again.

> **Listing 9.2   Showing a UI dialog box when an AJAX error occurs**

```
var errorDialog = document.querySelector('.error-dialog');

measly.on(500, function (err) {
  errorDialog.innerText = err.message;
  errorDialog.classList.add('error-dialog-open');

  setTimeout(hideErrorDialog, 3000);
});
function hideErrorDialog () {
  errorDialog.classList.remove('error-dialog-open');
}
```

querySelector is a native API for finding DOM elements using CSS selectors.

classList is a native API for manipulating the CSS classes found on a DOM element.

To be frank, this is a terribly uninteresting approach, and not something you couldn't accomplish. A more useful scenario would be in-context validation. In this case, watch out for `400 Bad Request` responses, which is the status code that should be assigned by the API to a validation failure response. Measly will set `this` in the event handler as the request object, allowing you to access important properties of the request, such as its DOM context element. The following code intercepts any `400 Bad Request` response and turns it into a validation message in the context of a piece of DOM. If you're binding Measly close enough to the visual context of the requests you create, humans won't have any trouble finding your list of validation messages:

```
measly.on(400, function (err, body) {
  var message = document.createElement('pre');
  message.classList.add('validation-messages');
  message.innerText = body.validation.messages.join('\n');
  this.context.appendChild(message);
});
```

The best part is that you get this almost for free! Because you're already using the context to make sure requests are aborted whenever you switch views, you may only have to declare a few child layers where it makes sense to do so, such as partial views or HTML forms. The last point I'd like to bring up is caching rules in Measly.

MEASLY CACHING RULES

Measly lets you cache two ways. First, it allows you to define an amount of time a response is considered fresh, meaning that subsequent requests for the same resource will result in the cached response for as long as the cached copy is fresh. The following listing shows how you can request to cache the response for 60 seconds, and then when a button is clicked Measly either uses the cached copy (if within 60 seconds since the last request) or makes a new request if the data has been updated.

Listing 9.3   Caching files with Measly

```
measly.get('/api/products', {
  cache: 60000
});
queryButton.addEventListener('click', function () {
  var req = measly.get('/api/products', {
    cache: 60000
  });
  req.on('data', function (body) {
    console.log(body);
  });
})
```

The other way you can avoid querying the server with an unwarranted HTTP request is to prevent it manually. The following listing is an example where a list of products is cached by hand.

Listing 9.4   Manually preventing unwarranted HTTP requests

```
var saved = []; // a list of products that you know to be fresh
var req = measly.get('/api/products');
req.on('ready', function () {
  if (computable) {
    req.prevent(null, saved);
```

```
  }
});
req.on('data', function (body) {
  console.log(body);
});
```

You'll find a quick demo into how Measly works in the accompanying code samples for this chapter, listed as ch09/01_a-measly-client-side-layer. In the demo I show how to create different contexts to contain different requests to a portion of the DOM.

All in all, `measly` may not be the answer you're looking for, but along with the rest of this book I hope it gave you something to think about!

9.5   Summary

That wasn't that hard, was it? We covered a lot of ground, and looked at many best practices along the way:

- Responsible API design follows the REST constraint model by providing conventional endpoints, sanitizing inputs, and also providing consistent outputs.
- Paging, throttling, and caching in a REST API are all necessary to provide a fast and safe API service.
- Documentation should be taken seriously to lower the friction introduced by your API.
- You should develop a thin API layer backed by a domain logic layer and a data layer.
- A thin client-side layer helps you assign a context to AJAX requests, validate responses, and render HTTP errors on the user interface.

appendix A
Modules in Node.js

This appendix covers things you need to know about modules and Node.js to use both effectively in your Grunt builds. Node.js is a platform built on top of the V8 JavaScript engine, the same engine that makes JavaScript in Google Chrome a reality. Grunt, the build tool you use in this book, runs on Node. Node is single threaded, as all JavaScript is.

Node comes with a nice little companion command-line interface (CLI) utility called npm, which is used to fetch and install packages from the node-packaged modules registry. Throughout the book, you'll learn how to use the npm tool as needed. Let's install Node.js first, since npm comes bundled with it!

A.1 Installing Node.js

You have a few options for installing Node. If you're the point-and-click type, then you might want to head over to their website, http://nodejs.org, and click on the big green Install button. Once the binaries are downloaded, unpack them if needed, and then double-click to install them. That's it.

If you prefer to install things in your terminal, consider nvm, a user-created Node version manager. To install nvm, you can type the following line into your terminal:

```
curl https://raw.github.com/creationix/nvm/master/install.sh | bash
```

Once nvm is installed, reopen your terminal window to get access to the nvm CLI. If you have any issues installing nvm, refer to their public repository at https://github.com/creationix/nvm. Once you have nvm you can install a version of Node, as shown in the following code:

```
nvm install 0.10
nvm alias default stable
```

The first command installs the latest stable version of Node in the `0.10.x` branch. The second command makes it so that any terminal window you open from now on will have access to the Node version you installed.

Great, now you have Node! Time for you to learn more about its module system, which is based on the CommonJS module's spec.

A.2 *The module system*

Node applications have an entry point that's specified when executing a node process. For example, if you run `node app.js`, your Node process will use `app.js` as the entry point. To load other pieces of code, you have to use the `require` function. This function takes a path and loads the module found in that location. The path passed to `require` can be

- A path relative to the script you `require` from, starting with `'.'`. For example, if you do `require('./main.js')`, you'll load a file that's in the same directory as the requiring script. We can also use `..` to get a script in a parent directory.
- A path to a directory. In these cases, `require` will look for a file named `index.js` in the provided directory and give you that.
- An absolute path. This one is rarely used, but you could provide an absolute file path, as shown in the following code:

```
require('/Users/nico/dev/buildfirst/main.js')
```

- The name of a package. Packages can be required by just providing their name; for example, to get the `async` package, you should use `require('async')`. Most of the time, this is effectively the same as doing `require('./node_modules/async')`.

A.3 *Exporting functionality*

Requiring modules wouldn't be useful if you couldn't interact with them. Modules can export functionality, effectively their API, by assigning to `module.exports`. As an example, consider the following module:

```
var mine = 'gold';

module.exports = function (pure) {
    return pure + mine;
};
```

If you fetched this module using `var thing = require('./thing.js')`, then `thing` would be assigned whatever `module.exports` ended up becoming inside `thing.js`. It is interesting to note that, unlike the browser model, where there are implicit globals assigned to `window`, the CommonJS module system keeps variables you declare in a module private unless you explicitly make them public by assigning to `module.exports`. Node has a `global` object you can assign to, which is called `global`, but using it is discouraged because that would break the modularity principle.

A.4   *Regarding packages*

Dependencies are kept in a `package.json` file, which is used by `npm` to figure out what packages you need to execute an application. When installing a package, you can provide a `--save` flag to have `npm` automatically persist that dependency to the `package.json` manifest, so you don't have to do that by hand. Dependencies in `package.json` get installed whenever you run `npm install` without any arguments.

Local dependencies are installed to a `node_modules` directory, which should be ignored in version control. In the case of Git, you can add a line containing `node_modules` to a file named `.gitignore`, and Git will know not to revision those files.

That's all you need to know about Node to use it effectively in your Grunt builds.

appendix B
Introduction to Grunt

Grunt is a tool that allows you to write, configure, and automate tasks—such as minifying a JavaScript file or compiling a LESS style sheet—for your application.

LESS is a CSS preprocessor, which is covered in chapter 2. Minifying is essentially creating a smaller file by removing white space and many syntax tree optimizations. These tasks can also be related to code quality, such as running unit tests (covered in chapter 8) or executing a code coverage tool such as JSHint. They could certainly be related to the deployment process: maybe deploying the application over FTP, or preparing to deploy it, generating API documentation.

Grunt is merely a vehicle to execute your build tasks. These tasks are defined using plugins, as explained next.

B.1   *Grunt plugins*

Grunt only provides the framework; you're in charge of picking the right plugins to perform the tasks you need. For example, you might use the `grunt-contrib-concat` to bundle assets together. You also need to configure these plugins to do what you want; for example, providing a list of files to bundle and the path to the resulting bundled file.

Plugins can define one or more Grunt tasks. These plugins are written and configured using JavaScript on the Node platform. The Node community developed and maintains hundreds of ready-made Grunt plugins, which you only need to configure, as you'll see in a moment. You can also create Grunt plugins yourself if you can't find one that suits your particular needs.

B.2   *Tasks and targets*

Tasks can be configured to conform to multiple targets, and each target is defined by adding more data when configuring the task. A common use of task targets is to compile an application for different distributions, as explained in chapter 3.

Targets are useful for reusing the same task for slightly different purposes. LESS is an expressive language that compiles to CSS. You might have LESS task targets that compile different parts of your application. Maybe you need to use different targets because one of them makes debugging easier for you by adding source maps that point to the original LESS code, while the other target might go as far as minifying your style sheet.

B.3 Command-line interface

Grunt comes with a command-line interface (CLI), called `grunt`, which you can use to run your tasks. As an example of how this tool works, let's analyze the following statement:

```
grunt less:debug mocha
```

Assuming you've already configured Grunt, which you'll learn about in a moment, this statement would execute the `debug` target for the `less` task, and, if that task succeeded, then any targets configured for the `mocha` task would get executed. It's important to note that if a Grunt task fails, Grunt won't attempt to run any more tasks. Instead, it will exit after printing the reasons why it failed.

It's worth mentioning that tasks are executed serially: the next task begins once the current task finishes. They don't run in parallel. Instead of giving the CLI a full task list every time, you can use task aliases: tasks that execute a list of tasks. If you use the special name `default` when creating an alias, then the tasks assigned to that alias will be run whenever the `grunt` CLI is executed without any task arguments.

Enough theory! Let's get our hands dirty with hands-on Grunting; you'll start by installing Grunt and expand on all of the areas we've discussed. To install Grunt, the first thing you'll need is Node, the platform Grunt works on. To install Node, head over to appendix A on Node, and then get right back here. I'll wait.

Okay, let's install the Grunt CLI. Using `npm` in your terminal, type the following command:

```
npm install --global grunt-cli
```

The `--global` flag tells `npm` that this isn't a project-level package install, but rather a system-wide install. Essentially, this will ultimately enable you to use the package from your command line directly. You can verify the CLI was installed properly by running the following command:

```
grunt --version
```

That should output the version number for the currently installed version of the Grunt CLI. Great! Everything you did so far was a one-time thing; you don't need to worry about doing any of those steps again. But how do you use Grunt?

B.4   *Using Grunt in a project*

Let's say you have a PHP web application (although the server-side language doesn't matter), and you want to automatically run a linter, which is a static analysis tool that can tell you about issues with the syntax you're using, whenever you change a Java-Script file.

The first thing you'll need is a `package.json` file in your project root. This is used by npm to keep a manifest of all the dependencies you have. This file doesn't need much; it needs to be a valid JSON object, so `{}` will do. Change the directory to your application's root directory and type the following into your terminal:

```
echo "{}" > package.json
```

Next, you'll have to install a few dependencies. You'll install grunt, which is the frame-work itself, not to be confused with `grunt-cli`, which looks things up and defers task execution to the locally installed grunt package. To get started, you'll also install `grunt-contrib-jshint`, an easy-to-configure task to run JSHint, a JavaScript lint tool, as a Grunt task. The `npm install` command allows you to install more than one pack-age at once, so let's do that:

```
npm install --save-dev grunt grunt-contrib-jshint
```

The `--save-dev` flag tells npm to include these packages in the `package.json` mani-fest, and tag them as development dependencies. It's a best practice to mark as a development dependency anything that shouldn't be executed in production servers. Build components should always run before executing the application.

You have the framework, the plugin, and the CLI; all that's missing is configuring the tasks, so you can start using Grunt.

B.5   *Configuring Grunt*

To configure Grunt, you need to create a `Gruntfile.js` file. That's where all your build task configuration and definitions will live. The following code is an example `Gruntfile.js`:

```
module.exports = function (grunt) {
  grunt.initConfig({
    jshint: {
      browser: ['public/js/**/*.js']
    }
  });
  grunt.loadNpmTasks('grunt-contrib-jshint');
  grunt.registerTask('default', ['jshint']);
};
```

As explained in appendix A on Node.js, where we discussed Common.JS modules, here the module exports a function, which Grunt will invoke, configuring your tasks. The `initConfig` method takes an object, which will serve as the configuration for all of your different tasks and targets. Each top-level property in this configuration object represents configuration for a particular task. For example, jshint contains the configuration for the jshint task. Properties in each task's configuration represent target configuration.

In this case, you're configuring the browser target for jshint to ['public/js/**/
*.js']. This is called a globbing pattern, and it's used to declare which files to target. You'll learn all about globbing patterns in a moment; for now it should suffice to say that it'll match any .js files in public/js or in a subdirectory.

The loadNpmTasks method tells Grunt, "Hey, load any tasks you can find in this Grunt plugin," so it's essentially loading the jshint task. You'll learn how to write your own tasks later.

Last, registerTask can define task aliases by passing it a task name and an array of tasks it should execute. You'll set it to jshint so it will run jshint:browser and any other jshint targets you might add in the future. The default name means that this task will be run whenever you execute grunt with no task arguments in the command line. Let's try that!

```
grunt
```

Congratulations, you've executed your first Grunt task! However, you're probably confused about the whole "globbing for files" thing; let's fix that.

B.6 Globbing patterns

Using patterns such as ['public/js/**/*.js'] helps quickly define what files to work with. These patterns are easy to follow, as long as you understand how to use them appropriately. Glob allows you to write plain text to refer to real file system paths. For example, you could use docs/api.txt without any special characters, and that would match the file at docs/api.txt. Note that this is a relative path, and that it'll be relative to your Gruntfile.

If you add special characters into the mix, things get interesting. For instance, changing your last example to docs/*.txt helps us match all text files in the docs directory. If you'd like to include subdirectories as well, then you need to use **, known as the globstar pattern: docs/**/*.txt.

B.6.1 Brace expressions

Then there's brace expansion. Suppose you want to match many different types of images; you might want to use something akin to the following pattern: images/
*.{png,gif,jpg}. That'd match any images ending in .png, .gif, and .jpg. It's not limited to extensions, although that's the most common use case. You could also use brace expansion to match different directories: public/{js,css}/**/*. Note that we're excluding the extension. That works fine; the star will match any file type and not be limited to one in particular.

B.6.2 Negation expressions

Last, there are negation expressions and these are somewhat tricky to get right. *Negation expressions* can be defined as "remove the matching results from what you've matched so far." Patterns are processed in order, so inclusion and exclusion order is significant. Negation patterns begin with an `!`. Here's a common use case: `['js/**/*.js', '!js/vendor/**/*.js']`. That says, "Include everything that's in the `js` directory, but not if it's in `js/vendor`." That's useful for linting code you've authored, while leaving third-party libraries alone.

There's one particular caveat of globbing I'd like to address; I often read people complaining about `['js', '!js/vendor']` "not working," and the reason for that is rather simple to understand now that you know how globbing works. The first globbing pattern will match the `js` directory itself, and the `!js/vendor` won't do anything. Later, the `js` directory will be expanded to every file in it, including those in `js/vendor`. A quick fix to this issue is to have the Globber expand the directories for you, using globstars: `['js/**/*.js', '!js/vendor/**']`.

There are two more topics for you to gulp down: configuring tasks and creating your own ones. Let's go ahead and see how we can configure Grunt to run a task from the ground up.

B.7   *Setting up a task*

Now you're going to learn how to set up a random task...by browsing the internet! As a quick-start trick, let's go back to the original example from section B.1. Remember how you configured it to run JSHint? Here's the code you used:

```
module.exports = function (grunt) {
  grunt.initConfig({
    jshint: {
      browser: ['public/js/**/*.js']
    }
  });
  grunt.loadNpmTasks('grunt-contrib-jshint');
  grunt.registerTask('default', ['jshint']);
};
```

Let's suppose you want to minify (covered in chapter 2) your CSS style sheets, and then concatenate them into a single file. You could Google around for grunt plugins to do that, or you might visit http://gruntjs.com/plugins and look around for yourself. Go ahead and visit that page and then type `css`. One of the first results you'll see is `grunt-contrib-cssmin`, and it'll link to the page for that package on the npm website.

On npm, you'll usually find detailed README files, and links to the complete source code on GitHub repositories. In this case, it instructs you to install the package from npm and add a `loadNpmTasks` to your `Gruntfile.js`, as shown in the following code:

```
module.exports = function (grunt) {
  grunt.initConfig({
    jshint: {
      browser: ['public/js/**/*.js']
    }
  });
  grunt.loadNpmTasks('grunt-contrib-jshint');
```

```
grunt.loadNpmTasks('grunt-contrib-cssmin');
grunt.registerTask('default', ['jshint']);
};
```

You'd also have to install the package from npm, the way you did with grunt-contrib-jshint earlier:

```
npm install --save-dev grunt-contrib-cssmin
```

Now all you need to do is to configure it. Grunt projects are usually well documented, giving you a few configuration examples on their home pages, as well as detailed lists of all the options available to them. Packages named grunt-contrib-* were developed by the team behind Grunt itself, so they should mostly work without any problems. When canvassing for the right package for a task, move on if something doesn't work, or isn't well documented. You don't have to marry them. Popularity (npm installs and GitHub stars) are good indicators of how good a package is.

It turns out that the first use example shows that you can also concatenate your CSS with this package, so you don't need an extra task to do that. Here's that example, showing how you can combine two files while minifying them using grunt-contrib-cssmin:

```
cssmin: {
  combine: {
    files: {
      'path/to/output.css': ['path/to/input_one.css', 'path/to/
      input_two.css']
    }
  }
}
```

You can easily adapt and integrate that with your needs. You'll also add a build task alias. Aliases are useful for defining workflows, as you'll see throughout part 1. For instance, chapter 3 uses them to define the debug and release workflows:

```
module.exports = function (grunt) {
  grunt.initConfig({
    jshint: {
      browser: ['public/js/**/*.js']
    },
    cssmin: {
      all: {
        files: { 'build/css/all.min.css': ['public/css/**/*.css'] }
      }
    }
  });
  grunt.loadNpmTasks('grunt-contrib-jshint');
  grunt.loadNpmTasks('grunt-contrib-cssmin');
  grunt.registerTask('default', ['jshint']);
  grunt.registerTask('build', ['cssmin']);
};
```

That's it! If you run `grunt build` in your terminal, it'll bundle your CSS together and then minify it, writing it to the `all.min.css` file. You can find this example, along with the others we've discussed so far, in the accompanying source code samples, under `appendix/introduction-to-grunt`. Let's wrap up this appendix by explaining how you can write your own Grunt task.

B.8   *Creating custom tasks*

Grunt has two kinds of tasks: multitasks and regular tasks. The difference, as you might suspect, is that multitasks allow consumers to set up different task targets and run them individually. In practice, almost all Grunt tasks are multitasks. Let's walk through creating one!

You'll create a task that can count words in a list of files, and then have it fail if it counts more words than what it expected. To begin with, let's glance at this piece of code:

```
grunt.registerMultiTask('wordcount', function () {
    var options = this.options({
      threshold: 0
    });
});
```

Here, you're setting a default value for the `threshold` option, which can be overwritten when the task gets configured, as you'll see in a minute. Because you used `registerMultiTask`, you can support multiple task targets. Now you need to go through the list of files, read them, and count the words in them:

```
var total = 0;
this.files.forEach(function (file) {
  file.src.forEach(function (src) {
    if (grunt.file.isDir(src)) {
      return;
    }
    var data = grunt.file.read(src);
    var words = data.split(/[^\w]+/g).length;
    total += words;
    grunt.verbose.writeln(src, 'contains', words, 'words.');
  });
});
```

Grunt will provide a `files` object, which you can use to loop through the files, filtering out the directories and reading data out of the files. Once you've computed the word counts, you can print the result and fail if the `threshold` was exceeded:

```
if (options.threshold) {
  if (total > options.threshold) {
    grunt.log.error('Threshold of', options.threshold, 'exceeded. Found',
      total, 'words.');
    grunt.fail.warn('Too many words');
  } else {
    grunt.log.ok(total, 'words found in total.');
  }
```

```
} else {
  grunt.log.writeln(total, 'words found in total.');
}
```

Last, all you have to do is configure a task target, the way you did before:

```
wordcount: {
  capped: {
    files: {
      src: ['text/**/*.txt']
    },
    options: {
      threshold: 3000
    }
  }
}
```

If the word count for all those files is more than 3,000, the task will fail. Note that if you hadn't provided a threshold, it would use the default value of 0, which you specified in the task. This is enough information to understand Grunt, which we introduced in chapter 1. In chapter 2, you'll get a deeper knowledge of build tasks themselves, how those should work, and how you can compose tasks to create a build workflow for development and another one for releases and deployments.

appendix C
Picking your build tool

Deciding on a technology is always difficult. You don't want to make commitments you can't back out of, but eventually you have to choose something. Committing to a build technology is no different in this regard: it's an important choice and you should treat it as such.

For the purposes of this book, I decided on Grunt as my build tool of choice. I made an effort to not go overboard on Grunt-specific concepts, but rather to explain build processes in the grand scheme of things, using Grunt as an accessory—the means to an end. I chose Grunt for several reasons; a few of these are shown in the following list:

- Grunt has a healthy community around it, even on Windows.
- It's widely popular; it's even used beyond the Node community.
- It's easy to learn; you pick plugins and configure them. No advanced concepts are used and no prior knowledge is needed.

These are all good reasons to use Grunt to teach build processes in a book, but I want to make it clear I don't think Grunt is the single best option out there; other popular build tools might fit your needs better than Grunt.

I wrote this appendix to help you understand the differences between the three build tools I use most often in front-end development workflows:

- Grunt, the configuration-driven build tool that you use throughout this book
- npm, a package manager that can also double as a build tool
- Gulp, a code-driven build tool that's somewhere between Grunt and npm

I'll also lay out the situations in which a particular tool may be better than the others.

You should read part 1 and appendix A of the book before going through this appendix. Grunt is introduced in appendix A and covered throughout part 1. I

284

assume basic knowledge of Grunt in this appendix. As a first step, let's discuss where Grunt excels.

C.1   Grunt: the good parts

The single best aspect of Grunt is its ease of use. It enables programmers to develop build flows using JavaScript almost effortlessly. All that's required is searching for the appropriate plugin, reading its documentation, and then installing and configuring it. This ease of use means members of large development teams, who are often of varying skill levels, don't have any trouble tweaking the build flow to meet the latest needs of the project. The team doesn't need to be fluent in Node, either; they need to add properties to the configuration object and task names to the different arrays that make up the build flow.

Grunt's plugin base is large enough that you'll rarely find yourself developing your own build tasks, which also enables you and your team to rapidly develop a build process. This rapid development is crucial if you're going for a build first approach, even when taking small steps and progressively developing your build flows.

It's also feasible to manage deployments through Grunt, as many packages exist to accommodate for those tasks, such as `grunt-git`, `grunt-rsync`, and `grunt-ec2`.

C.2   Grunt: the bad parts

Where does Grunt fall short? It may get too verbose if you have a significantly large build flow. It's often hard to make sense of the build flow as a whole once it has been in development for a while. When the task count in your build flows gets to the double digits, it's almost guaranteed that you'll find yourself having to run targets that belong to the same task individually, so you can compose the flow in the right order.

Because tasks are configured declaratively, you'll also have a hard time figuring out the order in which tasks get executed. In addition, your team should be dedicated to writing maintainable code when it comes to your builds. In the case of Grunt, you'll maintain separate files for the configuration of each task, or at least for each of the build flows that your team uses.

Now that we've identified the good and the bad in Grunt, as well as the situations in which it might be a good fit for your project, let's talk about npm: how it can be used as a build tool and its differences from Grunt.

C.3   npm as a build tool

To use npm as a build tool, you'll need a package.json file and npm itself. Defining tasks for npm is as easy as adding properties to a `scripts` object in your package manifest. The name of the property will be used as the task name, and the value will be the command you want to execute. The following snippet represents a typical package.json file, using the JSHint command-line interface to run a linter through your JavaScript files and check for errors. Using npm, you can run any shell command at your disposal:

> ### Grunt in a nutshell
>
> Grunt has the following benefits:
> - Thousands of plugins that do what you need.
> - Easy-to-understand and tweak configuration.
> - Only a basic understanding of JavaScript is necessary.
> - Supports cross-platform development. Yes, even Windows!
> - Works great for most teams.
>
> Grunt has a few drawbacks:
> - Configuration-based build definitions become increasingly unwieldy as they grow larger.
> - It's hard to follow build flows when there are many multitarget task definitions involved.
> - Grunt is considerably slower than other build tools.

```
{
  "scripts": {
    "test": "jshint . --exclude node_modules"
  },
  "devDependencies": {
    "jshint": "^2.5.1"
  }
}
```

Once the task is defined, it can be executed in your command line by running the following command:

```
npm run test
```

Note that npm provides shortcuts for specific task names. In the case of `test`, you can do `npm test` and omit the `run` verb. You can compose build flows by chaining `npm run` commands together in your script declarations. The following listing allows you to run the `unit` task right after the `lint` task by executing the `npm test` command.

Listing C.1 Chaining npm `run` commands together to make build flows

```
{
  "scripts": {
    "lint": "jshint . --exclude node_modules",
    "unit": "tape test/*",
    "test": "npm run lint && npm run unit"
  },
  "devDependencies": {
    "jshint": "^2.5.1",
    "tape": "^2.10.2"
  }
}
```

You can also schedule tasks as background jobs, making them asynchronous. Suppose you have the following package file, where you'll copy a directory in your JavaScript build flow and compile a Stylus style sheet during your CSS build flow (Stylus is a CSS preprocessor). In this case, running the tasks asynchronously is ideal. You can achieve that using & as a separator, or after a command, as shown in the following listing of your package manifest. Afterward, you can execute npm run build to process both steps concurrently.

Listing C.2 Using Stylus

```
{
  "scripts": {
    "build-js": "cp -r src/js/vendor bin/js",
    "build-css": "stylus src/css/all.styl -o bin/css",
    "build": "npm run build-js & npm run build-css"
  },
  "devDependencies": {
    "stylus": "^0.45.0"
  }
}
```

Sometimes a shell command won't suffice, and you may need a Node package such as stylus or jshint, as you saw in the last few examples. These dependencies should be installed through npm.

C.3.1 *Installing npm task dependencies*

The JSHint CLI isn't necessarily available in your system, and you have two ways to install it:

- Globally, when using it from your command line
- Adding it as a devDependency, when using it in an npm run task

If you want to use the tool directly from your command line, and not in an npm run task, you should install it globally using the -g flag in the following command:

```
npm install -g jshint
```

If you're using the package in an npm run task, then you should add it as a dev-Dependency, as shown in the following command. That allows npm to find the JSHint package on any system where the package dependencies are installed, rather than expecting the environment to have JSHint installed globally. This applies to any CLI tools that aren't readily available in operating systems.

```
npm install --save-dev jshint
```

You aren't limited to using only CLI tools. In fact, npm can run any shell script. Let's dig into that!

C.3.2 *Using shell scripts in npm tasks*

The following example is a script that runs on Node and displays a random emoji string. The first line tells the environment that the script is in Node.

```
#!/usr/bin/env node
```

```
var emoji = require('emoji-random');
var emo = emoji.random();

console.log(emo);
```

If you place that script in a file named `emoji` at the root of your project, you'd have to declare `emoji-random` as a dependency and add the command to the `scripts` object in the package manifest:

```
{
  "scripts": {
    "emoji": "./emoji"
  },
  "devDependencies": {
    "emoji-random": "^0.1.2"
  }
}
```

Once that's out of the way, running the command is merely a matter of invoking `npm run emoji` in your terminal, which will execute the command you specified as the value for `emoji` in the `scripts` property of your package manifest.

C.3.3   *npm and Grunt compared: the good and the bad*

Using npm as a build tool has several advantages over Grunt:

- You aren't constrained to Grunt plugins, and you can take advantage of all of npm, which hosts tens of thousands of packages.
- You won't need any additional CLI tooling or files other than `npm`, which you're already using to manage dependencies and your `package.json` manifest, where dependencies and your build commands are listed. Because `npm` runs CLI tools and Bash commands directly, it'll perform way better than Grunt could.

Take into account that one of the biggest disadvantages of Grunt is the fact that it's I/O bound. Most Grunt tasks read from disk and then write to disk. If you have several tasks working on the same files, chances are that the file will be read from disk multiple times. In Bash, commands can pipe the output of a command directly into the next one, avoiding the extra I/O overhead in Grunt.

Probably the biggest disadvantage to npm is the fact that Bash doesn't play well with Windows environments. Open source projects using `npm run` might run into issues when people try to fiddle with them on Windows. In a similar light, Windows developers will try to use alternatives to npm. That drawback pretty much rules out npm for projects that need to run on Windows.

Gulp, another build tool, presents similarities to both Grunt and npm, as you'll discover in a moment.

C.4   Gulp: the streaming build tool

Gulp is similar to Grunt in that it relies on plugins and it's cross-platform, supporting Windows users as well. Gulp is a code-driven build tool, in contrast with Grunt's declarative approach to task definition, making your task definitions a bit easier to read. Gulp is also similar to `npm run` in that it uses Node streams to read files and pipe data through functions that transform it into output that will end up written to disk. This means Gulp doesn't have the disk-intensive I/O issues you may observe when using Grunt. It's also faster than Grunt for the same reason: less time spent in I/O.

The main disadvantage to using Gulp is that it relies heavily on streams, pipes, and asynchronous code. Don't get me wrong; if you're into Node, that's definitely an advantage. But the issue with those concepts is that unless you and your team are well versed in Node, you'll probably run into issues dealing with streams if you have to build your own Gulp task plugins.

Gulp

There are a few things that are great about Gulp:

- High-quality plugins are readily available.
- Code-driven means your Gulpfile will be easier to follow than a configuration-driven Gruntfile.
- Faster than Grunt because it uses stream pipes rather than read and write to disk every time.
- Supports cross-platform development, the way Grunt does.

Gulp has drawbacks as well:

- It might be hard to learn if you don't have experience with Node.
- Developing quality plugins is hard for similar reasons.
- All of your team (current members and prospects) should be comfortable with streams and asynchronous code.
- The task dependency system leaves much to be desired.

When working in teams, Gulp isn't as prohibitive as npm. Most of your front-end team probably knows JavaScript, although chances are they're not that fluent in Bash scripting, and some of them may be using Windows! That's why I usually suggest keeping `npm run` to your personal projects and maybe using Gulp in projects where the team is comfy with Node, and Grunt everywhere else. That's my personal opinion; figure out what works best for you and your team. Also, you shouldn't constrain yourself to Grunt, Gulp, or `npm run` because those tools work for me. Do research and maybe you'll find a tool that you like even better than those three.

Let's walk through several examples to get a feel for what Gulp tasks look like.

RUNNING TESTS IN GULP

Gulp is similar to Grunt in its conventions. In Grunt there's a `Gruntfile.js` file, used to define your build tasks, and in Gulp the file needs to be named `Gulpfile.js` instead. The other minor difference is that in the case of Gulp, the CLI is contained in the same package as the task runner, so you have to install the `gulp` package from npm both locally and globally:

```
touch Gulpfile.js
npm install -g gulp
npm install --save-dev gulp
```

To get started, I'll create a Gulp task to lint a JavaScript file, using JSHint the way you've already seen with Grunt and `npm run`. In the case of Gulp, you have to install the `gulp-jshint` Gulp plugin for JSHint:

```
npm install --save-dev gulp-jshint
```

Now that you're fully equipped with the CLI that you globally installed, the local `gulp` installation, and the `gulp-jshint` plugin, you can put together the build task to run the linter. To define build tasks with Gulp, you have to write them programmatically in the `Gulpfile.js` file.

First, use `gulp.task`, passing it a task name and a function. The function contains all of the code necessary to run that task. Here you should use `gulp.src` to create a read stream into your source files. You can provide the paths to individual files, or use a globbing pattern such as the ones you've seen in your experiences learning about Grunt. That same stream should be piped into the JSHint plugin, which you can configure or use with the defaults it comes with. Then all you have to do is pipe the results of the JSHint task through a reporter and have it print the results to your terminal. All of what I described results in the following Gulpfile:

```
var gulp = require('gulp');
var jshint = require('gulp-jshint');

gulp.task('test', function () {
  return gulp
    .src('./sample.js')                          By returning the stream, Gulp knows to
    .pipe(jshint())                              wait until data stops flowing through it.
    .pipe(jshint.reporter('default'));
});
```

I should also mention that you're returning the stream so Gulp understands that it should wait for the data to stop flowing before it considers the task completed. You can use a custom JSHint reporter to make the output more concise and easier to read by humans. JSHint reporters don't need to be Gulp plugins, so you can use `jshint-stylish` for example. Let's install it locally:

```
npm install --save-dev jshint-stylish
```

The updated Gulpfile should look like the following code. It'll load the `jshint-stylish` module to format the reporting output.

```
var gulp = require('gulp');
var jshint = require('gulp-jshint');
```

```
gulp.task('test', function () {
  return gulp
    .src('./sample.js')
    .pipe(jshint())
    .pipe(jshint.reporter('jshint-stylish'));
});
```

You're done! That's all you have to do to declare a Gulp task named `test`. It can be run using the following command, provided you installed the `gulp` CLI globally:

```
gulp test
```

That was a trivial example. You can pipe the output of the JSHint linter through a reporter that will print the results of the linting test. You can also write output to disk using gulp.dest, which creates a write stream. Let's step through another build task.

BUILDING A LIBRARY IN GULP

To get started, let's do the bare minimum—read from disk with `gulp.src` and write back to disk piping the contents of the source file into `gulp.dest`, effectively copying the file into another directory:

```
var gulp = require('gulp');

gulp.task('build', function () {
  return gulp
    .src('./sample.js')
    .pipe(gulp.dest('./build'));
});
```

Copying the file is nice, but it doesn't minify its contents. To do that, you have to use a Gulp plugin. In this case you can use `gulp-uglify`, a plugin for the popular UglifyJS minifier:

```
var gulp = require('gulp');
var uglify = require('gulp-uglify');

gulp.task('build', function () {
  return gulp
    .src('./sample.js')
    .pipe(uglify())
    .pipe(gulp.dest('./build'));
});
```

As you probably realized, streams let you add more plugins while only reading and writing to disk once. As an example, let's pipe through `gulp-size` as well, which will calculate the size of the contents in the buffer and print that to the terminal. Note that if you add it before Uglify then you get the unminified size, and if you add it after, you get the minified size. You could also do both!

```
var gulp = require('gulp');
var uglify = require('gulp-uglify');
var size = require('gulp-size');

gulp.task('build', function () {
```

```
  return gulp
    .src('./sample.js')
    .pipe(uglify())
    .pipe(size())
    .pipe(gulp.dest('./build'));
});
```

To reinforce the point on the ability to add or remove pipes as needed, let's add one last plugin. This time you'll use `gulp-header` to add license information to the minified piece of code, such as the name, the package version, and the license type. To run the example shown in the following listing, enter `gulp build` in your command line.

Listing C.3   Using `gulp-header` to add license information

```
var gulp = require('gulp');
var uglify = require('gulp-uglify');
var size = require('gulp-size');
var header = require('gulp-header');
var pkg = require('./package.json');
var info = '// <%= pkg.name %>@v<%= pkg.version %>, <%= pkg.license %>\n';

gulp.task('build', function () {
  return gulp
    .src('./sample.js')
    .pipe(uglify())
    .pipe(header(info, { pkg : pkg }))
    .pipe(size())
    .pipe(gulp.dest('./build'));
});
```

As in Grunt, in Gulp you can define flows by passing in an array of task names to `gulp.task`, instead of a function. The main difference between Grunt and Gulp in this regard is that Gulp executes these dependencies asynchronously, while Grunt executes them synchronously.

```
gulp.task('build', ['build-js', 'build-css']);
```

In Gulp, if you want to run tasks synchronously you have to declare a task as a dependency and then define your own task. All dependencies are executed before your task starts.

```
gulp.task('build', ['dep'], function () {
  // here goes the task that depends on 'dep'
});
```

If you take anything away from this appendix, it should be that it doesn't matter which tool you use, as long as it allows you to compose the build flows you need in a way that doesn't make you work too hard for it.

appendix D
JavaScript code
quality guide

This style guide aims to provide the ground rules for an application's JavaScript code, so it's highly readable and consistent across different developers on a team. The focus is put on quality and coherence across different pieces of your application.

D.1 Module organization

This style guide assumes you're using a module system such as CommonJS,[1] AMD,[2] ES6 Modules,[3] or any other kind of module system. For a comprehensive introduction to module systems head over to chapter 5; I'll wait.

Module systems provide individual scoping, avoid leaks to the global project, and improve code base organization by automating dependency graph generation, instead of having to resort to manually creating tens of <script> tags.

Module systems also provide Dependency Injection patterns, which are crucial when it comes to testing individual components in isolation.

D.1.1 Strict mode

Always put "use strict";[4] at the top of your modules. Strict mode allows you to catch nonsensical behavior, discourages poor practices, and is faster because it allows compilers to make certain assumptions about your code.

---

[1] The CommonJS module specification hosts a wiki page at http://bevacqua.io/bf/commonjs.
[2] RequireJS has a comprehensive article on the purpose of AMD at http://bevacqua.io/bf/amd.
[3] Getting started with ES6 is much easier these days! See http://bevacqua.io/bf/es6-intro.
[4] The Mozilla Developer Network (MDN) has a great article explaining Strict Mode in JavaScript at http://bevacqua.io/bf/strict.

D.1.2   Spacing

Spacing must be consistent across every file in the application. To this end, using Editor-Config is highly encouraged. EditorConfig works by dropping an `.editorconfig`[5] file in your project root, and then you should install the EditorConfig plugin for your favorite text editor. Here are the defaults I suggest to get started with JavaScript indentation:

```
# editorconfig.org
root = true
[*]
indent_style = space
indent_size = 2
end_of_line = lf
charset = utf-8
trim_trailing_whitespace = true
insert_final_newline = true
[*.md]
trim_trailing_whitespace = false
```

EditorConfig can take care of indentation transparently, and everyone can consistently produce the right amount of tabs or spaces by pressing the tab key. Settling for either tabs or spaces is up to the particularities of a project, but I recommend using two spaces for indentation.

Spacing doesn't only entail tabbing, but also the spaces before, after, and in between arguments of a function declaration. This kind of spacing is typically highly difficult to get right, and it'll be hard for most teams to even arrive at a scheme that will satisfy everyone.

```
function () {}

function( a, b ){}

function(a, b) {}

function (a,b) {}
```

Try to keep these differences to a minimum, but don't put much thought into it either.

Where possible, improve readability by keeping lines below the 80-character mark.

D.1.3   Semicolons

Automatic Semicolon Insertion (ASI) isn't a feature. Don't rely on it.[6] It's super complicated[7] and there's no practical reason to burden all of the developers in a team for not possessing the frivolous knowledge of how ASI works. Avoid headaches; avoid ASI. Always add semicolons where needed.

---

[5]   Learn more about EditorConfig at http://bevacqua.io/bf/editorconfig.
[6]   Ben Alman has good advice about why you should use semicolons instead of omitting them at http://bevacqua.io/bf/semicolons.
[7]   A guide to the inner workings of automatic semicolon insertion (ASI) is available at http://bevacqua.io/bf/asi.

D.1.4 Linting

Given that JavaScript doesn't require a compilation step that would take care of unde-clared variables, linting is almost a necessity. Again, don't use a linter that's super-opinionated about how the code should be styled, like `jslint`[8] is. Instead use some-thing more lenient, like `jshint`[9] or `eslint`[10]. Here are a few tips when using JSHint:

- Declare a `.jshintignore` file and include `node_modules`, `bower_components`, and so on.
- You can use a .jshintrc file like the one below to keep your rules together:

```
{
    "curly": true,
    "eqeqeq": true,
    "newcap": true,
    "noarg": true,
    "noempty": true,
    "nonew": true,
    "sub": true,
    "undef": true,
    "unused": true,
    "trailing": true,
    "boss": true,
    "eqnull": true,
    "strict": true,
    "immed": true,
    "expr": true,
    "latedef": "nofunc",
    "quotmark": "single",
    "indent": 2,
    "node": true
}
```

By no means are these rules the ones you should stick to, but it's important to find the sweet spot between not linting at all, and not being super-obnoxious about coding style. If left unchecked, you may succumb to common mistakes such as missing semi-colons or improperly closing string quotes, but if you go overboard you may find that your team spends more time taking care of code style than writing meaningful code.

D.2 Strings

Strings should always be quoted using the same quotation mark. Use ' or " consis-tently throughout your code base. Ensure the team is using the same quotation mark in every portion of JavaScript that's authored.

---

[8] JSLint, the original JavaScript linter, can still be used online today at http://bevacqua.io/bf/jslint.
[9] JSHint is a modern alternative that's popularly observed in build processes. Find it at http://bevacqua.io/bf/jshint.
[10] ESLint is yet another lint tooling effort, aiming to be less concerned about style checking. Find it at http://bevacqua.io/bf/eslint.

BAD STRINGS
```
var message = 'oh hai ' + name + "!";
```

GOOD STRINGS
```
var message = 'oh hai ' + name + '!';
```

Usually you'll be a happier JavaScript developer if you hack together a parameter-replacing method such as `util.format` in Node.[11] That way it'll be far easier to format your strings, and the code looks cleaner too.

BETTER STRINGS
```
var message = util.format('oh hai %s!', name);
```

You can implement something similar using the following piece of code:

```
function format () {
  var args = [].slice.call(arguments);
  var initial = args.shift();
  function replacer (text, replacement) {
    return text.replace('%s', replacement);
  }
  return args.reduce(replacer, initial);
}
```

To declare multiline strings, particularly when talking about HTML snippets, it's sometimes best to use an array as a buffer and then join its parts. The string concatenating style may be faster but it's also much harder to keep track of:

```
var html = [
  '<div>',
    format('<span class="monster">%s</span>', name),
  '</div>'
].join('');
```

With the array builder style, you can also push parts of the snippet and then join everything together at the end. This is what string templating engines such as Jade[12] prefer to do.

D.2.1 *Variable declaration*

Always declare variables in a consistent manner, and at the top of their scope. Keeping variable declarations to one-per-line is encouraged. Comma-first, a single `var` statement, multiple `var` statements, it's all fine, but be consistent across the project. Ensure that everyone on your team follows the style guide, for consistency.

INCONSISTENT DECLARATION
```
var foo = 1,
    bar = 2;
var baz;
var pony;
var a
  , b;
```

---

[11] The documentation for Node's util.format can be found at http://bevacqua.io/bf/util.format.
[12] Learn more about templating in Jade by visiting their GitHub repository at http://bevacqua.io/bf/jade.

or

```
var foo = 1;
if (foo > 1) {
  var bar = 2;
}
```

Note that the following example is okay not only because of its style, but also because the statements are consistent with each other.

CONSISTENT DECLARATIONS
```
var foo = 1;
var bar = 2;
var baz;
var pony;
var a;
var b;
var foo = 1;
var bar;
if (foo > 1) {
  bar = 2;
}
```

Variable declarations not immediately assigned a value can share the same line of code.

ACCEPTABLE DECLARATION
```
var a = 'a';
var b = 2;
var i, j;
```

D.3 *Conditionals*

Brackets are enforced. This, together with a reasonable spacing strategy, will help you avoid mistakes such as Apple's SSL/TLS bug.[13]

BAD CONDITIONALS
```
if (err) throw err;
```

GOOD CONDITIONALS
```
if (err) {
  throw err;
}
```

Avoid using == and != operators; always favor === and !==. These operators are called the "strict equality operators," whereas their counterparts will attempt to cast the operands[14] into the same value type. If possible, try to keep even single-statement conditionals in a multiline format.

BAD COERCING EQUALITY
```
function isEmptyString (text) {
  return text == '';
```

---

[13] A detailed report on Apple's "GOTO Fail" bug can be found at http://bevacqua.io/bf/gotofail.

[14] Equality operators have a dedicated page on MDN at http://bevacqua.io/bf/equality.

```
}
isEmptyString(0);
// <- true
```

GOOD STRICT EQUALITY

```
function isEmptyString (text) {
  return text === '';
}
isEmptyString(0);
// <- false
```

D.3.1   *Ternary operators*

Ternary operators are fine for clear-cut conditionals, but unacceptable for confusing choices. As a rule, if you can't eye-parse it as fast as your brain can interpret the text that declares the ternary operator, chances are it's probably too complicated for its own good.

jQuery is a prime example of a code base that's filled with nasty ternary operators.[15]

BAD TERNARY OPERATORS

```
function calculate (a, b) {
  return a && b ? 11 : a ? 10 : b ? 1 : 0;
}
```

GOOD TERNARY OPERATORS

```
function getName (mobile) {
  return mobile ? mobile.name : 'Generic Player';
}
```

In cases that may prove confusing, use `if` and `else` statements instead.

D.3.2   *Functions*

When declaring a function always use the function declaration form[16] instead of function expressions.[17] If you try to use your function expressions before they're assigned to a variable, you'll get an error. In contrast, function declarations are hoisted[18] to the top of the scope, meaning they'll work regardless of where you place them in your code. You can learn all the details about hoisting in chapter 5.

USING EXPRESSIONS IS BAD

```
var sum = function (x, y) {
  return x + y;
};
```

USING DECLARATIONS IS GOOD

```
function sum (x, y) {
  return x + y;
}
```

---

[15] A few examples of ternary operator misuse in jQuery can be found at http://bevacqua.io/bf/jquery-ternary.

[16] StackOverflow has an answer that covers function declarations at http://bevacqua.io/bf/fn-declaration.

[17] You can find a concise definition of function expressions on MDN at http://bevacqua.io/bf/fn-expr.

[18] Variable hoisting is explained in the code samples found at http://bevacqua.io/bf/hoisting.

That being said, there's nothing wrong with function expressions that curry another function.[19]

CURRYING IS GOOD

```
var plusThree = sum.bind(null, 3);
```

Keep in mind that function declarations will be hoisted[20] to the top of the scope, so it doesn't matter what order they're declared in. That being said, you should always keep them at the top level in a scope, and always avoid placing them inside conditional statements.

BAD FUNCTIONS

```
if (Math.random() > 0.5) {
  sum(1, 3);
  function sum (x, y) {
    return x + y;
  }
}
```

GOOD FUNCTIONS

```
if (Math.random() > 0.5) {
  sum(1, 3);
}
function sum (x, y) {
  return x + y;
}
Or
function sum (x, y) {
  return x + y;
}
if (Math.random() > 0.5) {
  sum(1, 3);
}
```

If you need a "no-op" method, you can use either `Function.prototype`, or `function noop () {}`. Ideally a single reference to `noop` is used throughout the application. Whenever you have to manipulate the `arguments` object, or other array-likes, cast them to an array.

BAD ARRAY-LIKE LOOP

```
var divs = document.querySelectorAll('div');

for (i = 0; i < divs.length; i++) {
  console.log(divs[i].innerHTML);
}
```

GOOD ARRAY-LIKE LOOP

```
var divs = document.querySelectorAll('div');
[].slice.call(divs).forEach(function (div) {
  console.log(div.innerHTML);
});
```

---

[19] John Resig explains how to partially apply functions on his blog at http://bevacqua.io/bf/partial-application.
[20] Variable hoisting is explained in the code samples found at http://bevacqua.io/bf/hoisting.

However, be aware that there's a substantial performance hit[21] in V8 environments when using this approach on `arguments`. If performance is a major concern, avoid casting `arguments` with `slice` and use a `for` loop instead.

BAD ARGUMENTS ACCESSOR

```
var args = [].slice.call(arguments);
```

BETTER ARGUMENTS ACCESSOR

```
var i;
var args = new Array(arguments.length);
for (i = 0; i < args.length; i++) {
    args[i] = arguments[i];
}
```

Never declare functions inside of loops.

BAD INLINE FUNCTIONS

```
var values = [1, 2, 3];
var i;
for (i = 0; i < values.length; i++) {
  setTimeout(function () {
    console.log(values[i]);
  }, 1000 * i);
}
```

or

```
var values = [1, 2, 3];
var i;
for (i = 0; i < values.length; i++) {
  setTimeout(function (i) {
    return function () {
      console.log(values[i]);
    };
  }(i), 1000 * i);
}
```

BETTER EXTRACT THE FUNCTION

```
var values = [1, 2, 3];
var i;
for (i = 0; i < values.length; i++) {
  wait(i);
}
function wait (i) {
  setTimeout(function () {
    console.log(values[i]);
  }, 1000 * i);
}
```

Or even better, use `.forEach`, which doesn't have the same caveats as declaring functions in `for` loops.

---

[21] See a great article on optimizing manipulation of function arguments at http://bevacqua.io/bf/arguments.

EVEN BETTER, FUNCTIONAL ARRAYS WITH FOREACH

```
[1, 2, 3].forEach(function (value, i) {
  setTimeout(function () {
    console.log(value);
  }, 1000 * i);
});
```

NAMED FUNCTION VS ANONYMOUS

Whenever a method is nontrivial, make the effort to use a named function expression rather than an anonymous function. This makes it easier to pinpoint the root cause of an exception when analyzing stack traces.

BAD, ANONYMOUS FUNCTIONS

```
function once (fn) {
  var ran = false;
  return function () {
    if (ran) { return };
    ran = true;
    fn.apply(this, arguments);
  };
}
```

GOOD, NAMED FUNCTION

```
function once (fn) {
  var ran = false;
  return function run () {
    if (ran) { return };
    ran = true;
    fn.apply(this, arguments);
  };
}
```

Avoid keeping indentation levels from raising more than necessary by using guard clauses instead of flowing `if` statements.

BAD

```
if (car) {
  if (black) {
    if (turbine) {
      return 'batman!';
    }
  }
}
```

or

```
if (condition) {
  // 10+ lines of code
}
```

GOOD

```
if (!car) {
  return;
}
if (!black) {
  return;
```

```
}
if (!turbine) {
  return;
}
return 'batman!';
```

or

```
if (!condition) {
  return;
}
// 10+ lines of code
```

D.3.3   *Prototypes*

Hacking the prototype of native types should be avoided at all costs; use methods instead. If you must extend the functionality in a native type, try using poser[22] instead. Poser provides out-of-context native type references that you can safely build upon and extend.

BAD
```
String.prototype.half = function () {
  return this.substr(0, this.length / 2);
};
```

GOOD
```
function half (text) {
  return text.substr(0, text.length / 2);
}
```

Avoid prototypical inheritance models unless you have a good performance reason to justify yourself:

- They are way more verbose than using plain objects.
- They cause headaches when creating new objects.
- They need a closure to hide valuable private state of instances.
- Just use plain objects instead.

D.3.4   *Object literals*

Instantiate using the Egyptian notation {}. Use factories instead of constructors. Here's a proposed pattern for you to implement objects in general:

```
function util (options) {
  // private methods and state go here
  var foo;
  function add () {
    return foo++;
  }
  function reset () { // note that this method isn't publicly exposed
    foo = options.start || 0;
```

---

[22] Poser provides out-of-context native type references that you can safely build upon and extend. For more information, see http://bevacqua.io/bf/poser.

```
  }
  reset();
  return {
    // public interface methods go here
    uuid: add
  };
}
```

D.3.5 *Array literals*

Instantiate using the square bracketed notation []. If you have to declare a fixed-dimension array for performance reasons, then it's fine to use the `new Array(length)` notation instead.

Arrays in JavaScript have a rich API that you should take advantage of. You can start with array manipulation basics[23] and then move on to more advanced use cases. For example, you could use the `.forEach` method to iterate over all of the items in a collection.

The following list shows basic operations you can perform on arrays:

- Use `.push` to insert items at the end of a collection or `.shift` to insert them at the beginning.
- Use `.pop` to get the last item and remove it from the collection at the same time or use `.unshift` to do the same for the first item.
- Master `.splice` to remove items by index, or to insert items at a specific index, or to do both at the same time!

Also learn about and use the functional collection manipulation methods! These can save you a ton of time that you'd otherwise spend doing the operations by hand. Here are a few examples of things you can do:

- Use `.filter` to discard uninteresting values.
- Use `.map` to transpolate array values into something else.
- Use `.reduce` to iterate over an array and produce a single result.
- Use `.some` and `.every` to assert whether all array items meet a condition.
- Use `.sort` to arrange the elements in a collection.
- Use `.reverse` to invert the order in the array.

The Mozilla Developer Network (MDN) has thoroughly documented all of these methods and more at https://developer.mozilla.org/.

D.4   *Regular expressions*

Keep regular expressions in variables; don't use them inline. This will vastly improve readability.

---

[23] An introductory article on JavaScript arrays is available on my blog at http://bevacqua.io/bf/arrays.

BAD REGULAR EXPRESSIONS

```
if (/\d+/.test(text)) {
  console.log('so many numbers!');
}
```

GOOD REGULAR EXPRESSIONS

```
var numeric = /\d+/;
if (numeric.test(text)) {
  console.log('so many numbers!');
}
```

Also, learn to write regular expressions[24] and what they do. Then you can also visualize them online.[25]

D.4.1   *Debugging statements*

Preferably put your `console` statements into a service that can easily be disabled in production. Alternatively, don't ship any `console.log` printing statements to production distributions.

D.4.2   *Comments*

Comments aren't meant to explain what the code does. Good code is supposed to be self-explanatory. If you're thinking of writing a comment to explain what a piece of code does, chances are you need to change the code itself. The exception to that rule is explaining what a regular expression does. Good comments are supposed to explain *why* code does something that may not seem to have a clear-cut purpose.

BAD COMMENTS

```
// create the centered container
var p = $('<p/>');
p.center(div);
p.tcxt('foo');
```

GOOD COMMENTS

```
var container = $('<p/>');
var contents = 'foo';
container.center(parent);
container.text(contents);
megaphone.on('data', function (value) {
  container.text(value); // the megaphone periodically emits updates for
      container
});
```

or

```
var numeric = /\d+/; // one or more digits somewhere in the string
if (numeric.test(text)) {
  console.log('so many numbers!');
}
```

---

[24] There's an introductory article on regular expressions on my blog at http://bevacqua.io/bf/regex.
[25] Regexper lets you visualize how any regular expression works at http://bevacqua.io/bf/regexper.

Commenting out entire blocks of code should be avoided entirely; that's why you have version control systems in place!

D.4.3 *Variable naming*

Variables must have meaningful names so that you don't have to resort to commenting what a piece of functionality does. Instead, try to be expressive while succinct, and use meaningful variable names:

BAD NAMING

```
function a (x, y, z) {
  return z * y / x;
}
a(4, 2, 6);
// <- 3
```

GOOD NAMING

```
function ruleOfThree (had, got, have) {
  return have * got / had;
}
ruleOfThree(4, 2, 6);
// <- 3
```

D.4.4 *Polyfills*

A polyfill is a piece of code that transparently enables your application to use modern features in older browsers. Where possible use the native browser implementation and include a polyfill that provides that same behavior[26] to unsupported browsers. This makes the code easier to work with and less involved in hackery to make things just work.

If you can't patch a piece of functionality with a polyfill, then wrap all uses of the patching code[27] in a globally available implementation that's accessible from anywhere in the application.

D.4.5 *Everyday tricks*

CREATING DEFAULT VALUES

Use || to define a default value. If the left-hand value is falsy[28] then the right-hand value will be used.

```
function a (value) {
  var defaultValue = 33;
  var used = value || defaultValue;
}
```

---

[26] Remy Sharp concisely explains what a polyfill is at http://bevacqua.io/bf/polyfill.

[27] I've written an article on developing high quality modules that touches on the implementation-wrapping subject at http://bevacqua.io/bf/hq-modules.

[28] In JavaScript, falsy values are treated as false in conditional statements. Falsy values are '', **null**, **undefined**, and **0**. For more information, see http://bevacqua.io/bf/casting.

USING BIND TO PARTIALLY APPLY FUNCTIONS

Use `.bind` to partially apply[29] functions:

```
function sum (a, b) {
  return a + b;
}
var addSeven = sum.bind(null, 7);
addSeven(6);
// <- 13
```

ARRAY.PROTOTYPE.SLICE.CALL TO CAST ARRAY-LIKE OBJECTS TO ARRAYS

Use `Array.prototype.slice.call` to cast array-like objects to true arrays:

```
var args = Array.prototype.slice.call(arguments);
```

EVENT EMITTERS ON ALL THINGS

Use event emitters[30] on all the things! This pattern helps you to decouple implementations from messaging between different objects or application layers:

```
var emitter = contra.emitter();
body.addEventListener('click', function () {
  emitter.emit('click', e.target);
});
emitter.on('click', function (elem) {
  console.log(elem);
});
// simulate click
emitter.emit('click', document.body);
```

FUNCTION.PROTOTYPE AS A NO-OP

Use `Function.prototype` as a "no-op:"

```
function (cb) {
  setTimeout(cb || Function.prototype, 2000);
```

---

[29] John Resig, of jQuery fame, has an interesting article on partial JavaScript functions at http://bevacqua.io/bf/partial-application.

[30] Contra provides an easy-to-use event emitter implementation at http://bevacqua.io/bf/contra.emitter.

index

MORE TITLES FROM MANNING

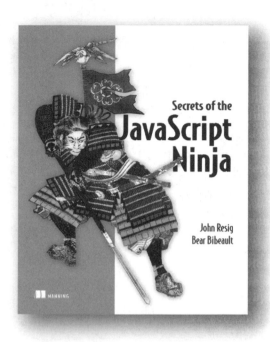

Secrets of the JavaScript Ninja
by John Resig and Bear Bibeault

ISBN: 9781933988696
392 pages
$39.99
December 2012

Single Page Web Applications
JavaScript end-to-end

by Michael S. Mikowski and Josh C. Powell

ISBN: 9781617290756
432 pages
$44.99
September 2013

For ordering information go to www.manning.com

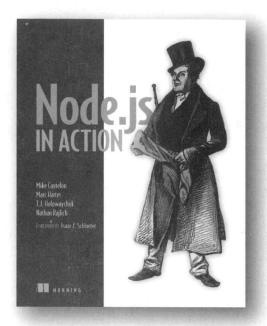